MARCEL BREUER

A Memoir

MARCEL BREUER

A Memoir

Robert F. Gatje

Foreword by I. M. Pei

THE MONACELLI PRESS

First published in the United States of America in 2000 by
The Monacelli Press, Inc.
10 East 92nd Street, New York, New York 10128.

Library of Congress Cataloging-in-Publication Data
Gatje, Robert F.
Marcel Breuer : a memoir / Robert F. Gatje ;
foreword by I. M. Pei.
p.   cm.
Includes index.
ISBN 1-58093-029-8
1. Breuer, Marcel, 1902- . 2. Breuer, Marcel, 1902- —
Criticism and interpretation. 3. Architects—
United States—Biography. I. Title.
NA737.B68 G38 2000
720'.92—dc21
[B]   00-033961

Printed and bound in Singapore

Designed by Abigail Sturges

Cover: Marcel Breuer in his office, mid-1970s.
*Back cover: Study for the bell banner and church of
Saint John's Abbey, Collegeville, Minnesota, mid-1950s.*
Frontispiece: Marcel Breuer, 1960.

Contents

Marcel Breuer at
La Gaude, 1963.

Preface and Acknowledgments

I worked with Marcel Breuer for twenty-three years, eleven of them as one of his partners, until his retirement in 1976 and eventual death in 1981. At the peak of his career in the late 1960s, Breuer was one of the best-known, most admired and beloved members of his profession. Today, he has been largely forgotten by a fickle public, except in the case of his beautiful chairs. He was one of the most remarkable men I have ever met and I owe much of the joy, satisfaction, and rewards of my forty years of architectural practice to him. This book is a frank gesture of affection and thanks and an attempt to convey what it was like to work by his side in his several offices. My hope is that it will help remind the world of a great man.

Responsibility for the accuracy of these words rests with me and the friends and colleagues who have taken the time to share their memories with me. These individuals are acknowledged as part of my *dramatis personae* at the back of the memoir, and their names are identified, when they first appear, in bold type. I have also spoken at length with James Marston Fitch, Ken Frampton, Robert Geddes, I. M. Pei, Paul Rudolph, and Ezra Stoller. Aside from the taped interviews, I have refreshed my own memory by reading, sometimes for the first time, a number of books I had originally added to my library for their excellent pictures, or because they were presented to me by Breuer with characteristic inscriptions.

When I approached Breuer's widow, Connie, for guidance in preparing this manuscript, she explained that, although she greatly valued my friendship and appreciated the strong feelings that I have for her husband and his work, she also knew that he had many times expressed disinterest in a personal biography, preferring to be judged by his architecture. Yet she wished me well, and I, in turn, have limited my narrative to events associated with the professional life that I and my friends shared with him.

Breuer was very sensitive to criticism, and he was thus very careful not to criticize the work of others. His oft-stated position was that no one who had not lived through the whole production of a building was in a position to pass judgment on the outcome. The original program, discussions with the client, government requirements had all shaped the building in a more fundamental way than that last "one percent art" that he claimed to control. I never agreed with him in rejecting the right of intelligent critics to form their opinions based on the result rather than on knowledge of its formation. And I never saw Lajkó anything but pleased when someone said or wrote something positive about his work.

Marcel Breuer's middle name was "Lajos," the Hungarian form of "Louis." His parents had followed the Austro-Hungarian fashion of giving him a French first name, Marcel, but he never used it except as a signature. "Lajkó" is the diminutive form, or nickname, derived from "Lajos." It is pronounced somewhere between "*Loy*-ko" and "*Lai*-ko." It has been spelled any number of ways, as witness many letters from his friends, which are now preserved in the Special Collections of the Syracuse University Library and in the Marcel Breuer papers at the Archives of American Art, Smithsonian Institution, in Washington, D.C. However one chooses to spell it, what is certain is that all his friends used this nickname in addressing him and would immediately recognize as a poseur anyone who referred to "My friend, Marcel . . ."

Unless otherwise identified all the drawings are mine, based as noted "after" iconic photographs of Breuer's work. The title of my center chapter, "The Taste of Space . . . The Juice of Stone," comes from Breuer's one and only poem. It used to be repeated as a mantra around the office.

The thanks customary to a preface go to all those interviewed, my editors Stephanie Salomon and Andrea Monfried, graphic designer Abigail Sturges, and especially my best friend, Susan Witter, who has supported the writing of this book in every way possible, even though she never knew Lajkó.

Foreword

I. M. Pei

Although I knew Lajkó Breuer for forty years, I am neither the oldest nor the closest among his friends. I did not study under him during my years at Harvard, but he was an inspiring presence among his peers. During his years at the Bauhaus he embraced the credo of "machine civilization" and the potential of industrial technology. His seminal contribution to furniture design was an expression of his belief in the beauty inherent in mass production.

Breuer arrived in the United States in 1937 and spent the next nine years teaching at Harvard. Although he built very little, a generation of architects emerged under his influence. History has to take note of this when it passes judgment on the man and his work.

Breuer left Harvard for New York in 1946, and I, in 1948. His reputation ensured him several commissions of consequence, while I was still trying to find my way. Subsequently he became the architect of choice for residential work among the more avant-garde clients. I, on the other hand, was engaged mostly in the field of urban planning and low-cost housing. This was fortuitous, as our non-parallel paths brought us closer together as friends and colleagues. As Bob Gatje has pointed out in this book, Breuer disliked criticism of his work and hence eschewed critique of the work of others. This contributed to his loneliness, in spite of his warm and sympathetic personality. Through the years of our friendship, he asked for my opinion of his work only once, when he was confronted with the important design challenge of building on top of Grand Central Terminal.

He was genuinely fond of my wife, Eileen, who briefly studied design with him as a landscape major at Harvard. Breuer, his wife, Connie, and Eileen and I sailed the Greek islands together twice, in 1958 and 1967. During those two-week holidays we promised each other not to have alcohol on board and to avoid discussion of architecture. But we consumed copious amounts of ouzo on shore and marveled at the play of sunlight on form. Is that not the essence of architecture?

The work of Breuer's mature years illustrates the cubist sensibility of this sculptor-architect. He left behind a large volume of work, much of which is meticulously documented in this book. It confirms beyond question that Breuer was one of the most important form-givers of our time.

MARCEL BREUER

A Memoir

An Introductory Biography of Marcel Breuer: 1902–1953

Marcel Breuer was born in 1902 in Pécs, an important city near the southern border of Hungary, where Croatia and Serbia meet each other. He always described his father as a doctor and the family as comfortably well off. He rarely spoke of his childhood but he did mention his first movie— seen when a traveling entrepreneur set up a tent in his neighborhood— which inspired a lifelong devotion to the cinema. When I once tried to convince him of the benefits of "key-man" insurance, he referred to his chagrin upon learning that all the insurance his father had set aside for the security of his family had been wiped out in the ruinous inflation that swept Europe after World War I.

Marcel Breuer on an early ski holiday.

With Europe in an economic shambles after the end of that war, it cannot have been an easy time to consider entry to a university as Breuer came of age. He was helped when he won a scholarship to the Academy of Fine Arts in Vienna, and in 1920 the eighteen-year-old set off with the intention of becoming a painter or sculptor. **Paul Weidlinger,** an old friend of Lajkó's, has said of his own upbringing in the intellectual hothouse of Vienna in those days: "We were so instilled with a love of learning that we didn't know that one could not go to college."

Something about the academic atmosphere in Vienna did not appeal to Breuer and he stayed at the academy for only a very short while. In the next few months he heard from a friend about a unique new school called the Bauhaus devoted to arts and crafts. When he inadvertently ruined the blade of a carpenter's plane he was using at a temporary job, he left Vienna for Weimar in haste and enrolled as a student/apprentice at the Bauhaus under its founder/director Walter Gropius an architect already famous, who was to become one of the best-known teachers of architecture in the twentieth century.

The world of modern art was quite small at the time, and whether it was Paris, Munich, or Berlin, "everyone" knew each other. Gropius was able to assemble an arts faculty from among his closest friends including Johannes Itten, Oskar Schlemmer, Wassily Kandinsky, and Paul Klee. It is honored and remembered to this day.

Weimar during the 1920s was not only the new capital of postwar Germany but became the eventual home of Theo van Doesburg and the group of artists and architects associated with de Stijl. They were, at times, rivals to the Bauhaus. The city was a vibrant center of experimental ferment and radical politics—very much more to Breuer's taste than Vienna. It is important to keep in mind, however, that these Bauhaus giants were already mature, adult achievers when the eighteen-year-old Marcel Breuer arrived on their doorstep in 1920, and although many were to become his close friends, there was in many cases a significant age gap. Gropius, Kandinsky, and Klee were, respectively, nineteen, thirty-six, and twenty-three years older than he was, and Josef Albers, who, like Breuer, eventually rose from student to faculty "master" was nevertheless fourteen years older. In their eyes, Breuer must have seemed a child—albeit a wunderkind.

The Bauhaus was in no sense a regular school. There were informal classes, but most of the work was done in the studios where Breuer devoted himself to the carpentry shop, designing and building with his own hands much of the furniture for which he quickly became famous. Although he put in some time as a draftsman/apprentice in Gropius's architectural office, which coexisted with the Bauhaus in Weimar (and was criticized for its conflict of interest), there were no courses in architecture, a fact that later proved to be an obstacle to Breuer becoming registered as a professional. His teachers were artists—mostly painters—and some of the imagery he developed as part of his personal architectural vocabulary can be directly traced to the painting and graphics that surrounded him in the Bauhaus and at de Stijl. As a self-styled young bohemian, Breuer couldn't understand how it was possible for Paul Klee to paint his wonderfully inventive canvases between certain rigidly observed morning hours of work, while wearing a jacket and tie. But then, Klee was half-Swiss and Breuer was always troubled by Swiss self-discipline. Breuer's Bauhaus memories dealt mostly with parties, which he enjoyed, and academic intrigue, which he tried to avoid.

At a time when everyone was writing manifestos, Breuer kept clear of publication. But when he had to declare himself, as he did during certain critical moments in the history of the Bauhaus, he did so most eloquently, always trying to steer clear of the political violence of Weimar Germany. His experiments in what were truly radical furniture designs involved not only the introduction of new materials, such as the chromed-steel tubing of his bicycle handlebars, but also concepts such as nesting tables, wall-hung modular storage units, and the use of freestanding cabinetry as space dividers. He also began his practice the way many young architects begin their careers— by designing interiors for his friends.

Gropius clearly recognized the talents of this wunderkind and took him under his wing. Breuer was helped through his certification process as a journeyman after being assigned by Gropius to design the principal interiors of an experimental house—the "Haus-am-Horn"—that the school built as part of the first Bauhaus exhibition in 1923. Breuer left the Bauhaus in 1924 at a time when right-wing pressure in the city council of Weimar plus Gropius's own demonstrated financial mismanagement forced the school to look elsewhere for municipal support.

Undoubtedly Lajkó felt that he had "graduated" and needed the professional experience of working in an architect's office, which he did for a year in Paris (1924–25). He often related the story of arriving at the Gare du Nord weighed down by one enormous suitcase (guarding it with his life since he'd heard that Paris was full of thieves) and looking for the Latin Quarter because he'd been told that that was where the cheap hotels were. He lugged that suitcase for miles because everyone he spoke to had a different idea of the exact location of the Latin Quarter.

This was for him the beginning of a lifelong love affair with Paris, which I was to share forty years later. While there, he lived a very frugal life and spoke later of far from affluent artists gathering at the Hôtel Pont-Royal long before it had been remodeled to its present splendor. It was during this time that he first met the architect Le Corbusier, beginning a friendship that was to last for thirty years.

Meanwhile, Gropius had found a new home for the Bauhaus in Dessau and designed a very handsome new building to house the school,

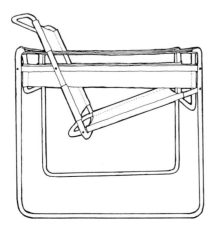

The Wassily. The first tubular steel chair designed by Breuer, or anyone else for that matter, was later named after his friend the painter Wassily Kandinsky.

15

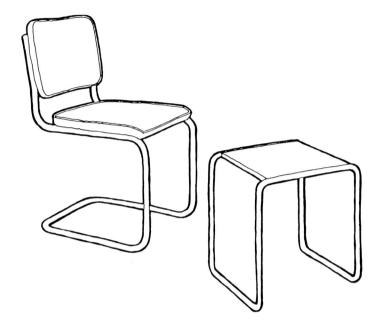

The Cesca. Breuer's first cantilevered chair, named after his mother, was inspired by one of his side tables.

which opened in 1926. He convinced Breuer to return by making him a master and giving him the commission to design the principal interiors of the new group of buildings. The three years that followed were most eventful for Breuer. His competition entry for a multistory housing scheme sponsored by a German magazine was widely published and admired. He perfected and patented his first tubular steel chair—the marvelous cube of air defined by leather straps and shiny metal that is known today as the "Wassily." This was followed by over fifty different pieces of furniture—chairs, tables, tea-carts—all mass-produced by Thonet Brothers. He worked on the idea of a cantilevered two-legged chair at the same time that other architects—notably Mies van der Rohe and the Dutchman Mart Stam—were shaping their own versions of the same concept. Stam won the race to the patent office but most people believe Breuer's account, which is that he gave Stam the idea by turning his tubular steel-legged table on its side to demonstrate its resiliency and potential use as the base of a chair.

Lajkó held off building a prototype himself while looking for chromed tubing with a stronger, thicker wall. He preferred the tight turns he had used in the Wassily chair but knew that they would be overstressed by the forces of a resilient cantilevered chair. Stam ignored the problem by using rigid pipe, and Mies gave the legs of his version a long slow curve to avoid the weakness at the tight bend in the tubing. Years of legal patent controversy followed, but history awards Breuer the authorship of the ubiquitous chair that he later named after his mother, Francesca—the "Cesca."

The conflict surrounding the design and production of his furniture eventually led Breuer to get out of the business and to hope that he would become better known for his architecture. At the time, however, the publicity attending the lawsuit certainly helped to launch his career, and he was the interior designer of choice for many figures of the avant-garde such as the great Berlin theatrical producer Erwin Piscator. Throughout the 1930s, when most architects were starving for work, the royalties dutifully paid by Breuer's manufacturer, Thonet Brothers, kept him going.

In 1927 there was an enormously influential demonstration of modern architecture built in the form of housing units on the grounds of the Weissenhof estate in Stuttgart. Mies van der Rohe had been responsible for choosing the thirty modern architects whose work was to be shown. Perhaps because of Breuer's youth (he was sixteen years Mies's junior) he did not include Breuer. Gropius found this unfair and arranged for Lajkó to design interiors for two of the houses—his own and Mart Stam's—that are today better known than most of the houses themselves. I never heard Breuer speak of Mies, although he certainly knew him and must have admired his work. There may have been some professional jealousy between the two. Breuer (a Hungarian) had exhibited with the Deutscher Werkbund at Gropius's invitation in Paris in 1930; Mies (a German) had not. Mies invited Breuer to design a house only at the last minute for the Berlin Building Exhibition of 1931. Breuer's opened on time; Mies's was late. It is also possible that Breuer was resentful of Mies's willingness to negotiate with the Nazis in a vain effort to save the Dessau Bauhaus in 1932 before moving it, largely at his own personal expense, to Berlin, where it finally died.

Elaine Hochman's fascinating 1997 study of the school, entitled *Bauhaus: Crucible of Modernism*, uses recently uncovered documents from the former East Germany to highlight as never before the incredible political and financial tensions that surrounded Gropius and his faculty in Weimar Germany. Unfortunately, readers of her book may come away with an impression of violent unhappiness that overshadows the frequent carefree and joyous memories that Breuer and others have chosen to recall.

Several key members of the faculty had left the Bauhaus with Gropius in 1928, or shortly thereafter, and Breuer decided it was time to open his own architectural office in Berlin. Gropius again lent a hand in the attempt, which was ultimately successful, to persuade the authorities of the German Association of Architects to admit Lajkó as a member despite his absent diploma.

In 1932 he received his first commission for a stand-alone house. The client was Paul Harnischmacher, an industrialist from Wiesbaden who had approached Gropius about a factory in 1928. When the commission was

The first Harnischmacher house. At its core, this was a white box not unlike those being built at the same time by many of Breuer's contemporaries. It takes on special, human characteristics with its striped awnings and curtains plus glass windscreens and nautical rigging.

watered down to the simple remodeling of an existing apartment, Gropius passed it on to Breuer. While working on the apartment, a positive relationship developed, and when the Harnischmachers decided to build in Wiesbaden what was to become a very famous house, they turned to Breuer.

Lajkó told me that he was familiar with the name Harnischmacher from national advertising but unsure of the exact product line. He guessed it was mouthwash, but it turned out to be shoe polish. At any rate, the site was a large green hillside, and the house that was built there resembled many of the white boxes that European modernists were designing in Germany, Switzerland, and Czechoslovakia. Breuer, however, extended and embellished the three-story structure with the decks, stairs, railings, and sun-control devices that were to reappear again and again in his formal vocabulary—many of which were adopted from the nautical vernacular that modern architects came to admire.

It is impossible to imagine that the young architect was unaware of the beautiful house that Mies had designed for the Tugendhats in Brno, Czechoslovakia, only two years before or, for that matter, of the strikingly similar house at Garches, near Paris, that Le Corbusier had built for the Steins at about the same time. Such speculation is, of course, ultimately academic. All the architects of a certain standing knew one another and one another's work. And although each eventually drifted away from the common canon to develop his own "style," there *was* a magical moment when they all seemed to be working toward the same end with similar means and virtually no jealousy—considering how little work there was to be had.

When the Harnischmacher drawings were complete and ready to be bid, Lajkó asked his client whether he had any favorite contractors who should be consulted. Harnischmacher said he knew nothing of the building trades but had heard the name Philipp Holzmann. Breuer pointed out that they were the largest builders in Germany and unlikely to be interested in a house, however grand. On the other hand, things were slow all over Europe in the early 1930s and it was decided to include them on the list of bidders. Holzmann was not only interested, it submitted the lowest bid and built the house to everyone's great satisfaction. It was widely published and admired, especially as the first completed work of a young up-and-coming architect. Unfortunately, it was destroyed in a British air raid in the closing months of World War II and only photographs remain.

In 1954, shortly after I went to work for Breuer, the Harnischmachers, who had held onto their bomb site in Wiesbaden, approached Breuer about designing a second house there to be used in their retirement. Even though he was at the time trying to move away from residential work, Lajkó was so touched by their loyalty that he designed another, smaller house in his 1950s style—a one-story composition of glass and masonry planes. When the question of the selection of a contractor came up, Harnischmacher suggested including Philipp Holzmann again, despite Breuer's feeling that the company was probably already overloaded with post–World War II reconstruction projects. Hansgert Schmitz, whose father had been on the board of Philipp Holzmann at that time, later described the surprise and pleasure with which this bid request had been received. It was immediately bumped up to top management, despite a very heavy schedule of construction projects. The company submitted the lowest bid and even pulled the original job superintendent out of retirement to supervise construction of the second house, which, so far as I know, still stands.

Lajkó had closed his office in Berlin in 1931 for lack of work and during the next few years he toured southern Europe and North Africa, sometimes by means of a Ford motorcar, of which he was very proud, sometimes by bicycle, and occasionally in the company of the architect and graphic artist Herbert Bayer, who had left the Bauhaus with him. His travels reinforced his admiration for vernacular architecture, which he thought remained immune to the dictates of fashion in the same way that he hoped contemporary design might pursue a rational, non-fashionable path.

By the end of 1932 his travels landed him in Zurich, where he was able to benefit directly from the patronage of his friend Sigfried Giedion. Giedion had established two Swiss furniture stores called "Wohnbedarf," which were a major outlet for Breuer's furniture as well as the designs of Aalto, Le Corbusier, and other prominent designers. He would later become well-known to my generation of architects for his 1938–39 Charles Eliot Norton lectures at Harvard, which were subsequently published as *Space, Time and*

Architecture. Giedion commissioned Breuer to redesign his stores in Basel and Zurich. Shortly thereafter, Giedion introduced Breuer to two Swiss architects, Emil and **Alfred Roth,** who were already working on a housing scheme for property that Giedion's family owned in the fashionable Doldertal district of Zurich. The pair of four-level apartments that resulted from their collaboration are among the most famous products of European modernism of the 1930s.

The first Harnischmacher house and the Doldertal apartments, looked at as pure architectural volumes, strongly resemble other white boxes of the International Style. One feature that sets them apart is the striped awning material that "humanizes" these buildings and helps to control the sunlight. Such a practical offering to the occupants was natural to Breuer, even though it may have offended the purist sensibilities of the other architectural giants of the era. From my visit to Doldertal in 1953, I remember the awnings as blue and white, but the only original photos are in black and white and it is possible that Lajkó was influenced by the awnings of the

Breuer and Alfred Roth. The two, who met through Sigfried Giedion, became close friends and often skied together. Roth later recommended several of his students at the ETH for apprenticeship in Breuer's office.

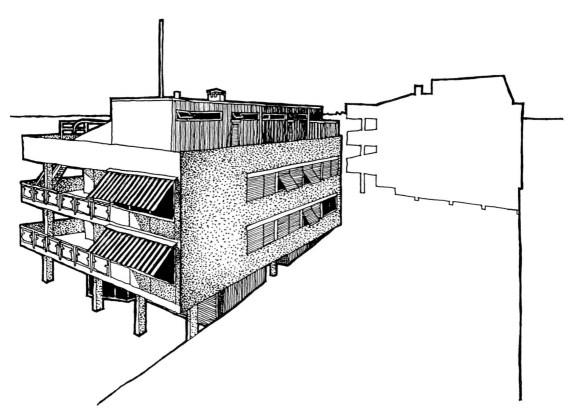

Palais Royal gardens in Paris, one of his favorite haunts, where the material has always been gray and white.

Encouraged by Giedion, Lajkó continued his work in furniture design and had just patented some new ideas for chairs made from flat bars of aluminum when an international competition was launched by France's largest aluminum manufacturer. Breuer submitted his designs to two juries—one made up of representatives from industry and the other nominated by the Congrès International d'Architecture Moderne (CIAM), which included Giedion, Gropius, and possibly Le Corbusier. Lajkó's work was selected unanimously for first prize by each of the juries. None of these chairs ever became as popular as his tubular steel and wood furniture, and their production was eventually halted by the aluminum shortages of World War II.

Gropius had moved to London in 1933, where he formed a partnership with Maxwell Fry and became an adviser to Jack Pritchard, the founder of Isokon, a company that promoted good modern design in buildings and eventually, in furniture. Gropius put Breuer in contact with a young London architect/author, F. R. S. Yorke, and after half-completed English lessons, Lajkó

The Doldertal apartments (after Finsler). Breuer's Swiss collaborators, Alfred and Emil Roth, had determined the site plan for Sigfried Giedion's housing project, but the buildings are pure Breuer.

21

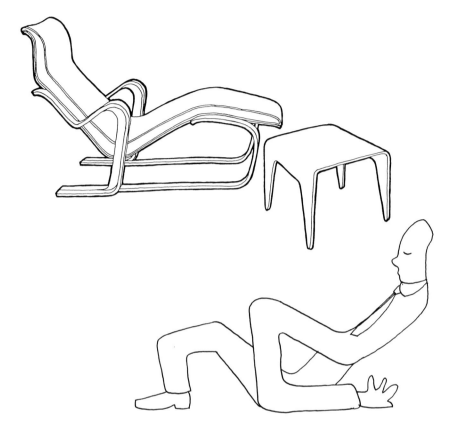

The Isokon lounge chair and side table. The laminated-wood frame was derived from earlier experiments using steel and aluminum bands, but the warmth of its final shape and material established this as a domestic classic.

A later commentary on the Isokon chair. This appeared in the office's "Marcel Breuer Coloring Book" of Christmas 1963.

this is so restful color my suit a restful charcoal brown; put a martini in my hand, add a bit of hair,

moved to London in 1935 with the promise of a partnership with Yorke. Breuer moved into the Lawn Road Flats, the first modern apartment development in England, designed for Isokon by one of its other founders, the Canadian Wells Coates. Breuer already had many social friends in London, acquired during travels and while skiing in Europe. He was welcomed as an immediate force in the Modern Architectural Research Group (MARS), where he met new friends who were to remain with him for the rest of his life.

When Isokon decided to move into furniture production, it was Gropius once again who championed Breuer and suggested that he consider making plywood variants of his aluminum reclining chairs. Of the models that resulted, two have established themselves in design history— a plywood nesting table and a reclining armchair, appropriately named the "Isokon chair."

Among the architectural commissions that Breuer and Yorke received were several renovation jobs including a 1936 flat in the famous Highpoint Apartments for a Mrs. Ventris and her architect son Michael, who was later to be renowned as the decoder of Minoan B, a Cretan script that had puzzled scholars for centuries. They also remodeled a house in Bristol for Crofton Ganes, another furniture distributor, who then commissioned the partners to design a show house for his furniture line at the Royal Agricultural Show of 1936 in Bristol. This small, temporary building was a free composition of full-height rubblestone walls with wood-framed glass infill under a strong, horizontal roof plane. It clearly appears to have been influenced by contemporaneous work of both Mies and Le Corbusier, and yet, even today, it represents the first, best example of what would become a typical Breuer building.

In 1936 Breuer and Yorke were asked to design a "Civic Center for the Future" for the British Cement and Concrete Association as a showpiece for what this material might be capable of. Breuer chose to design a form of collage that would illustrate some of his best ideas. The model photographs show buildings he had designed for unsuccessful competitions as well as prototypes for many buildings that were later to be built successfully.

In the spring of 1937 Dean Joseph Hudnut of the Harvard Graduate School of Design (GSD) brought Walter Gropius to the United States as a professor of architecture. At Gropius's invitation, Breuer followed, in time to join the faculty for the fall term. The two of them revolutionized the teach-

The Bristol Pavilion. This show house for Crofton Ganes, an English furniture distributor, at an agricultural fair shows Breuer's first use of his trademark planes of rubblestone.

ing of architecture in America by introducing the Bauhaus function-based approach to design at the GSD. Prior to this time, most schools organized their curriculum according to principles developed at the Ecole des Beaux-Arts in Paris for architecture education in the classic mode. (By the time I went to Cornell in 1948 "Beaux-Arts" had become a term of opprobrium). Among the distinguished architects who studied under them were **Edward Larrabee Barnes, Eduardo Catalano,** Ulrich Franzen, Robert Geddes, **John Johansen,** Philip Johnson, Elliot Noyes, Paul Rudolph, **Harry Seidler,** and Richard Stein. Gropius also invited Breuer to join him in an architectural partnership in Cambridge, Massachusetts, that was to last for four years.

Bill Landsberg, with Noyes, Stein, and others from the first graduating class, was hired to work in the new Gropius/Breuer office. Landsberg remembers Gropius during the Harvard years as having been "a respected, rather austere figure," as opposed to Breuer, "who was more approachable and very soon on friendly terms with his students." Ed Barnes wrote in the fall 1995 *GSD News* that he considered his friend an "absolute artist" and a great teacher who was best one-on-one and encouraged his students toward freedom and experimentation: "Why *not* to do it?" The first time they had met was in Breuer's bachelor apartment in Cambridge: "I saw snow-white walls, Japanese matting, low lighting, somewhere a brilliant blue, a mirror, candles, and a mixture of materials—wicker, fur, and bright chrome. I felt I was inside a Paul Klee painting." Barnes went on to write of his friend's view of himself: "I don't think he ever gave a damn about what others said. Breuer went his own way."

John Johansen wonders whether Lajkó really enjoyed teaching any but the very brightest of his students and remembers him humbling one of the slower ones by critiquing a drawing with "What do we make of this? Trouble in your love life?" In talking with me shortly before his death in 1997, Paul Rudolph, who was in Gropius's class and saw Breuer only in open critiques and at parties, remembered him as being "remarkably agreeable and available. He gave of himself so endlessly that he had to be an effective teacher. There was not the least bit of pomposity and we were never aware of his ego, except for his power. He was the great European architect who was somehow, miraculously, found among us." **Stan Abercrombie,** who became a distinguished writer and editor after leaving Breuer's office, told me of Philip Johnson's simple statement, "Breuer was the *real* artist of the Harvard GSD."

The Gropius and Breuer partnership in Cambridge produced a number of extraordinary houses as well as a pavilion at the 1939 New York World's Fair and some defense-industry housing. Two of the houses they designed were for themselves and one, the 1940 Chamberlain cottage in Weyland, Massachusetts, while little more than a one-room weekend residence,

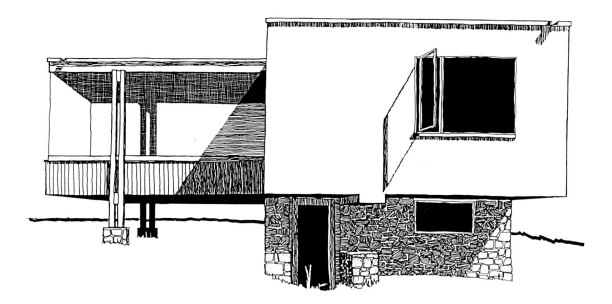

became an icon of modern American architecture, immortalized in a now-famous photograph by Ezra Stoller.

Although Breuer and Gropius were able to work together in harmony within the same architectural idiom, the two men were very different. Gropius, an urbane socialite and organizer of artists and educators, was a careful creature of the modern movement who always surrounded himself with bright young designers. **Carl Stein** reports that his late father, Dick, had told him that Gropius, if in charge of a project, would spend all the time and most of the fee in researching the proper solution and then rush out the drawings in haste. Breuer, on the other hand, was an intuitive designer who reached decisions quickly and spent most of *his* time in developing the details of his original conception. However, Dick Stein remembered Lajkó coming along to check on progress on a competition at Wheaton College. He rejected the shape of the driveway that they had worked out according to the functional program, drew another that was more attractive, and said, "We'll figure out how to make it work after we win the competition." (They didn't win.)

Few architectural practices were as single-minded as Gropius and Breuer's. Bob Geddes told me of visiting Philip Johnson's new New York office while looking for a summer job in 1948. Philip admired his Harvard portfolio and suggested, "I'm a Mies man, myself. Landis Gores over there is a Wrightian. You can be our Breuer."

The Chamberlain cottage (after Ezra Stoller). The facade of this tiny structure in Weyland, Massachusetts, has become an icon of the modern house and demonstrates Breuer's uncanny eye for shape.

25

Constance Leighton, from Salem, Massachusetts, had seen and admired a publication of Lajkó's work. While living and working in Boston, she interviewed for and landed a job as secretary in the Gropius/Breuer firm. Lajkó was known to say, "Connie was a pretty good secretary but I thought she'd make an even better wife." They were married in 1940.

Christopher Wilk, the author of the Museum of Modern Art's 1981 catalog of a show of Breuer's furniture and interiors, has told me that he heard from several students, who happened to be passing by in a corridor of the GSD, of the exact moment when the partnership with Gropius broke up in 1941. Both men were shouting most uncharacteristically about some missed appointment. Reginald Isaacs tells a slightly different story in his biography of Gropius, but whatever the details, the parting would seem to have been foreordained. Anyone looking at the projects produced by the partnership (even Gropius's own house) and comparing them to the later work of the two men can appreciate the frustration Breuer must have felt in seeing his designs credited to his very much older mentor, whatever respect he had to feel for Gropius.

The rupture must have been traumatic for both men. Gropius had been a father figure to Lajkó since they met at the Bauhaus and went far out of his way to promote the career of his young protégé on a great many occasions. The friendship that Breuer felt for Gropius and his wife Ise is recorded in their long correspondence on file in the Archives of American Art in Washington, D.C. It is possible that, consciously or unconsciously, Lajkó may have tried to make up for his abrupt departure from Gropius by becoming himself the mentor to a whole new generation of young architects, of which I was eventually proud to be one.

Breuer stayed on in Cambridge and at Harvard for five more years. He started a delicate wooden summer cottage in Wellfleet on Cape Cod in 1943 that Connie and their son still use every summer. Similar cottages on adjacent land in the pine forest were built by and for his friends Serge Chermayeff, Paul Weidlinger, Georgy Kepes, and Edgar Stillman.

Chermayeff and Breuer had met during Lajkó's two years in England, where Serge was in partnership with Eric Mendelsohn and was founder of MARS. Their subsequent friendship was frequently punctuated by outbursts of seeming conflict. **Ivan Chermayeff,** a prominent graphic designer and Serge's son, remembers Lajkó hiring him one summer to ferry blocks of ice across the lake that separated the two friends' houses because the unpaved track in the sand ended at the Chermayeffs and the ice man wouldn't deliver to the Breuers. Ivan was all of twelve years old at the time and called *freshling* by Breuer. (In German, *frischling* means piglet and *fröschling* means tadpole. When I asked Ivan which it was, he said, "Neither. Breuer made it up.") Serge, realizing that the ice would melt unless promptly delivered, loudly accused Breuer of knowing that he would have to help Ivan carry the

Serge Chermayeff with Lajkó, 1972. The two old friends are near their vacation cottages in Wellfleet, Massachusetts.

heavy blocks to his rowboat twice a week, and felt put upon. There are stories of arguments over shampoo suds, when someone washed his hair in the small lake, and of the time Serge, in making a rhetorical point, slammed his finger down so hard on Lajkó's dining room table that it was broken and Breuer couldn't help roaring with laughter.

As the war ended in 1945, Breuer designed a Serviceman's Memorial for Cambridge, which never was built but remained one of his favorite conceptions and seems clearly to have been derived from the work of Mies, van Doesburg, and Mondrian while remaining at the same time completely his own. That was also the year for two marvelous houses: one for the Tompkins family in Hewlett Harbor, New York, and the other for Bert Geller, the shoe manufacturer, in Lawrence, Long Island. Bert and his wife, Phyllis, were absolute Breuer fans and would come back later for a second, smaller house. Lajkó furnished and laid out the entire house for the Gellers. He appreciated their devotion but was furious when he returned a year later to find every ashtray exactly where he had put it: "I've never been so insulted in my life! I designed this house for you to *live* in, not to keep as some sort of a shrine!"

Breuer moved to New York in 1946 with very little work on the horizon but undoubtedly with the hope that the big city would offer him more opportunities than Cambridge. He rented most of a townhouse on East Eighty-eighth Street near the East River, lived on the second floor with Connie and their infant son, Tamas, and had his office on the third. He was without any staff when Harry Seidler, who had known Lajkó when he was a

The Robinson house (after Robert Damora F.A.I.A.). The design is a brilliant display of some of Breuer's favorite themes—butterfly roof, binuclear plan, vertical siding, and rubblestone—in Williamstown, Massachusetts. Lajkó told me this was his favorite house.

student at the Harvard GSD, stopped by to say hello and to see about getting a job. Seidler had come to Harvard from Vienna via England and Canada and had admired Breuer, as he told me, not only for his great "crits" (design critiques) but as "an outgoing man, full of fun, who liked to give parties at his bachelor apartment."

He found Breuer at work on a drawing. Lajkó insisted that there was nothing for Seidler to do and no way to pay him. Harry said he could draw whatever Breuer was working on—and probably draft it better—and was willing to wait for a salary. Suddenly, there was an office.

Seidler drew up the great Robinson house of 1947 in Williamstown, Massachusetts, among other designs, and made models into the night. Connie sometimes dropped by to ask, "Don't you ever go home?" His duties included looking after Lajkó when he came down with the flu while Connie was out of town. This earned him the nickname "Mädchen für alles" (the maid of all work); the two often spoke German together. The ministrations included going out for medicines and salami sandwiches.

Soon they were joined in the office by Margaret Firmage, who was to serve Lajkó for many years as secretary and bookkeeper. One day, she ushered in a dignified older woman—Marion Thompson, the widow of the president of the Pennsylvania Railroad, who was wealthy enough to keep the taxi that had driven her from Pittsburgh waiting on Eighty-eighth Street during a three-hour interview with Breuer. They agreed on a commission to design her large house in Ligonier, Pennsylvania, and several weeks later her son, Rollo, a GSD alumnus, joined the staff. The house kept the office going for quite a while. It was big enough to include a five-car garage. Mrs. Thompson, however, did not always see eye-to-eye with her architect son and his professor and proved to be a difficult client. When the house was finished she brought in a decorator friend who shared her taste for chinoiserie. When I visited the house ten years later, the very gracious woman gestured to a long, elegant, wood-siding wall adjacent to the entry and declared, "Look at that! It's taken me ten years to grow enough ivy to cover it. You'd think it was meant for a Coca Cola sign!"

Just as Harry was making plans to leave the office in 1948, Breuer met Bill Landsberg, his former student, on Madison Avenue and offered him a job. He stayed on for seven years and at times, when things were really slow, was the only member of the drafting staff. Later that year, another GSD graduate appeared on the scene and on the letterhead as "Elliot Noyes, Industrial Designer." Noyes had studied architecture at Harvard but his talents ran to graphic and industrial design. "El," as he was known, was starting his own successful career and agreed to share office space with Lajkó, who hoped that Noyes's commercial clients might produce some architectural commissions. During World War II El had been a bomber pilot in England and Thomas J. Watson Jr., the son of the founder of IBM, flew many missions with him as his bombardier. The two became friends and Noyes began to needle Watson about the enormous responsibility he would have in taking over control of the IBM Corporation from his father after the war. He zeroed in particularly on the design aspects of corporate policy—graphics, products, and architecture. This association was later to prove most profitable for IBM, Noyes, and Breuer.

The early years in New York seem to have been somewhat chaotic. The office was small, the practice sparse, and Lajkó was frequently out of town. There was a moment in the late 1940s when Breuer was in South America following up business leads given to him by his Argentinean graduate student, Eduardo Catalano, while Seidler and Noyes, with Rollo Thompson, were trying to keep things together at the office. Connie Breuer was preparing to move into their first, celebrated New Canaan house with her young son when its very audacious cantilever began to sag. This triggered frantic letters from El to one South American capital city after another in an attempt to find Breuer. The office was eventually referred by Lajkó to his old Hungarian engineer friend Nick Farkas in Brooklyn who, after shaking his

Breuer's first house for his family in New Canaan (after Robert Damora F.A.I.A.). Fascinated with the strength of balloon-frame construction, Lajkó pushed it to, and probably beyond, reasonable limits by hanging his porch off what was already a daring cantilever.

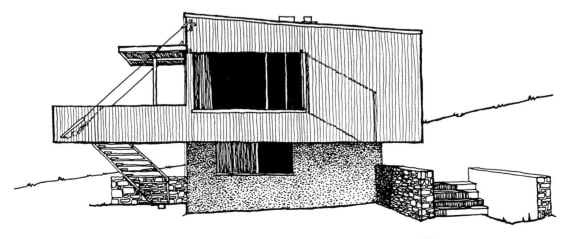

head at the balcony hanging off the cantilever, made some suggestions. Then Harry had to catch up with Breuer again to explain what had to be done to correct the sag and to ask for the transfer of funds so that the contractor could be paid. Even after the structural corrections were made, I. M. Pei has described it to me as "a delightful house, but always bouncy." Louisa Calder was quoted by Murray Drabkin as warning her husband Sandy, "Don't conga on the cantilever!"

Considering the crazy pressures on the young and inexperienced staff during those first few years in New York, the serene series of notable houses they were able to produce with Lajkó seems nothing short of miraculous—from the Robinson house in Williamstown, Massachusetts (perhaps his best house, and certainly his favorite), to the House in the Garden of the Museum of Modern Art (MoMA) in New York. I first saw the MoMA exhibition structure in 1948 and it made a great impression on this young student. Its present occupants are descendants of Nelson Rockefeller, who bought the house from MoMA after the exhibition, sawed it in half, and rebuilt it as a guest house in Pocantico Hills, the Rockefeller estate in Westchester County, New York.

Breuer was soon at work on the first of three houses in Litchfield, Connecticut, for **Rufus Stillman,** a corporate public-relations executive. Rufus eventually became Lajkó's closest friend and most productive client. He and his wife, Leslie, had been living in a Milton, Connecticut, colonial when the couple decided to build their own house on property in nearby Litchfield. Not knowing anything about contemporary architecture, they went to MoMA to get advice and to study work that had been constructed in the museum's garden. They visited the Breuers' house in New Canaan for an interview. Though charmed by their initial meeting, the Stillmans found Lajkó's house "odd" and had tentatively chosen another architect, an Ivy League American like themselves. When it came time to tell Lajkó of their decision, they simply couldn't do it. Returning to the house that they had at first found awkward, Rufus told me of rounding a corner at its approach and saying, "Oh, Leslie, it looks so *marvelous*."

After discussions, Breuer sent his client drawings that Rufus found "dry and unconvincing." Rufus made a small cardboard model in order to better understand the design. When he showed the model to Lajkó he was assured that the house "wouldn't look like that at all!" Rufus had hoped that his house might have a balcony suspended on cables, like Breuer's, but Lajkó said simply, "The wires don't work." The house ended up with a vestigial canopy supported by cables.

The 1950 house included a white concrete-block wall at one end of the swimming pool. Leslie's father, Harry Caesar, commissioned a mural by Alexander Calder for this wall and paid him $350 for it. It was finally agreed that the cartoon that was to serve as its layout contained too many

The House in the Garden of MoMA. The first truly modern house I ever saw drew more visitors than any previous exhibit at the museum. It is still in use on the Rockefeller estate in Westchester County, New York.

Breuer's second New Canaan home (after Ben Schnall). Built just four years after his first, famous residence, he lived in this calm and comfortable masonry monument for twenty-five years.

embarrassing silhouettes and Calder then produced another that was executed. When the Stillmans sold the house, the new owners wouldn't buy the mural and it was painted out. Upon repurchasing this house after selling the second and third, the Stillmans finally had the first, funny Calder executed.

Lajkó's own sense of humor ran to the ribald rather than the intellectual. The Breuers and the Ivan Chermayeffs were holiday dinner guests of the Stillmans some years after they had met when conversation between Sarah Chermayeff and the Stillmans got onto the subject of her pottery and their Queen Anne silver, with Breuer "bored as hell" according to Rufus. Lajkó finally interjected, "If I wasn't sitting here with some of my oldest friends, and if it wasn't Christmas, and if there wasn't a fine snow falling outside, I think I might say 'Shit on Queen Anne!'"

By 1950 Breuer had moved his office to a brownstone on East Thirty-seventh Street, where he kept a pied-à-terre on the third floor, and the staff had begun to take on the personality of the people I was to meet a few years later. Drawings for Breuer's second house in New Canaan were produced in 1951, and it was about as different from the first as two small houses could be. Unlike its high-flying predecessor, the new structure hugged the ground with massive planes of rubble fieldstone and resembled Breuer's 1936 pavilion for Crofton Ganes in England. Lajkó and Connie lived in it until Breuer retired and the couple moved to New York City. Several times he confided to friends that he had made twenty mistakes in designing the second house, but he never told them what those mistakes were. After he sold the house to a wealthy stone contractor, and the office designed for it an elegant expansion and retrofit, he expressed his pleasure at the changes. Perhaps his twenty reservations had mostly to do with the fact that he didn't have enough money to make the house bigger initially.

In three of his early houses in the United States, a remarkable development in Breuer's architectural vocabulary and instinct is evident. The very large Frank house, which he designed with Gropius in 1939 for Pittsburgh, Pennsylvania, was a classic stuccoed "white box" in the European International Style. By 1947 his first house in New Canaan was pushing the limits of taut New England "balloon framing" by using gravity-defying can-

32

The UNESCO advisers on a lunch break during project development in Paris. Gropius is second from left, Breuer is opposite him, and Le Corbusier is behind his trademark eyeglasses.

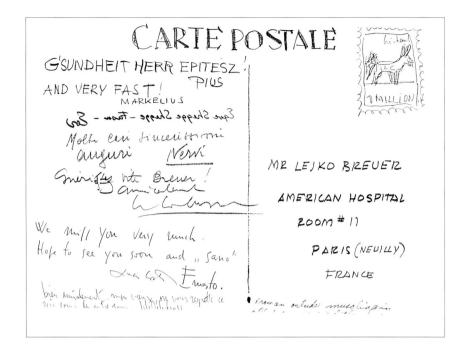

A get-well card from the UNESCO advisory board. It was written on the back of a menu from the Paris restaurant Lapperouse.

tilevers with wire-supported canopy and porch. His final home in 1951, while small by late-twentieth-century standards, is monumental in its massing and execution. Rough and powerfully textured with deep dark shadows, it is the work of the sculptor he once set out to be.

Although the small office followed its string of high-quality houses with Breuer's first institutional buildings at Sarah Lawrence and Vassar Colleges, together with a public library in Grosse Pointe, Michigan, business was slow in the spring of 1952 and Lajkó decided to take a short vacation in Europe. Bill Landsberg was the only one left in the office. He offered to work without pay while he finished the drawings for his own house in Port Washington, New York, and Lajkó readily agreed.

In 1951 the United Nations Scientific, Economic, and Cultural Organization (UNESCO) chose Paris as the site of its new headquarters and a distinguished French architect, Pierre Beaudoin, to design it. To act as its professional advisers in dealing with the architect, UNESCO had assembled a blue-ribbon panel that included Eero Saarinen, Walter Gropius, Sven Markelius, and Le Corbusier. In early 1952 the advisers met in Paris to view Beaudoin's preliminary designs, and by the end of the afternoon had come to two conclusions: they didn't like his design, and they couldn't imagine that they would be satisfied by *anything* that he might come up with.

Someone suggested a drink, and apparently minus Corb, they were all lined up at little café tables under the awning of the Deux Magots when

Breuer came walking down the Boulevard St. Germain. Gropius shouted, "Lajkó, what the hell are you doing here?" Breuer joined them and talked about his sluggish practice and his plans to continue on to Rome the next day. After he left, the group discussed its problem further, and a consensus developed in favor of awarding the commission to an international trio (to ease the slap at Beaudoin). Envisioned were Breuer as design architect, the well-known Italian Pier Luigi Nervi as structural engineer, and Bernard Zehrfuss of Paris as the project administrator.

The next hurdle was how to contact Breuer. No one knew where he was staying. Hurried phone calls to his office in New York the next day enabled the group to track him down and get his agreement to meet with Nervi in Rome, where the two began a collaboration that Lajkó was often to characterize as the most productive association of his life.

Whenever Lajkó and I were later in Paris together, he would suggest a drink at the Deux Magots, "for luck." (Bill Landsberg has pointed out that Breuer's loyalty to that venerable café actually went back much further: "In 1939, after the Frank house was completed, there was very little work at the Gropius and Breuer office. Out of a job, I decided to take my first European trip. I asked Lajkó if there were any places in Europe I should be sure not to miss. His first recommendation was the Deux Magots.")

When Le Corbusier heard that the UNESCO panel had passed over the obvious candidate—himself—he was furious and in protest launched a bitter letter campaign through CIAM that was to destroy whatever friendship Breuer still felt for him from their Paris days in the 1920s. Gropius was once again instrumental in finally securing the commission for Breuer and his team. Rufus Stillman was with Lajkó when Corb died in 1965 and the *New York Times* called for Breuer's contribution to the obituary. He muttered to Stillman: "Oh, I suppose I can think of *something* to say about him . . ." I don't know what he finally contributed to the *Times*, but Bill Landsberg quotes Lajkó as saying earlier of Corb, "He never ate his functionalism as hot as he cooked it"—probably a rough translation of an old Hungarian proverb.

Marcel Breuer at home, 1952.

The Office on Thirty-Seventh Street: 1953–1956

In most of the United States, a young graduate of a professional architecture school must work in the office of one or more licensed architects for three years before he or she can sit for a grueling exam. If passed, it allows the licensee to open an independent practice or, at the very least, to use the title "architect." It is quite usual, particularly in large cities where there are many architectural offices, for such interns to move about from one office to another in order to broaden the range of their own experience. In 1952 I had just returned from a year of study at the Architectural Association in London on a Fulbright Scholarship that followed my 1951 graduation from Cornell's College of Architecture. After working for almost a year in the office of Percival Goodman, the dean of Columbia University's Graduate School of Architecture, I was getting restless.

The Blueprint Company sent a messenger to Goodman's office several times a day for pickup and delivery of drawings that were to be reproduced, and the messenger had several regular customers on his route. One day he inadvertently left a roll at our office that was labeled for delivery to "Marcel Breuer Architect 113 East 37th Street." I stared at the sticker in blank astonishment. It was a little like seeing a package addressed to God. Not only was there a real office bearing Breuer's name, but it was in the neighborhood—and it sent out for blueprints just like we did. The process of demythologization began then and there.

A few months later, in early 1953 when I gave my notice, I made up a list of the offices I would apply to and Breuer was at its head. I didn't really expect to get in, assuming that his staff would be crowded with the top

113 East Thirty-seventh Street. Not much has changed since I first climbed these steps for a job interview many years ago.

graduates of Harvard, but I decided to give it a try. My telephone call was answered by a rather deep female voice with an elegant British accent telling me that Mr. Breuer was in Europe but that I could stop around at any time to drop off a résumé.

One-thirteen East Thirty-seventh Street was, and is, a very ordinary old brownstone on a tree-shaded block between Park and Lexington Avenues. The entrance to the office was off a landing at the top of a long flight of outside stairs behind tall glass doors. Seated behind a busy reception desk was Margaret Firmage, Breuer's secretary, bookkeeper, guardian angel, and eventually, mother to us all. She had a somewhat imposing air as she peered over the eyeglasses alternatively perched on the end of her nose or dangling from a runaway ribbon around her neck. Her voice was, if anything, more elegant in person than over the phone. Peg, or Peggy, as she was known about the office, had been with Breuer since shortly after his move to New York and served him faithfully until retiring to Florida in 1958.

Whenever I walked in—and I think it was the middle of the afternoon—there must have been a lull in the workday. At least Mrs. Firmage had more time on her hands than was required simply to accept my résumé, and we talked. I learned that "Mr. Breuer" divided his time between the New York office and the special office that had been set up in Paris to handle his biggest ongoing commission, the design of the UNESCO headquarters. She had the impression that he might be looking for additional staff on his return in a week's time and promised to show him my résumé. I was to call back after the following week, and as I headed down the brownstone stoop, I thought that this was probably as close as I would ever get to seeing Marcel Breuer. I didn't even have a letter of recommendation from anyone he knew.

When I called back, I expected to have to jog Mrs. Firmage's memory: "You remember, the tall guy with dark curly hair and glasses." Instead, she recognized my name and assured me that Mr. Breuer would like to interview me at my earliest convenience. I have always thought that, whatever might have caught Breuer's eye in my résumé, much more important must have been some nudge of recommendation from Peggy. When I suggested this several years later, she chuckled and denied it.

At any rate, with heart in throat, a fresh haircut, and portfolio in hand, I climbed the brownstone steps again the next day and waited nervously while surveying the busy comings and goings of the seven staff members who used the big front parlor as drafting space, plan room, and reception area in a friendly, informal manner. I was eventually ushered back to Breuer's private office and conference room (through which everyone had to walk on the way to the one bathroom at the rear of the brownstone).

Breuer was just over fifty years old at that time, stood about five feet eight inches tall, and weighed slightly more than he wished. His dark hair was combed carefully in bangs over his high forehead, and his kindly face was already lined with an intricate pattern of creases that radiated from his pale blue eyes. He put me immediately at ease with a few remarks in his soft German-Hungarian accent. (It was hard not to notice the accent but a little difficult to place it, and although Breuer had been speaking English since his move to London almost twenty years earlier, it remained with him for the rest of his life. People in the drafting room often tried to mimic it in an affectionate way but few were ever able to master it.)

He began with "Mrs. Firmage says that you would like to work here" and followed with his favorite phrase of punctuation, "Is it?" (which I always took to be a near-literal translation of the German "Nicht wahr?" or "Not true?"). After assuring him that he had indeed been properly informed, I opened my portfolio and he slowly turned its pages and drawings while carrying on a totally unrelated conversation about my training and European travels. I like to believe that I resisted the normal applicant's impulse to draw the interviewer's attention to the finer points of what he was supposed to be looking at, and it did seem to me that, after all my care in the preparation of my drawings, he spent most of the time looking straight at me rather than at them. At any rate, after one more requested reassurance that I really wanted to work in his office, he said, "Why not?," and I was hired.

B.J. Barnes. This photo dates from her work in the U.N. Headquarters design office.

Since I was free to start work, we agreed on the following Monday. Breuer then introduced me to Bill Landsberg, his "chief draftsman" and principal assistant. Bill transmitted Breuer's salary offer, which I accepted with no discussion. I was walked around the office and met everyone on the staff that very afternoon. In addition to Landsberg, they included **Belva Jane (B.J.) Barnes, Hamilton (Ham) Smith, Herbert (Herb) Beckhard,** and **Jack Freidin.**

Bill was clearly the senior person in the office and claims to have been the first person to speak to Lajkó when Breuer arrived in the GSD drafting room in 1937. B.J. was acid-tongued and had almost as much experience as Bill. She would only take orders from Lajkó and not always from him. When I referred to B.J. as a "maiden lady" recently, Bill said that he would hesitate about that term since "her propensity for telling raunchy jokes in mixed company seemed inconsistent with that description." He went on to say that, although he liked her, "her acerbic personality put off many people" and remembered Breuer once muttering under his breath, "There are times when I could cheerfully strangle her."

B.J. maintained a position of respect based principally on her ability as a drafting machine. **Bobbie Neski** says, "She would arrive in the morning, carefully roll up the neatly pressed sleeves of her Brooks Brothers blue shirt, and start drawing at the upper-left-hand corner of a sheet of drawing paper and, while lobbing verbal bombshells around the drafting room, never stop until the paper was filled with her exquisite linework."

Ham had joined the office only a few months before I did, having been hired on Eero Saarinen's recommendation to direct a new project for Saint John's Abbey in Collegeville, Minnesota. Herb had been in the office a bit longer than Ham and was working on house drawings.

I had picked a good time to apply to the office. Breuer's practice was on a roll that would carry it for another twenty years of great productivity. A number of staff members had recently left. (Rollo Thompson set up his own office; Dale Byrd took his fabulous rendering skills elsewhere; and Beverly Green, the first woman and first African-American to be licensed in her home state of Illinois, had become sick and died shortly after her departure.)

Within the following few months, the size of the staff almost doubled. Dave Crane was later to become known as one of America's principal city planners, but he didn't last long in the office. (I remember Bill, almost ashen-faced, informing me after Breuer had rushed out the door to catch a plane to Europe, "Lajkó just told me to fire Dave Crane. I don't get it. He's one of the best draftsmen we've got." We never did get it, but there was a rumor

Dave Crane, Herb Beckhard, and Ham Smith at the corner of Park Avenue and Thirty-seventh Street in 1954. This was even before construction of the Pan Am Building.

41

that Breuer had heard that Dave had made some slighting remark about the office at a cocktail party. If there was one thing Lajkó couldn't stand it was disloyalty. Herb thought that Crane had probably not followed orders on the second Harnischmacher house.) We were also joined by Phil Thiel, who eventually became a distinguished professor of architectural theory in Seattle. Bobbie and **Joe Neski** turned up at about the same time.

As I soon learned, the Breuer office was considered one of the best places for a young architect to work in New York City. The salaries were somewhat lower than in the bigger shops, but the work was stimulating and the company very entertaining. Breuer had a good eye for people and treated them fairly. The old creaky floors and walled-off fireplaces gave the office a real feeling of "home," and it was easy to stay on after hours and get to know all these new friends.

Jack Freidin described our employer about as well as anyone when he said to me, "Breuer expressed in his person, as in his work, a certain economy. Everything about him had a meaning at one level or another—nothing extraneous. He was soft-spoken and reticent, which made you pay attention to what he said, and what he said was significant. This quality even extended to the way he looked and dressed, the way he combed his hair—making the most with the least—nothing wasted."

I hadn't had much inclination to examine the contents of Breuer's office during my interview but I later noted that it contained several items of special interest. On a prominent corner of his desk was an exquisite model of the recently completed lakeshore cottage for Leslie Stillman's father, Harry Caesar, in Lakeville, Connecticut. It was clearly one of Lajkó's favorites, and a later visit on my part confirmed to me the simple brilliance of its design.

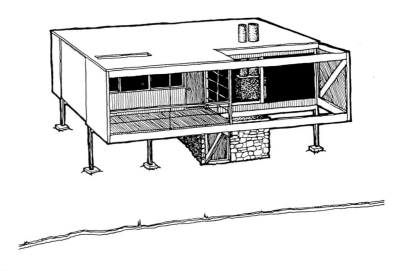

The Caesar cottage. Its shuttered view of the lake is shielded from nearby neighbors. A model of this Lakeville, Connecticut, retreat always sat at the corner of Breuer's desk.

The Neumann house. This brilliant house in Croton-on-Hudson is my personal favorite. Its red, blue, and white concrete-block walls glide out to, and sometimes beyond, the edge of the roof plane and are placed on a flag-stone platform defined by undulat-ing rubblestone.

On a side table stood a thick piece of frosted Plexiglas into which a staggered pattern of round lenses had been ground. It was meant to recall a dazzling window from Breuer's Heinersdorff house in Berlin of 1929.

On the wall was a colored floor plan of Breuer's new house for George and "Scarves by Vera" Neumann in Croton-on-Hudson, New York. The composition of rigorous orthogonal planes of brilliant red-, blue-, and white-painted concrete block contrasted with the graceful curved retaining walls of rubblestone and resembled the paintings of Kandinsky and Mondrian, from which it may have drawn inspiration. (Of all of Breuer's houses, the Neumann house, with its unbroken wall planes that slid out to the edge of the overhanging roof plane above, had the greatest influence on my own personal vocabulary.)

The conference table in Breuer's office was a slab of granite on a set of stainless-steel legs joined at top and bottom into a continuous X-frame. Although it resisted force applied directly to either side, it had a disconcerting tendency to twist if pushed on an angle, after which it would swing back in recovery with a barely audible hum. Joe Neski called it the "tuning fork" table and once teased Lajkó about it, who replied, "But it's very interesting." Elsewhere were various knock-off versions of the cantilevered tubular-steel chair, since no one made the original anymore (Wohnbedarf in Switzerland was the favored supplier). Each seat was carefully covered with a loose, flat Naugahyde cushion; Breuer was tired of wearing holes in his trousers on the abrasive caning. There were also several prototypes of laminated-wood side chairs and tables that had never gone into production. (I discovered one of the side tables in a "modern antique" store in New York's

Soho in the mid-1990s, and the proprietor was ecstatic at my confirmation of its provenance. Most of the other laminated chairs are in storage in **Christine Benglia**'s loft, salvaged from the trash heap of an office move. The Caesar model is in the Bauhaus-Archiv, and Herb Beckhard has the Neumann floor plan.)

On the third floor, where Breuer maintained a small apartment for nights when he couldn't get home to New Canaan, there were two very special short Isokon reclining chairs. When Lajkó had left England, he brought along the design drawings but no example, and the chairs were not in production in the United States. Wanting a pair for his first house in Cambridge, he had them fashioned by hand with great difficulty, considering that factory jigs were normally necessary to bend the laminated frames. This unique pair, which had ebonized rather than natural wood frames, made its way to New York and then to Breuer's Thirty-seventh Street apartment. When Breuer later gave up the apartment, he offered these museum pieces to Herb Beckhard and myself. I still have mine, several times refinished; the frame of Herb's broke and he threw it away.

When I turned up for work on that Monday in May 1953, I was assigned by Bill Landsberg to a drafting table next to Ham Smith, who began to fill me in on Saint John's Abbey, the project he had been working on for the previous month and that was to occupy him on and off for almost ten years.

Saint John's Abbey and University, in Collegeville, near Saint Cloud, Minnesota, about an hour's drive northwest of Minneapolis, is the largest Benedictine abbey in the world. It was founded by monks from the Abbey of Maria Laach in the Black Forest just after the American Civil War. They found the beautiful Minnesota countryside, with its low hills and frequent lakes, to be similar to what they had left behind in Germany. Over the course of a century, the monks erected severe brick buildings in a stiff Romanesque style. The abbey and its men's university prospered, although building restrictions during World War II and a conflict within the community over what should be built had stopped new construction for twenty years. Then came the G.I. Bill, and by the 1950s the buildings were straining a tight series of interlocking courtyards that had outgrown the vision of their founders. There had been a few attempts at grafting on modern additions designed by local architects, but it was clear that a radical solution was needed.

Abbot Baldwin Dworschak was not unmindful of the historic role of the Benedictines in the development of Gothic architecture, starting with Abbot Suger at St. Denis. He was advised by a building committee that was headed by Father John Eidenschink; guided by its one architect member, Father Cloud Meinberg; and prodded by **Frank Kacmarcik**, a graphic designer then working at the college who eventually became a brother in the order. Letters of invitation were sent to a dozen architects from around the world who either had specific experience in the design of churches or an ability to handle comprehensive planning. Five were eventually invited for interviews: Breuer, Gropius, Richard Neutra, Barry Byrne, and Joseph Murphy. Breuer was selected for the job in April 1953 and was told much later that it was his apparent humility that had won the hearts of the religious community. Breuer was mild-mannered, kind, and could be gentle, but they were wrong about the humility. Stanley Abercrombie told me, most pointedly, "He hid his ego behind a screen of shyness, but he liked the idea that he was the best."

In addition, I was told by Frank Kacmarcik on a recent trip to the abbey that Gropius, during his interview, and once more the mentor, had said, "I'm too old to see this thing through to completion. I really came out here to urge that you choose Breuer." Kacmarcik went on to say that Barry Byrne had volunteered at the time, "You've got a good group of architects here, any one of whom could handle your commission with distinction, but only one is a true artist—Breuer." Lajkó really was an architect's architect.

Saint John's asked first for a master plan that would allow it to break out of its self-imposed straightjacket. It was a planning challenge that took us months to resolve, and the ultimate solution was described by Breuer in terms of the classic Chinese puzzle in which one piece must be moved before getting at the next. There was a great deal of programmatic data that had to be digested and analyzed, and Ham and I divided it up between us. The existing church was a huge roadblock, physically and emotionally. The abbey was a leader in the liturgical reform movement, which was to culminate in Vatican II, and many members of the community felt that something totally new was needed. We met less opposition than expected to our suggestion that the old church would have to be replaced. By early July there was an elaboration, at scale, of Breuer's first sketch for the pattern of growth, and versions of it were being mailed back and forth to New York, Paris, and Collegeville.

Lajkó was living in France with Connie and their young son Tamas (Tom) at the time, since the UNESCO job was very demanding and it gave the family a chance to sample life in Breuer's favorite city. When I had a similar opportunity ten years later, Lajkó gave me two pieces of advice: "Don't rent a summer house in Normandy—it rains all the time" and "If you are to pick up your child after school, don't forget."

He was referring to this oft-told tale: Connie was quite sick one morning shortly after the Breuers' arrival in Paris and Lajkó was assigned to drive Tom across town to the French-American school in his jazzy new MG. Promising to return promptly at 3:30, he proceeded to the office and a demanding first day of work with Pier Luigi Nervi. When he next looked at his watch it was 5:00! Connie's reaction to his telephone call was pre-

The UNESCO drafting room in Paris. Breuer is at the drawing board on the left.

dictably frantic, and Lajkó quickly drove to the school where the cute little boy in a sailor suit was nowhere to be found. Returning home, he notified the police, who asked Breuer to stay by the phone and await their report. After hours of agonizing uncertainty, Lajkó returned to his car, parked two blocks away, intent on conducting his own search. There, sitting by the car at the curb, was Tom—who didn't remember exactly where he lived but recognized the bright new MG as he had ambled back across town, over a bridge, and into familiar territory.

Breuer would turn up in New York every month or so, but in between, in those days before faxes and electronic mail, we had to rely on airmail, very infrequent phone calls, and telegrams. We would compose long careful letters to accompany the Friday night shipment of the latest sketches and then wait for over a week before the annotated letter and drawings were returned. Breuer didn't have an English-speaking secretary in the Paris office so he relied upon handwritten notes to convey his intent. Meanwhile, the planning process had to continue and we would turn our attention to other aspects of the master plan and try to avoid the occasional and inevitable crossing of comments. Eventually Lajkó, and Ham (who made trips to Minnesota when Breuer was unavailable), brought the community around to a course of action that, when finally and formally presented in January 1954, was wholeheartedly approved.

Travel back and forth to Europe in pre-jet times usually involved up to eighteen hours in a propeller plane, and Bill Landsberg would drive out to

Idlewild Airport to pick up Breuer after each grueling flight. According to Bill, "Despite the weariness of such an exhausting trip, Lajkó always wanted a complete rundown on everything that had transpired during his absence, which I would give him on the drive back to the city."

It was during one of Breuer's mid-1950s absences in Paris that the office received a telephone call from a young woman in Canada asking whether Lajkó would be available for an interview the following week. It concerned an office building in New York and Philip Johnson had given her Breuer's name. The logistics could not be worked out. The woman's name was Phyllis Lambert, and it was Mies van der Rohe who designed the Seagram Building.

Breuer's method of design was, and remains for me, rather mysterious. It began, usually after studying the needs of the client, with an inspiration as to form that sprang from his particular instinct. To this would be gradually added refinements and changes developed during his discussions and sketches at our drafting tables. It is very difficult to sort out, particularly many years later, who contributed what, when, and how to the final mix. I remember working on the plan of the new Saint John's Abbey church, particularly the Brothers' Chapel in its lower level and the chapter house next door. Ham worked closely with Lajkó on the form of the church and the development of the great concrete bell tower, or "banner," as it came to be shaped. Breuer's notes from Paris were addressed sometimes to one of us, sometimes to the other. In any case, those first eight months in the office were dominated by the study, design, and preparation of what was to become a monument of modern architecture. It was one of the most exciting moments in my professional career; at the time, we took it as routine.

Designing is one thing; salesmanship is another. Breuer never felt comfortable selling himself, but he was remarkably successful at selling his ideas. He frequently cloaked his argument in favor of a particular shape or form in functional justification; clients appreciated the latter and admired the former. With his instinct for how best to convey architectural concepts to laymen, Breuer was not content to present the diagrams or block model that might have satisfied the requirements of the master-planning assignment he had been given. We developed a fully thought-out architectural and structural concept for the church (Lajkó had asked for preliminary structural input from Pier Luigi Nervi in Rome), and the building today is very similar to the model that was shipped west in late December 1953. It generated great support, which was certainly needed during the years of fundraising and construction that followed.

One of the brilliant features of the church is the banner, which had its origins in purely functional requirements. It was intended to stand as a campanile for the abbey's five great bells and was to reflect sunlight through the

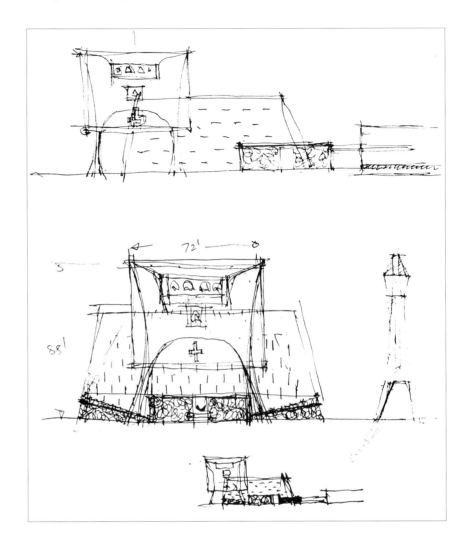

The Saint John's Abbey church banner. These are a few of Breuer's early studies for the structure, which was to support the bells of the church and reflect sunlight back through the north-facing stained glass.

stained glass of the main facade of the building, which, because of the orientation imposed by the master plan, faced north. After sketching many intriguing forms, including one that looked like a very robust, squared-off ping-pong racquet, Breuer settled on a concrete banner that appears stretched between extensions of four huge legs. These join in arches below the banner and serve as a symbol of entry. The banner heralds the abbey as seen from great distances across the flat Minnesota farmland. Shortly before his death in 1996, Abbot Baldwin told me that Lajkó had said that the inspiration for the banner had come from the churches he had seen on his sailing trips through the Greek islands, in which the bells are often hung in wall openings.

The north facade of the church is made up of a deep hexagonal grid of concrete, framing individual fields of stained glass. But long before that, as we were finishing the drawings for the model maker, I had laid out for Lajkó's approval a larger grid of staggered rectangles and, as a further choice for him to make, filled each one symmetrically with a different pattern of window mullions. Despite my urging, and to my great surprise, he refused to narrow the choice and said the model and drawings should include my entire patchwork of textures. He may have used one of his favorite expressions, "You know, Bob, zis *could* be very nice . . . is it?" (Of this frequent turn of phrase, **Allen Cunningham** wrote me recently that it "covered every possibility; e.g: it *could* be very nice if you work on it for, say, ten more years . . . or it may not. Depending on your mood the comment could leave you either totally devastated or walking on air!")

Abbot Baldwin described Breuer as being a very good listener who absorbed everything while Ham "scribbled" furiously to capture it all for the written record. Apparently Ham kept good minutes, for the abbot went on to say that Breuer was only an occasional visitor later on since "he learned everything from Ham's reports." On one of their early trips to the abbey, Ham and Lajkó found their connecting flight from Minneapolis canceled by a snowstorm and were fortifying themselves in the bar of the railroad station while waiting for the next train. An aggressive hostess tried to make conversation with Lajkó, asked his name, and was told "Smith." When Ham's turn came, he repaid the favor with "Breuer."

We were in the last stages of refining the shape of the church when a much folded and sketched-over print of its floor plan arrived by mail from Father Joachim, a member of the abbey's building committee. He announced with triumph that he had discovered the proportional system that was obviously governing the design: the center line of the high altar was at the "golden mean" of the length of the nave. He also demonstrated that the length of the north facade bore exactly the same "golden" proportion to that of the south facade and that the angles of the sides of our trapezoid were within two degrees of Pythagoras's magical, pentagonal thirty-six degrees. (The "golden mean," or "section," can be constructed geometrically and approximates the Fibonacci sequence of additive numbers whereby most living things such as sunflower pods and snail shells grow: 0, 1, 1, 2, 3, 5, 8, 13, 21, 34, and so on until it smooths out at 1 is to 1.62 as .62 is to 1. Architects and mathematicians have long contended that this natural proportion is inherently beautiful to the human eye.) We were astonished, since nothing was further from our thoughts, but sure enough, when we made measurements, it was clear that he was almost exactly right. Breuer was extremely amused when this was reported to him and we changed the dimensions so that the calculation would be exact.

Once the master plan was approved in the spring of 1954, the monks decided to move ahead with the first stage of construction, the monastic wing, which was to be attached to one corner of the existing monastic quadrangle. I worked with Ham on the drawings and eventually helped out on the building's interior design by selecting a large series of liturgical images that we enlarged as black-and-white photo-murals for important walls throughout the building. They are still in place, slightly yellowed and sometimes torn, but treated with continuing respect by the community.

Originally, the building was to be defined by a deep concrete frame three stories high, with an infill of windows and red brick to match the existing brick buildings of the monastery. But one of the abbey's nearby neighbors, the Cold Springs Granite Company, had offered to supply split-face granite block, which was left over from the production of more monumental slabs. Red brick was kept for some inside floors and walls but everyone welcomed the virtual gift of this noble material, which was used in the end walls and spandrels of the monastic wing. The monks began to move into the almost completed building at the start of the following academic year, in the fall of 1955.

There was one point in the composition at which a concrete wall, probably determined by the future church, was destined to meet a granite wall at what both Ham and I felt would be an awkward corner. Ham wanted to extend the concrete wall beyond the intersection and let the granite hit it from behind. I suggested a slit window to separate the two materials. When we couldn't agree, we referred the question to Lajkó. Breuer suggested, "Why don't we just let them meet at the corner?" I burst out with, "You can't do *that.*" After an awkward pause, Lajkó smiled and said, "Of *course* I can." In one beautiful small room of the monastic wing used as the abbot's chapel, measuring only eleven by thirteen feet, Breuer contributed a magical mixture of some of his favorite themes, which often involved the surprising juxtaposition of the fine with the ordinary: a waxed, red-brick floor, white-painted concrete-block walls, a gilded rough concrete-slab ceiling, bright blue doors, custom-designed furnishings of solid teak, and a "stained glass" window in shades ranging from gray to white by his old friend Josef Albers. Further design work on the abbey church was put off until January 1956 when its structure could be joined to the newly completed monastic wing.

By 1953 the sister institution of Saint John's in Bismarck, North Dakota—a convent and girls' school called the Annunciation Priory—had outgrown its temporary quarters in downtown Bismarck and had been offered a handsome price for its real estate. The sisters decided to invest in a barren, windswept hillside well out of town. Since many of the nuns had come from Minnesota and were familiar with Breuer's work there, they needed little added encouragement to recruit the modern master, but they did get it from Frank Kacmarcik, who had become an independent art consultant, and Ray Hermanson, a local architect, who asked Breuer on behalf of the sisters if he would be interested in adding to his Catholic portfolio. This was quite brave

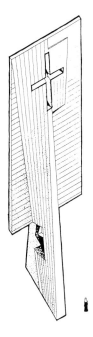

The bell tower at the Annunciation Priory in Bismarck, North Dakota. Ham Smith's drawing of the complex sculptural composition shows the twisting planes in concrete.

of them since their local bishop, a former plumbing contractor, was opposed to modern design. Breuer accepted the commission, and Ham and I began work on its master plan just as the drawing phase of the monastic wing for Saint John's was winding down. The program was quite detailed and I paid at least one visit to the convent as I tried to understand the difference between a student, a novice, and a postulant. While there, I learned of another, subtle distinction in the housing pattern. Whenever any girl attending the secondary school indicated an interest in becoming a nun, she was quickly moved in with other girls who had indicated a similar interest.

In 1954 we produced the master plan of what was to be one of Lajkó's most romantic compositions: a cruciform series of interlocking wings forming a rectangular acropolis astride the North Dakota hills that was identified for miles around by a tall, magnificent bell tower defined in part by warped surfaces of rough concrete. I had left the project by the time it came to designing the tower and church and I see Ham's fine hand in each, but he gives all the credit for the design of their form to Breuer. To the extent that architectural collaboration can ever be understood, Breuer's method began with his ideas, which, after being carefully drawn up for his review as best we could understand his intention, could then be elaborated or even amended by suggestions from the staff. His critique of our ideas became the teaching tool whereby we all learned his language. Remarkably, he even used some of the same phrases my own father employed as I was growing up: "We don't do that" and "That's very nice."

51

Sometime during my first year in the office, Lajkó received a commission to design a house from a family named Snower in Kansas City, Kansas. What made the challenge interesting, but ultimately defeating, was the site, which was located on a street corner in a posh residential development with a very tight set of design guidelines, a design review board, and the stated intent to maintain the "traditional" architectural character of the neighborhood. The Snowers wanted to know whether it was possible to design a Breuer house that could meet all the community requirements of steep roofs, small windows, and so forth. Breuer accepted the challenge in the spirit in which it was offered, and after Dave Crane was unexpectedly fired, I ended up finishing the working drawings. It was a fine house but not famous, one of those "closet jobs" that never got published.

In 1956 Breuer was asked by the Tile Council of America to design a "Bathroom of the Future," which would use lots of ceramic tile and be featured in full-color industry ads in the architectural press. Lajkó designed a bathroom far more spacious than any he tried to sell to his house clients, and it was built in a photographer's studio near the office. It had a full-height sliding glass door that led out to a patio filled with flowers and shrubs. No one had been particularly interested in this blatantly commercial venture until Bill Landsberg mentioned casually as he was leaving the office to observe the shoot that Lajkó had suggested that a nude model be on call to enliven interest in the proposal. Suddenly there was a rush of volunteers to "help" Bill with his assignment, and he took a few of the staff along. For years the office photo files contained several eight-by-ten-inch color transparencies of the model posed in such a way that the mullion of the sliding window covered enough of her to render her charmingly decent as she stepped in and out of the walled patio.

The office was small enough that anyone might be asked to pitch in and help on a project that was short on time and faced with a deadline. B.J. Barnes and Joe Neski were working with our Dutch associate architect— addressed only by his last name, Elzas—on a new department store to replace the bombed-out De Bijenkorf in downtown Rotterdam. I became quite friendly with Elzas, who sat at a drafting board right next to mine, and years later, at his request, I designed the parking garage that De Bijenkorf built as an adjunct to the store. For some reason, perhaps because I'd mentioned my interest in graphic design, I was asked to create a cover for the spiral-bound booklet of drawings that became our standard method of presentation to clients. Since De Bijenkorf means "beehive" in Dutch, and Lajkó had already employed its hexagons to determine the stone pattern on the facade of the building, I combined the title of the project with a hexagonal symbol that we used later as an etched device on the glass doors. For the letterform of the title, I chose a shadowed Egyptian type style with heavy slab serifs that was popular in one of my favorite magazines, the *Architectural Review* of London. As the working drawings of the project progressed, Lajkó decided to use the same letterform as building signage over the store's main entrance on the Coolsingle and I made the drawing for its execution in heavy three-dimensional back-lit letters of teak, each about two feet tall.

The Coolsingle was a new, monumental boulevard laid out by the post-war Rotterdam city planners to traverse a war-ravaged wasteland. A new stock exchange had already been built across from the De Bijenkorf site. It conformed to a building line that included a rectangular jog that narrowed the street to create some concept of urban gateway. Lajkó's plan for the department store was a grand travertine box, and he had no intention of adding a projecting "bump," as he called it, just to satisfy the city planners. Instead, he turned to his old friend, the sculptor Naum Gabo, and asked for a piece of heroic sculpture that would project from the wall. The final version actually stands on the sidewalk in front of the building and has been accepted as a Rotterdam landmark—although architect and critic Bob Geddes told me that some who were more sensitive to the delicate urban fabric of the surroundings were not particularly pleased by it.

A portion of the north facade, which was not blocked by adjacent structures and was used for offices, was sheathed in an elegant glass curtain wall that Lewis Mumford singled out in *The New Yorker* as one of the most successful creations of its type. Printed praise from America's dean of architectural critics delighted Lajkó.

Signage at the main entry to De Bijenkorf (after Frits Monshouwer). The huge back-lit teak letters were derived from one of my suggestions.

De Bijenkorf. This department store in Rotterdam is sheathed in travertine slabs, some of which are cut to a pattern of hexagons suggested by the beehive from which the store takes its name.

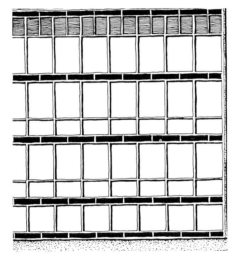

De Bijenkorf office facade (after Frits Monshouwer). Lewis Mumford singled out this subtle curtain-wall composition for special praise. It is tucked away behind the big travertine box.

Among my pleasures in reading the *Architectural Review* were the regular articles by Nicolete Gray about building signage in which she often noted the unexpected quirks that sometimes occurred due to a sign-painter's personal whim. She included a photo of our big teak letters in her 1960 book *Lettering on Buildings* and was amused by my report that the carpenter who made the letters had "improved" on my execution drawing by adding a serif to the bottom point of the *N*, which, obviously, the architect had forgotten.

54

Herb Beckhard had completed the design work on the Levy house in Princeton, New Jersey, and was in charge of a series of projects stimulated by visits that Andy Gagarin, president of the Torrington Manufacturing Company, made to Rufus Stillman's house. Rufus served as vice president for personnel of Torrington at the time. There was a factory for Torrington in Oakville, Ontario, a high-school gym in Litchfield, Connecticut, and two elementary schools in Bantam and Northfield, Connecticut, near the factory, where Rufus and Andy had political clout. And finally, there was a huge new house in Litchfield for Andy Gagarin himself.

The Connecticut schools were built in association with O'Connor & Kilham, a large firm located in the "Architects' Building" at 101 Park Avenue and specializing in school design. Jack Freidin was assigned to work in their office as our representative while the working drawings were being prepared and has written to me, "I felt like the advance guard defending the sacred designs from the depredations of the Philistines; and how proud I was when Breuer would pay his periodic visit to that vast drafting room and come directly over to my desk to review the project's progress and development."

The Gagarin house was budgeted at the then palatial cost of twenty-five dollars per square foot, and Andy had given Lajkó virtual carte blanche in its design. It is a grand house in every way and I remember the awe with which a group of the staff first saw it just before completion. With its teak floors, apparent miles of rubblestone walls, bush-hammered concrete fireplace, and signature steel-slat suspended stairway descending to the swimming pool deck, it was almost too much in those Calvinist times. There is a peculiar "kink" in the glass wall at the entry that Breuer had improvised in response to a request by the client. According to Herb, it is one of the strengths of the design. But that kink, and even the lavishness of the house itself, provoked muttered criticism that was very rare in the drafting room. We felt somehow that artists like Breuer worked best under some sort of imposed discipline.

I helped Jack Freidin draft a revised version of Breuer's Wellfleet cottage in 1953 for Edgar Stillman, Rufus's brother. (Jack doesn't remember that I worked with him on the project but I recognize my scale figures in the published elevations.) Jack recalls, "One morning, Breuer came over to my drafting table and showed me the back of an envelope with some shaky marks that at first glance looked like chicken scratches. He said it was a plan for a cottage to be built on the dunes in Wellfleet. It looked like he drew it while driving over a rocky road, and when the drawing was getting too close to the envelope's edge he just shrunk things. There were a few basic dimensions included. I drew it up following the dimensions and was amazed to see how it all fitted together and worked. The cottage was one of my favorite projects. It was mine alone to develop and detail, and I drafted it with tender loving care. I composed each sheet carefully and was intent on the quality of the linework. To this day, I can feel the bite of the lead on the white tracing paper; it wasn't plastic 'lead' on slippery plastic 'paper' then. I remember selecting the 6H lead I used for the cross-hatch work to represent the screening on the elevations." (Herb Beckhard used to call Freidin "Jack the ripper" because his needle-point leads frequently sliced through the tracing paper.)

When it came time for the cottage to be built, Bill Landsberg wandered around the changing dunes trying to get a fix on where the property lines were in the wild pine forest, which Lajkó had described only verbally. According to Bill, "The clue that helped us was the remains of a barbecue fire the Stillmans had left on the previous weekend." The contractor concluded that this "indicated the client's preference for the location of the house." Apparently he was right, for there it was built.

The office was very pleased to see our boss honored with the first comprehensive publication of his work in 1955: *Sun and Shadow,* which was edited by his friend Peter Blake, who had also written MoMA's catalog of the House in the Garden when he was the institution's curator for architecture and design. Things were moving so fast in the rapidly expanding practice that we lost track of all that was going on and who was responsible for what. Breuer came up with solutions so quickly and sold them so effectively that projects progressed through the various stages of production with a speed that would be astounding in other offices and led to a very efficient, and profitable, operation. Herb remembers him saying "You don't talk about architecture, you *do* it." With hindsight, I realize this was a unique moment in architectural history. But at the time, it was just a most enjoyable job.

In the summer of 1955, I took a vacation on Nantucket Island with Don Claudy, a good friend from junior college and high-school days. Don had finished law school and service in the Air Force and was working in Washington, D.C. I proposed that we drop in on the Breuers in Wellfleet, since I had an open invitation. We had lunch with Connie and Lajkó on the screened porch of their beautiful summer home, which I knew very well from drawings but was seeing for the first time. Lajkó was decked out in his summer American weekend costume—chambray shirt and chino slacks—quite a change from his elegant hand-tailored suits. Although Don knew nothing about architecture and Breuer had a well-known aversion to lawyers, I was struck by the ease with which the conversation flowed and the genuine good spirits that surrounded those few hours out of context. As we were driving off after saying goodbye, I remember Don exclaiming, "Boy, are you lucky! That is one helluva boss."

The Alworth (Starkey) house. The main living areas are bracketed between huge laminated-wood beams above and below that define an uninterrupted view of Lake Superior in Duluth, Minnesota.

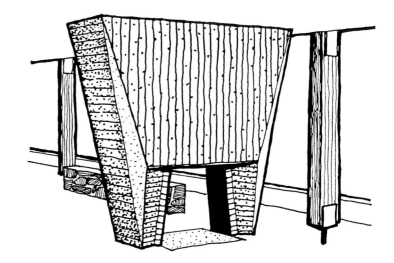

The Alworth (Starkey) house (after Arthur Siegel). Lajkó gave me undeserved credit for the shape of this outdoor fireplace, which supports the main one in the living room above.

Roy Halvorsen was the wealthy self-made "Christmas Tree King" of Duluth, Minnesota, thanks to his discovery that a perfect little freezable tabletop tree could be found at the very top of the otherwise useless, twisted evergreens that grew in the frozen marshes of northern Minnesota where he loved to hunt. His daughter, June Alworth, had been widowed in the early 1950s and left with two young children; Roy thought the design and construction of a new house might lighten her sadness. They chose a steep hillside with a panoramic view of Lake Superior, and Lajkó conceived one of his most spectacular binuclear houses. The living section was bracketed between huge laminated wood girders above the roof and below the floor. The girders were, in turn, visibly bolted to laminated wood columns that touched the open terrace below on delicate steel pins. The two-story bedroom section rested on the ground, and the whole was tied together with bridges and railings. The house, often identified with June's second married name, Starkey, was published in *Time* and the professional press.

Herb had started work on the Alworth house when Lajkó added the Gagarin and second Harnischmacher residences to his load, and I was asked to help out on Alworth. I must have been feeling more secure in the office by that time for, when differences arose between Herb and myself, I asked Bill Landsberg to clarify our roles: "It's either his job or mine!" Herb withdrew to his other projects and I finished the working drawings. After that, Lajkó rarely asked two of his associates, as we were soon to be named, to try to work together. It was difficult enough for each of us to satisfy him, and each project from then on was usually structured as a partnership between just one of us and Lajkó.

The lower terrace of the house needed some concrete to support a massive masonry fireplace in the living room above. Lajkó suggested that perhaps the clients could use an outdoor barbecue, and the support quickly became one more distinctive Breuer fireplace. Searching for a formal precedent for some architectural element years later, Lajkó said to me, "You know, Bob . . . like that fireplace you designed for under the Starkey house." It happens that I have a very vivid memory of the sketch he left at my board for that fireplace, but I was pleased that he would give me credit.

Florence Knoll, design chief for the famous husband-wife furniture firm of Knoll Associates, had been hired in 1953 by J. Robert Oppenheimer, the director of the Institute for Advanced Study in Princeton, New Jersey, to do the interiors of a new group of townhouses planned for visiting scholars. She had once worked in the old Gropius/Breuer office in Cambridge, and in 1954 she suggested Breuer as architect to Oppenheimer. There were to be about one hundred units in one- and two-story buildings, with enough land for a gracious setting but not enough money for more than rather spartan living quarters. Ham had worked on the site plan but the architecture was turned over to me—my first job with Lajkó that started from scratch. The project moved smoothly. I was responsible for the organization of all the drawings, as well as for drafting most of them with **Jay Ritchie,** who had just joined the firm and was to stay for three years. I decided to arrange the pages of details in what I thought a logical and useful way, combining vertical strips of sections with alternating partial elevations interrupted by detailed plan sections. It was the sort of nuance that only an architect could appreciate. I was, therefore, more than pleased when Lajkó, reviewing them, turned to me and said, "This is a very beautiful set of drawings. I wish I could draw as well."

Gabriel Sedlis, who worked for Breuer from 1956 until 1959, remembers that whenever Breuer took soft black pencil to tracing paper at someone's board he was very careful in making later erasures: "He always put a piece of paper over the lower part of the drawing as he gently used the eraser so as not to smudge the rest of the drawing."

John Johansen said, "He couldn't draw worth a damn. I could draw better than he could with my left hand—but it was *all* in his mind's eye!" Lajkó made a similar but not identical point when he once, rather self-deprecatingly, explained to Allen Cunningham, "I just have a good eye." Allen disagrees with Johansen about Lajkó's drawing ability: "I see a drawing style that Herb adopted along with Richard Meier and others which is a wobbly line (action drawing?) technique which is evocative, highly descriptive and epitomizes for me a characteristic akin to 'thinking aloud.' It has a potency and directness which communicates an idea in progress rather than one fully resolved and therein lies the attraction . . . Breuer drew like an artist; he was not a draftsman."

The Princeton townhouses used Breuer's residential vernacular plus the red brick of the Georgian institute across the road. We tried hard to give them the feel of a home, despite the fact that they would house transient occupants, and each apartment had a fireplace and private terrace or balcony. I sat in on a few of the review sessions and it was clear that Lajkó and Oppenheimer got along well.

During construction, Jay Ritchie reported a building code requirement that would have put an ugly gooseneck vent pipe in the middle of every terrace. A meeting was arranged with the contractor, the building department, the mechanical engineer, and the client to hash things out. Sewer-pipe venting was discussed in confusing and acrimonious detail, and Oppenheimer followed the discussion with the same attention that he must have used in directing the making of the atomic bomb. At the end, with everyone at wit's end, he quietly summed up the two opposing viewpoints and announced, "Under the circumstances we will have no option but to sue the borough of Princeton." The building department backed down.

Another construction problem developed concerning sand in the pipes that were used for hot-water radiant heat under the floor slabs. The contractor was at fault for not having put protective covering over their ends while stored at the job site prior to installation. Breuer used the occasion to ask for a full-time project representative, or "clerk o' the works" (CO'W) as they were called in those days, and taught me a lesson I've never forgotten: "I want a clerk with so much spare time on his hands that he will poke around the site and discover problems before they happen, rather than running around at the contractor's beck and call putting out fires and checking only those things that the contractor wants him to see."

Breuer was unhappy with the appearance of the era's commercially made "gravel stop"—the band of metal that tops the fascia or edge of a flat roof and seals the edge of the waterproof roofing. We specified a bent profile of stainless steel with hidden expansion joints, and Jay, who had been enlisted as CO'W, had noticed a great deal of "oil canning," or visual crinkling, on the sunny side of each building as it was nearing completion. He did some calculations and reported to Lajkó on his next site visit that the thermal expansion of stainless steel in the sunlight was more than our expansion joints had allowed for. Without acknowledging any concern, Breuer, who always trusted his own "hands-on" experience rather than mathematical calculations, apparently observed the same phenomenon during the day as the sun moved to the opposite side of each building. Still, he could only bring himself to say, at the end of his visit, "Well, Jay, I suspect you are right in theory but that's not the way it works." Nevertheless a few days later, our standard specification, or "spec," was changed to corrugated stainless steel, which looked better and allowed an accordion-like expansion.

Another standard detail that Breuer was always refining was his sliding window, which did away with the clunky frames then manufactured, replacing them with a single, elegant teak pull bar cemented to the glass near the center of each window. The sliding portion rode on stainless-steel ball-bearing hardware that had been designed by the hardware industry for other purposes. In the process of refinement, however, other problems arose and in house after house the detail was subtly changed to improve on previously observed difficulties. B.J. Barnes reported that when a client in Baltimore—who was otherwise delighted with her house—complained to Breuer that heavy wind-driven rain, and sometimes even just plain condensation, would pool in the gutter behind the windows, he suggested that she get out a sponge and a bucket to sop up the water. Many of the original installations have been subsequently replaced, but Ham used the original detail in his own beach house in East Hampton and it is still there. He told me once of being in the house during a storm as water was projected into his dining room in a regular series of jets through hardware holes along the underside of the window. The slider pane cracked during the same storm but the teak pull was so well cemented in place it has held the glass together ever since.

Revisiting the Institute for Advanced Study townhouses in Princeton forty years after their construction, in connection with the effort by one of its professors to undo some of the damage done by intervening administrations, I was very disheartened to see peaked roofs on all the flat-roofed buildings—an overreaction to roof leaks of many years ago. I saw a peaked roof on the Levy house during the same visit to Princeton.

In early 1955 Breuer was commissioned by the New York City Board of Higher Education to design a new library and classroom building for the Bronx campus of Hunter College, largely upon the recommendation of its scholarly president, George N. Shuster. The site was a fine one, on the shore of the Bedford Park Reservoir. It had been left empty during the Depression when the city had run out of the funds needed to complete the otherwise handsome Collegiate Gothic campus of limestone and irregular earth-toned ashlar masonry. I was named job captain and had just begun my analysis of the detailed program when Breuer introduced me to Eduardo Catalano, who was to work in the office for the summer before going on to what would become an illustrious career as professor of architecture at the Massachusetts Institute of Technology (MIT). He had been working in Mexico for the well-known structural engineer/architect Felix Candela and was very familiar with Candela's breathtaking experiments in the use of thin concrete membranes (two to three inches in thickness) to roof over large areas with great economy of material. Lajkó seemed captivated by Eduardo's use in his own house of one variant—the hyperbolic paraboloid (H.P.) shell.

The H.P. shell is a "warped" plane that is difficult to describe. It can be imagined as a square rubber sheet with four straight and rigid edges. If one

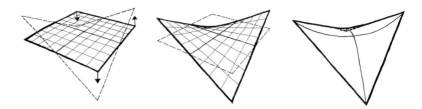

The birth of a hyperbolic paraboloid. Lines originally parallel to the edges remain straight, while diagonals are beautiful curves.

edge were twisted ninety degrees relative to its opposite, the two other edges would remain straight but inclined lines, and curiously, so will any other line on the sheet perpendicular or parallel to the rigid edges. From every other point of view, however, the sheet would be beautifully curved, and it was surely this sculptural shape that caught Lajkó's fancy. Another of its mathematical properties is that a line drawn on the diagonal between opposite corners will in one case be a catenary parabola and in the other—a hyperbolic arch. If the sheet were frozen in its deformed, or "warped" shape, it would be remarkably stiff and resistant to flattening or further bending—much more so than the original flat sheet, even if it had likewise been frozen. As long as the edges are kept stiff and straight, the sheet in between will support itself together with any snow, rain, or wind loads, even if it is very thin. H.P. segments can be combined with mirror images along one or more of their sides to create marvelous, useful shapes, and Breuer was about to do just that.

A flue-tile sunscreen (after Ben Schnall). Breuer used this to wrap the sunny sides of both buildings at Hunter.

The program for the classroom building, which also contained faculty offices, was quite conventional and was to be housed in a simple three-story bearing-wall structure around a square courtyard, sheathed in limestone to match its neighbors. Its windows were shaded from the sun by a three-dimensional grille, which Lajkó had made from one-foot-long sections of terra-cotta flue tile placed on their sides and stacked with offset joints. The tile was decorative and practical, with a color that ranged from buff to red-orange and slight irregularities of shape that came from its being fired in the furnace: an industrial product with the appearance of hand-crafting whose color resembled the earth hues of the ashlar masonry used in other parts of the campus. This was one of Lajkó's many felicitous inventions, which he used elsewhere to equally happy effect.

The Hunter library was rather more specialized: although the classroom building could be served with fixed interior walls and partitions, the main library reading room needed to be open and unencumbered to allow for later rearrangement of the seating and bookstacks that shared its floor area. In my analysis of the program I found that we could put all the required closed bookstacks in a partial basement essentially equal in area to the main reading room above. Eduardo began testing various arrangements of H.P. shells to see what spans were possible. Our desks were next to each other in the back of the second floor in front of an abandoned fireplace so that our stools rocked on and off the marble hearth. Everyone passed by behind us en route to the washroom, which extended out back alongside the garden behind the brownstone. We worked well together, and Breuer would stop by once a day or so with his characteristic "What is news?"

In order to keep columns, which would interfere with rearrangements, to a minimum, Eduardo and Lajkó worked out a structural unit that started with a fat, cruciform column from which four square H.P. shells sprang almost like an umbrella that has been blown inside-out. By allowing six of these units—two in one direction, three in the other—to be arranged side by side, bracing one another, a floor area measuring 120 by 180 feet was covered, and

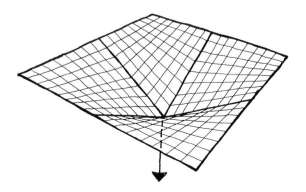

An umbrella made up of four H.P. shells. The shells spring from one point of support but need to be braced against any overturning motion.

63

there were only six interior columns. The building was then wrapped in a light glass curtain wall, just strong enough to stiffen the outer edges of the shells, which was in turn shielded from the sun on two sides by terra-cotta flue-tile screen walls. Since the roof shapes were generated by straight lines, the plywood sheets making up the formwork into which the concrete was to be poured and the strips that covered their edges could be straight, flat, and ordinary, despite the soaring curves that would result. We hoped in this way to be able to build a dramatic structure within the limited budget of the city. By the time Eduardo left for Cambridge in the fall, the buildings were essentially designed, and after appropriate approvals, it remained only to produce the working drawings, which took the balance of the year.

Breuer wanted the curtain wall around the library to come down as close as possible to the floor, so that the drama of the interior could be seen from outside. He left a band of stone about two feet high above the floor, which masked some heating ducts and a low range of bookshelves and functioned as a continuous seat all around the perimeter. The head librarian, always on the lookout for additional shelf space, asked whether this band under the windows couldn't be raised to six or seven feet, calculating that thousands more books could in this way be housed. Breuer gently argued against such a change, and after running through a set of practical reasons (of which he always had many), he admitted that it was really a matter of the proportion between the height of the stone and the glass above. "Ah hah," said the librarian, "then it is *just* a matter of aesthetics!" At this point, President Shuster, who had been keeping a neutral distance from the fray, jumped in and saved the day: "We want a beautiful building as well as a practical one. I read once that Cleopatra was thought a famous beauty but that if her nose were just an eighth of an inch longer it might have spoiled everything. We do care about aesthetics and we must let our architect be the judge of that." We could have hugged the man.

Around this time, Bill Landsberg left the office to set up his own practice on Long Island. He collaborated with Breuer on two later projects—the Westchester Reform Temple and the O. E. McIntyre plant on Long Island. Bill was replaced as chief draftsman and office manager by **Murray Emslie,** who had been introduced to Breuer by Ham Smith. They had worked together some years earlier in another office.

Working on Hunter posed a number of daunting problems. The city of New York was and is a notoriously difficult client. Years of internal bureaucratic scandals have led to layer upon layer of control by bigger and bigger bureaucracies. Because it is so hard to work for, the city is frequently stuck with incompetent architects; in addition, architects long ago lost the role of field supervision to an internal city department. When the better contractors stopped bidding on such tough and slow-paying jobs, those who replaced them were not above beating up their subcontractors, ruthlessly renegotiating prices after the award of the contract. This led to New York State's infamous Wicks Law, which is still on the books and requires that the bids for general construction be separate from those covering the mechanical and electrical installations. This has added countless millions of dollars to public works constructed by the city of New York and greatly waters down the control that general contractors should otherwise be able to exert over their subcontractors.

Then there was the Building Department, the Bronx branch of which was rumored to be corrupt and awkward to deal with. Our fee was low, the contract was onerous in its requirements, and we were likely to be thrown into an adversarial position in relation to the contractor as well as the city.

The day came when Murray and I had to take the subway to the Bronx to meet the chief of the Building Department in order to file our plans for preliminary examination. The chief had a terrible reputation, but Murray assured me from previous personal experience that behind the gruff manners was a very fair and decent public servant. At first whatever he said to me seemed barked rather than spoken and I had a sinking feeling that this was not getting off to a good start. As it turned out, Murray was right and the chief had our plans examined promptly and efficiently. Since the theory of H.P. shells was unknown to anyone in his department, the chief retained Mario Salvadori, a distinguished member of the New York structural engineering fraternity and a professor at Columbia, to review our design calculations. Maybe it was because we took the time to walk our plans through the department personally rather than rely upon the usual expediters (and their suspected palmgreasing) that we were treated most professionally. It was an important lesson.

When it came time to put the documents—drawings and specifications—out for bid, we learned that there was no possibility of a "prequalification" of bidders for city work, despite the extraordinary care needed in pouring our delicate H.P. shells. The procedure was to be an open one in which any contractor with adequate financial resources would be permitted to submit a bid. The low bidder for general construction was the Leon D. DeMatteis Construction Company, an old firm with considerable experience in dealing with the city as a client but that specialized in low-cost housing and had no credentials that would lead Breuer to expect the sophistication that his design required. I met Leon himself for the first time at the job site. He was dressed in a long dark overcoat and was smoking a large black cigar. He introduced Breuer and me to his son Fred, who was about my age and also a Brooklyn boy, and said he would be running the job in the field. Breuer took an immediate liking to the father, as he frequently did in meeting practical men in the industry, and I developed a good working relationship and friendship with Fred that lasts to this day. After his father's retirement, Fred and his brother built the DeMatteis Orga-

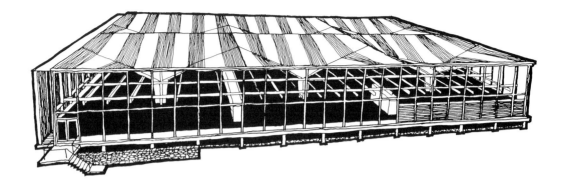

The Hunter College Library (after Ben Schnall). Stripes of gray and black roofing serve to dramatize the undulating surface of the shell structure.

nizations into a firm of international developers that finished work on the MoMA Tower and constructed many prominent buildings throughout New York City and in Saudi Arabia.

Even though we were not paid for most of the time I spent in the field, Lajkó encouraged my regular visits to the site, and a bond developed between the contractor, the city's inspector, and our office that seemed inspired by the challenge of the fascinating project we were building. The work went well and we were proud of the results, which received critical praise, extensive publication, and several design awards.

Lighting a library reading room presents a number of problems whenever the arrangement of tables and bookstacks needs to remain flexible. Lamps on the tables won't work if they are to be free to move away from electrical outlets, and ceiling fixtures won't work if, as was the case at Hunter, there is no ceiling. Breuer devised an open grid of lightweight rectangular metal tubes that was suspended at intervals from the H.P. shells above and through which the overarching structure was clearly visible. Spanning between these tubes was a staggered pattern of fluorescent lighting fixtures providing the level of illumination required for the tabletops below.

Lighting levels came from a chart published annually by a trade association that included electrical engineers and lighting-fixture manufacturers. Few in our profession had noticed that the recommended light levels rose slightly each year while the human eye did not seem to be changing; nor did we recognize that the trade association might have a vested interest in selling more and more fixtures and bulbs. By the late 1950s library reading rooms were recommended to be lit at 150 foot-candles, which is at the very bright end of any scale. As the library neared completion, we were all quite pleased by the appearance of the lighting grid but had never seen it in operation. I was on the floor of the reading room with Lajkó one fall afternoon as the outside light began to fade, and he suggested to the contractor that the grid be turned on. We were almost blinded by the light that exploded overhead, and as our eyes adjusted to the situation it was clear that there was no way to see the structure above through the brilliant plane that had been created. Breuer was furious and demanded recalculation and remeasurement by our electrical engineer, which showed that we had what had been specified: 150 foot-candles. At that point, Lajkó took matters into his own hands and ordered the removal of one of every two fluorescent tubes, over the objections of the librarian, who knew the "official" recommendations. They were never replaced and generations of Hunter College readers never complained. It remained for Dick Stein in his 1977 book *Architecture and Energy* to expose the phony charts and decry the waste of energy in America's over-lit interiors. The charts have subsequently been significantly revised downward.

The New Haven Railroad had, in 1955, a very dynamic new president, Patrick J. McGinnis, who launched a number of dramatic projects to update the image of "his" railroad. He began with a brilliant new logo by Breuer's friend the Swiss graphic artist Herbert Matter and hired Lajkó, again on the recommendation of Florence Knoll, to design two railroad stations for New London, Connecticut, and Rye, New York. Lajkó worked with Herb Beckhard on the Rye station and with Eduardo on the one in New London, in which H.P. shells appeared as canopies for the railroad platforms. **Val Michelson,** who had followed me from Percival Goodman's to Breuer's office, recalls Lajkó describing his intent regarding a bridge that he envisioned crossing the railroad: "You know, something like Maillart would do." Robert Maillart was a great designer of bridges throughout Switzerland, and it was Breuer's only reference—as far as anyone can remember—to the work of another creative genius. In the end, neither of the stations was built.

There were, however, three experimental high-speed trains that did get built, by Talgo of Spain, Budd, and the Pullman Company. Herb and Ham directed the design of the trains, which included an exterior paint treatment by Breuer's old Bauhaus friend Herbert Bayer and featured the vermilion, black, and white colors of Matter's logo. The office also designed the interiors, which were fitted out with all the care of an airliner.

Trial runs were conducted and the trains performed perfectly, but the roadbed between New York and Boston was too bumpy to permit use at the high speeds for which the trains were designed. Some of the beautiful trains still remain, abandoned on obscure sidings.

Herb remembers Lajkó's presentation of preliminary sketches of the stations to McGinnis and his assistant, Harry McGee, in their suite at the Roosevelt Hotel: "McGinnis arrived late and was bombed out of his mind. Lajkó didn't know how to proceed with an audience that was clearly having trouble focusing on anything and the presentation was finally concluded as McGinnis waved to his assistant and said, 'I know you can Harry it, handle.'" McGinnis was eventually eased out of the company by unhappy stockholders but later surfaced as president of the Boston and Maine Railroad, for which Matter designed another logo, this time in blue, black, and white, and the office designed another train.

For reasons that were never explained but were somehow connected to McGinnis, Lajkó asked me to go up to the Avery Architecture Library at Columbia University and do some research on the building of Grand Central Terminal. I summarized the story in a report to Breuer together with fascinating newspaper photos of the era showing Park Avenue with its on-grade steam engines. The paper was passed on to McGinnis and promptly forgotten. What McGinnis had in mind can only be guessed, but I thought of him years later when the Grand Central Tower project was offered to Lajkó.

The year 1956 saw the practice booming. Lajkó moved out of his third-floor apartment to make room for more drafting tables and because the long climb up those stairs was beginning to bother his back. New draftsmen and -women seemed to be arriving every week. The brownstone was full to overflowing.

Ray Matz, my Cornell classmate, had joined the staff, and Lajkó loved to discuss cars with him—Ray owned a classic bottle-green MGB and Breuer had just bought a bat-winged Mercedes that would be followed in later years by equally spectacular Jaguars. Hilary Hultberg was hired to help Peg Firmage as secretary. She had been recently divorced from her well-known artist husband, John, and later left the office to marry Peter Morton when he was assigned to The Hague as clerk o' the works for Breuer's U.S. Embassy, which he had helped to design.

During the summer of 1955, Lajkó had started a custom of taking on students as apprentices to help out around the office when many of the regulars were on vacation. One of the first was Charles Rathbone, who came from the University of Liverpool under the sponsorship of Philip Goodwin of MoMA. The Liverpool connection continued in 1956 with Allen Cunningham and in 1957 with John Meunier, now the dean of the architectural school at Arizona State University. Geoff Jarvis, a Scot, was with us for the summer of 1955. One morning toward the end of his stay, the *New York Times* carried a story about the election of a Reverend Jarvis as the head of the Church of Scotland. Geoff had a rakish reputation, so I didn't expect his answer when I asked if he was related. Furrowing his brow, he said, "Yes, he's my father."

Lajkó offered another summer job to Jan Rowan, a student from Pratt Institute who came highly recommended by Sybil Moholy-Nagy, the widow of one of Breuer's oldest friends from the Bauhaus—the artist László Moholy-

Nagy—and a member of Pratt's faculty. He was assigned to work with me, and I considered him to be an untalented, ostentatious poseur whose nomination seemed to be based on a rumored romantic liaison with his professor. At my suggestion, he was fired before the end of the summer. We were somewhat chagrined to see him turn up just a few years later as editor of *Progressive Architecture* and understood that *P/A* was unlikely to publish our work during his tenure at the magazine.

Life in the old brownstone was very much that of a family, with all of its joys and tensions. The office was small enough so that most of us—seven or eight at a time—would usually have lunch together, including Breuer if he was in town. We had a number of favorite spots. The Shelburne Hotel on Lexington Avenue was for formal luncheons and used by Lajkó and those he would eventually ask to become his associates. More often, we would go to a small luncheonette down half a flight of stairs off Third Avenue where we could hear the elevated subway rattling overhead. Herb describes Lajkó's method of eating as being more an act of breathing in than chewing; it was very swift and left the rest of us to finish many minutes later. One of Breuer's secret favorites was pig's knuckles and he always prefaced their consumption with "I hope you'll forgive me for this . . ."

Lajkó felt that, in coming to America, he had left his European persona behind, and despite his charming accent, he affected everything American that he could: big checked "lumber" shirts on the weekend, casual profanity when it suited the discourse, first names around the office, with nicknames preferred (except for "Mrs. Firmage"—she always called him "Mr. Breuer," so he usually returned the courtesy). He used to take those of us who were senior aside and say, "People are starting to call me 'Mr. Breuer' again—spread the word about 'Lajkó.'" Even with this clear directive, there were young draftsmen who simply couldn't bring themselves to use "Lajkó." John Johansen remembers being asked "Vaht's news?" so often that he finally decided to unburden himself of a long list of personal concerns only to see Breuer's crinkly blue eyes glaze over about halfway through the litany.

According to Herb, Lajkó walked the city streets like a native New Yorker, assuming, correctly as it turned out, that he would be protected by some enveloping cloud of divine intervention. He chose to cross against the light since that way he wouldn't be sideswiped by a taxi making a right turn.

Sometime during the spring of 1956—a year in which I also passed my licensing exam to practice architecture in New York and was married to Barbara Wright—Lajkó approached five of his employees individually with a remarkable offer. The five were Herb, Ham, Murray, Joe, and myself. The proposal was that, in return for our agreement to stay in the office for ten years with the title of associate, he would make each of us an equal partner at the end of that time. There was no need to raise capital to buy into the firm; our loyalty was the price of admission.

Breuer remarked, "You know, Bob, I don't think we're ever going to make a lot of money in this business. I'm not a very good 'salesman.' My philosophy has always been something close to your American expression about building a better mousetrap . . . But we'll have some fun." Considering that Breuer, like many renowned architects then and now, had a justified reputation for paying low salaries, his proposition was unbelievably generous and one that was without precedent. It also worked for him—he bought loyalty and stability in the management of his firm for twenty years, during a time when most of his competitors had to deal with associates and partners on a revolving-door basis. And he was overly modest in describing his talents as a businessman. As for us, we were partners of the legendary Marcel Breuer, shared credit for a long line of remarkable buildings—and certainly did have fun.

The one person who did not accept the offer was Joe Neski. I remember discussing the pros and cons of the offer with Joe and Bobbie at length. Bobbie argued eloquently in favor of the independence that would allow her very talented husband to make his own name in the world, and he eventually agreed. The other surprise was that B.J. was not offered the same deal. She was very hurt, having considered Lajkó a true friend, and left the office very unhappily within the month to join Wallace Harrison, who was working on the Metropolitan Opera House. Breuer was frank in saying, without recognizing how patronizing it must have sounded even then, that he couldn't count on B.J.'s long-term loyalty: "She could leave to get married at any time."

Lajkó was unremittingly old-world in his professional dealings with women. When Bobbie cornered him on the stairway to complain that she had received only a five-dollar-a-week raise when all the guys had gotten ten dollars, he replied: "Oh Bobbie, you don't need the money." In handing another female member of the staff her bonus one year, he said, "Now, I want your promise that you'll not get pregnant." And yet, for all that, when Herb had joined the office, two out of the four "draftsmen" were women; and years later, when Rita Reif wrote a scathing *New York Times* article about the way in which women were treated in our profession, the photographs accompanying the report included five out of the six women from our architectural staff. Six out of thirty was a far higher proportion than in almost any other office in New York City.

Another example of Lajkó's generosity was recalled by Jay Ritchie, who had left the office in July 1957 after two and a half years. He received a letter from Breuer in December thanking him for his service, informing him that the year had been a good one, and enclosing a check for $1,000 as his share in the profits. Most employers don't give Christmas bonuses to someone who has left even a month before the holidays; considering the buying power of a thousand dollars in 1957, this was a most open-hearted gesture.

The New York Times, *April 1971. A photo taken in connection with an article about women in architecture showed Lajkó* *surrounded by Tara Dahran, Jane Yu, Susi Strohbach, Francesca Ventura, and Sharon Grau.*

201 East Fifty-seventh Street. This street corner has changed a lot in the intervening years. Schrafft's is gone but the Sutton theater is still there.

The Office on Fifty-Seventh Street: 1956–1960

In 1956, the northeast corner of Fifty-seventh Street and Third Avenue was occupied by a five-story building with a Schrafft's restaurant on the ground floor, right next to the Sutton movie theater. The building is still there, as is the Sutton, but Schrafft's has moved on. Breuer rented the third floor, which had large windows facing south and west and space for the twenty to thirty staff members who eventually filled it. The neighborhood featured good restaurants (there were two "Original Joe's" and one just plain "Joe's" within three blocks of one another), furniture showrooms, art galleries, photo shops, convenience stores to suit all our needs, and Bloomingdale's.

The space was laid out in a free and open fashion, with cubicles lined up along the Fifty-seventh Street windows for the four new associates. The cubicles were separated by partitions made of brightly painted perforated Masonite "pegboard" trimmed in natural birch that touched neither the floor nor the ceiling. The only door that could be closed led to Breuer's office, which also served as a conference room and was located immediately off the entry in the southeast corner of the space. A ceiling was implied by an open grid of lighting fixtures in a white wooden frame that also served to steady the partitions. The placement of the building's columns suggested a front and rear drafting room, although there was never any functional distinction between the two. Artwork by some of Lajkó's friends—Tino Nivola, Moholy-Nagy, Bayer, and Albers—was scattered about along with black-and-white photos, large and small, of architecture, either his own or old favorites.

Breuer commuted regularly to his second house in New Canaan via Grand Central Terminal and kept very regular hours, punctually arriving just before nine and rarely remaining long after five. He kept a small apartment on the floor above the office. (John Meunier remembers coming into the office one morning to find that a sleepless Lajkó had crept down into the drafting room during the night; many tables had handwritten notes attached to their drawings.) During the summer, once the family had moved back from Paris, his weekends were spent in Wellfleet. One of his secretaries remembers his regular parting words as he dashed out of the office on Friday afternoon as a mischievous and somewhat garbled "I leave you now, flat."

After my marriage I lived for four years thirty-four blocks north at Ninety-first Street and Park Avenue in a rent-controlled one-bedroom walk-up before designing and building my own home in Bedford, New York, and join-ing Lajkó as a regular Grand Central commuter. Herb and Ham each lived on Long Island and had to fight their way crosstown to and from Pennsylvania Station. Murray lived within easy walking distance on the Upper East Side.

For many alumni of the firm, Fifty-seventh Street was the most pleas-ant and productive of Breuer's many offices. There was no segregation between the floors, as at Thirty-seventh Street, no partitioned hierarchy, as was later the case on Madison Avenue. The character of most drafting rooms is set at architecture school, where students are trained in large, messy barn-like spaces in which the walls are covered with drawings and accumulated graffiti. Drafting boards and reference tables are open for all to see and com-ment on, and strong personalities tend to dominate the rumble of conver-sation. Cooperative chatter is constant and very much a part of the learning experience. In actual architectural offices, the high-jinks and clutter tend to be more controlled, depending upon the severity of the boss and the impres-sion he or she wants to give clients. But there is always an undercurrent of incipient anarchy that can easily burst forth after hours and during weekend charrettes when radios are played and food is ordered in. (The term *char-rette* denotes a state of maximum panic and fear of being late in delivering a product on schedule. The fabled derivation of the concept comes from artists at the Ecole des Beaux-Arts who had not yet finished their painting or sculpture when the wagon, or charrette, came by to pick it up for delivery to the salon where it was to be displayed. The work had sometimes to be completed *en charrette*.)

Breuer liked young people and encouraged informality in the drafting room, probably a nostalgic hangover from his years as a professor. Joe Neski's fine sense of humor and facility as a mimic, combined with Val Michelson's Russian accent and Gabby Sedlis's Polish-Lithuanian one, made for an explosive conversational mixture that regularly brought down the house. Allen Cunningham used to love doing Churchill to Joe's Eisenhower. The repetitive work involved in architectural drawing—dots and textures that don't require much attention—meant that talk wasn't much of an interruption.

Among all the nationalities represented, there were quite a number of people who had played soccer in their youth. Bragging led to the need to show prowess, and one day someone made a ball of crumpled tracing paper bound by drafting tape to demonstrate some nicety of footwork. Soon a regular ritual developed around a tight circle of players. The game was to keep the ball (or sometimes a paper cup) in the air (cheers) by kicking it (plunk) and not letting it hit the floor (groans). The chorus could be heard all over the drafting room, in response to which Lajkó came over during one such match, surveyed the scene, smiled, and passed through with no comment as the game continued. Although sometimes played at lunchtime, the game was more often a relief valve in the middle of an all-night charrette.

Don Bolton thought that we didn't appreciate the products of his native Canada, so we taped a long strip of yellow tracing paper to the wall near his desk. Every time he would remind us, someone would leap up with a magic marker to add yet another name to the list of "famous people you didn't know were Canadian." This was later joined by another list, "famous people you didn't know were architects."

This spirit was not limited to the drafting room. Isabelle Pack, later **Isabelle Hyman,** served Breuer as a dignified private secretary after Peg Firmage retired. She shared the front office with Mary Louise Wilson, our receptionist, a truly talented comic who would later become a well-known character actress and author. She could break Isabelle up with off-the-phone commentary and was a great favorite of the staff as they passed to and from the elevator.

It became a tradition to present Lajkó with a birthday gift designed and made in the office. Allen Cunningham recalls "a jigsaw puzzle of Queen Nefertiti's head (with whom Connie Breuer shared a remarkable likeness). **Dick Meier** cut the puzzle itself and I was delegated to make a container, which emerged as a tubular object covered with mink. Breuer was very appreciative."

A young Japanese architect named Yoshinubu Ashihara was in the office for a year or so and worked, in part, on the design of the gardens at either side of the abbey church at Saint John's. He was very quiet, unassuming, and totally underestimated while he was with the office. He moonlighted one spring at MoMA helping to reassemble the intricately precut pieces of "the Japanese House in the Garden." We knew so little about Yosh at the time that no one realized he had left a wife behind in Tokyo while he gained what he considered the priceless opportunity to work with Breuer. We were all proud and more than a little surprised to learn of his subsequent career in Tokyo, where he had one of the most active offices of architecture while holding down a professorship at Tokyo University and becoming president of the Japanese Society of Architects.

Christine Benglia, who joined the firm in 1963, observed years later,

"Lajkó knew how to pick very good people—but then, very good people were attracted to him." The character of the office was so formed by the personality of Breuer, by his choices and those that were made on his behalf, that it seemed the most natural thing in the world to be surrounded by brilliant, supportive people who worked together in a genuinely productive way. **Peter Samton** arrived in 1960 and has remarked, "Everyone submerged their own egos to follow the father who had succeeded so early in his own life."

I took a three-month leave of absence from this growing hothouse of talent in the spring of 1957 for a delayed honeymoon trip to Europe. Lajkó encouraged, and even helped finance, the trip that was to be key to my later, international share of his practice. Toward the end of our trip, we were visiting the great chapel designed by Le Corbusier at Ronchamp. I was composing a photograph when a voice with a familiar Brooklyn accent asked, "Ya wouldn't have any extra Kodachrome on ya, woodja?" I did and loaned a roll to Norton Juster, who then hitched a ride in the back of our convertible Volkswagen down to the Côte d'Azur, where we parted after lunch with one of his University of Pennsylvania architecture professors. Norton kept us enthralled during the drive with stories he had "made up." He later published many of them, some with illustrations by his roommate, Jules Feiffer, including such children's classics as *The Phantom Tollbooth* and *The Dot and the Line*. Norton came to work for Breuer after Barbara and I returned from Europe.

A year after the move to Fifty-seventh Street, Breuer received the commission to prepare a master plan for the Bronx campus of New York University (NYU). NYU was then the largest private university in the country, and its faculty was divided between the buildings surrounding Washington Square, in Greenwich Village, and the "Hall of Fame" campus high on a bluff overlooking the Harlem River, which separated the Bronx from Manhattan. The latter had been laid out at the turn of the century by the most famous American architectural firm of the day—McKim, Mead and White. The buildings were three and four stories in height and built of an elegant, long "Roman" brick, yellow-orange in color, which was trimmed in classical limestone ornament. The central library was crowned by a green copper dome that could be seen from miles away. From two of its sides radiated graceful curving colonnades in which were placed heroic busts of America's most famous citizens—the original Hall of Fame.

Since space was so tight downtown on Washington Square, the university had decided that if it was to expand, and that was certainly what all universities were doing then, it had to be at the uptown campus (never "the Bronx campus"; the neighborhood was even officially "University Heights" to the post office). The McKim, Mead and White plan had never been fully implemented, so there was space for a new six-hundred-person dormitory as well as for classrooms and laboratories for the engineering faculty. I worked with Ham under Lajkó's direction on the master plan, and after its approval later that year, we divided up the architectural commissions between us.

Technology I (later named Gould Hall) was Ham's domain and housed teaching and research facilities in four stories topped by a large penthouse containing mechanical equipment. Its entry was marked by a soaring canopy in the form of a hyperbolic paraboloid shell. The most dramatic structure, however, was on the opposite side of the rectangular wing, on a plaza that it shared with the campus center and dormitory beyond.

The Technology I program called for two steep-floored lecture halls that would not fit comfortably into the main building. Breuer joined them together at their lower edges, where the demonstration tables were located, with an entry corridor between and then raised them off the ground on three massive "legs." The resultant shape was sheathed in rough "board-form" concrete, patterned and jointed to great sculptural effect. Breuer had never done anything like it, and it was the talk of the office and the larger architectural community. Some called it, jokingly, the "bird" or worse, but it served its aesthetic purpose, which was to celebrate the public, special spaces as opposed to the modular offices, classrooms, and laboratories that made up the rest of the program. It remains, to my eye, one of Breuer's most successful inventions and a monument to his constant search for programmatic "accidents" that would justify the articulation of one part, as opposed to the whole. More than thirty years later, the architect/critic Robert A. M. Stern called for it to be landmarked (although Stern hates it) as a strong example of the unusual shaping of architectural form at

The NYU lecture halls (after Ben Schnall). Breuer's keen eye for contour and contrasting surface texture is evident.

77

*The NYU lecture
halls. The dormitory
is in the background
behind this landmark
structure.*

which Lajkó excelled. Today, the lecture-hall wing is named Begrisch Hall, after a donor.

Below the hilltop on which Technology I was built, the campus falls away in a steep hillside; McKim, Mead and White despaired of ever using it for their classical building vocabulary, and it remained, as a result, the largest empty acreage on campus. Breuer adopted the architects' color scheme of yellow Roman brick, with unpainted concrete standing in for carved lime-stone. Then he decided to terrace what he could of the hillside with a series of rubblestone retaining walls that had their color and material precedent in the ashlar stone base on the downhill side of the Hall of Fame.

One terrace formed in this way became a rooftop plaza resting atop new dining rooms and their kitchen. The plaza included an entry pavilion complete with reception desk and student lounges. From the pavilion, two bridges shot out into space and grabbed our seven-story dormitory, which sat at the bottom of the hillside, at its middle floor. In this way a previously unusable site became home to the largest dormitory on campus, and since no one had to walk up or down more than three stories, the need for ele-vator service was minimized. There were alarmed doors on every floor between the men's and women's dormitories, but I suspect that they were removed long ago. The structure of the dormitory wing began with massive legs, or "pilotis," as their Corbusian predecessors were called. Despite my attempt to express the overly complex structure on the facades, the dormi-tory finally had none of the visual drama of the rest of the hillside composi-tion. The building was bent in the middle, which created the sort of concave facade that Lajkó loved and found to be "welcoming." Seen from the Major Deegan Expressway below, however, the opposite, convex facade is less convincing and rather dull.

Bernie Marson joined the staff as CO'W for the NYU job, and one of his non-project-related activities in the office was service on the office soft-ball team. The architectural softball league brought (and still brings) young professionals together in Central Park for an alternate form of competition, and even some senior partners were known for their prowess on the field. In recent years, at least one woman is required on each team. Our team had beaten several big offices, such as Skidmore, Owings & Merrill, and was aggressively coached by Herb Beckhard. One day an important game was scheduled with Philip Johnson's team, which turned up one man short. Rather than have the game canceled, Herb, as our captain, asked Bernie to play on the Johnson team. Marson had a good day and his adopted team won. Herb was furious and protested that the game was invalid because Bernie didn't work for Johnson.

Bernie found Lajkó (though, like many others in the office, he had dif-ficulty calling the great man by his nickname) very interested in the details of the American construction process and someone who could take infinite pains when it came to crucial and even minor decisions. Bernie was checking shop drawings in the office one Saturday when Lajkó came in and spent a fascinated hour poring over the highly complex, large-scale drawings, which the contractor uses to show the architect exactly how it intends to execute what is understood to be the architect's intent. It was apparently foreign to his earlier European experience.

Bernie mentions another memorable moment at the drafting board when Breuer was choosing a color for the NYU door bucks (the frames that surround a door opening). There were five very similar shades of gray, and Lajkó lingered over them for many minutes before a hushed group of impressionable draftsmen until he felt sure of his choice. Breuer rarely explained why he made a particular choice and his presence at any drafting board tended to draw a small crowd—something he never discouraged. Still, if we were eventually to start making choices for him, those of us who had been around long enough to have the guts did ask why, and sometimes got revealing answers. They were usually based on practical considerations since Breuer was uncomfortable discussing aesthetics. Ed Barnes quotes Lajkó, even back in his teaching days at Harvard, as saying, "Talking about it will spoil it."

In the field at NYU, Bernie was hugely grateful for the support that Breuer extended to him as his representative in the field. Lajkó at one point overruled and then secured the demotion of the client's senior inspector, who had thought the "young kid" was getting out of line.

On another occasion, Lajkó was leading a delegation of VIPs on what was planned as a ceremonial visit. When he got to the H.P. shell that formed the entry to Technology I, he noticed an interesting widening of the joints between the flat rectangular form boards as they conformed to the warped shape. He left his distinguished guests to cool their heels while he got involved in a discussion with a carpenter about how best to treat the joints.

Having adopted rubble fieldstone as one of his signature materials, Lajkó took infinite pains in explaining to the draftsmen who had to draw it, and to the masons who had to lay it, exactly what he wanted. Once, Lajkó looked up at the job site as he drove by in his Jaguar on the Major Deegan Highway below and saw some bad masonry. He took the next exit and pointed it out to Bernie: "You can't make him rip it out. Just try to get the mason to make it better as he goes along. Always tell the workman what to do, carefully." (Joe and Bobbie Neski were with Lajkó at the UNESCO job site one day while they were on vacation when he excused himself to chew out an Italian stonemason who was doing equally unacceptable work.) Nevertheless, Breuer had great respect for the contributions that thoughtful, experienced workers could make to a building and was always willing to listen to their opinions.

Ham Smith continued to work on a succession of University Heights buildings for a satisfied NYU until the campus was sold and it became Bronx Community College. In retrospect, the project demonstrates the two strongest, albeit unacknowledged, influences on Breuer's work: Le Corbusier and Mies van der Rohe. The repetitive, modular facades of the dormitory and classroom wings derive from a broad modernist tradition to which Mies was one of the earliest and strongest contributors. The campus center pavilion is more directly and uniquely related to the Miesian planar vocabulary that Lajkó spoke so well. The structure housing the lecture halls looks like nothing that Le Corbusier ever designed, or anyone else for that matter, but it has forebears in Corb's pioneering work in rough, sculptural concrete, which established a precedent for Lajkó's design. What Breuer did was to use somewhat disparate elements from the broad spectrum of European modernism to more "human" effect than their single-minded originators were capable of.

And then there is the question of how much the personal preferences of Ham and myself may have determined the final form of this large and complex project. Once we'd finished collaborating on the master plan, neither Ham nor I ever consistently consulted each other about the two NYU buildings that were growing up alongside each other. We each worked directly with Breuer, who was the common, unifying link. I think that he applauded the minor differences in style as enriching the whole.

Living in monuments, and his houses in New Canaan were certainly that in the eyes of architects around the world, presented problems of privacy to Lajkó and Connie. Connie recalls living in the first, cantilevered wood house,

Lajkó and Connie on the balcony of their first New Canaan home.

81

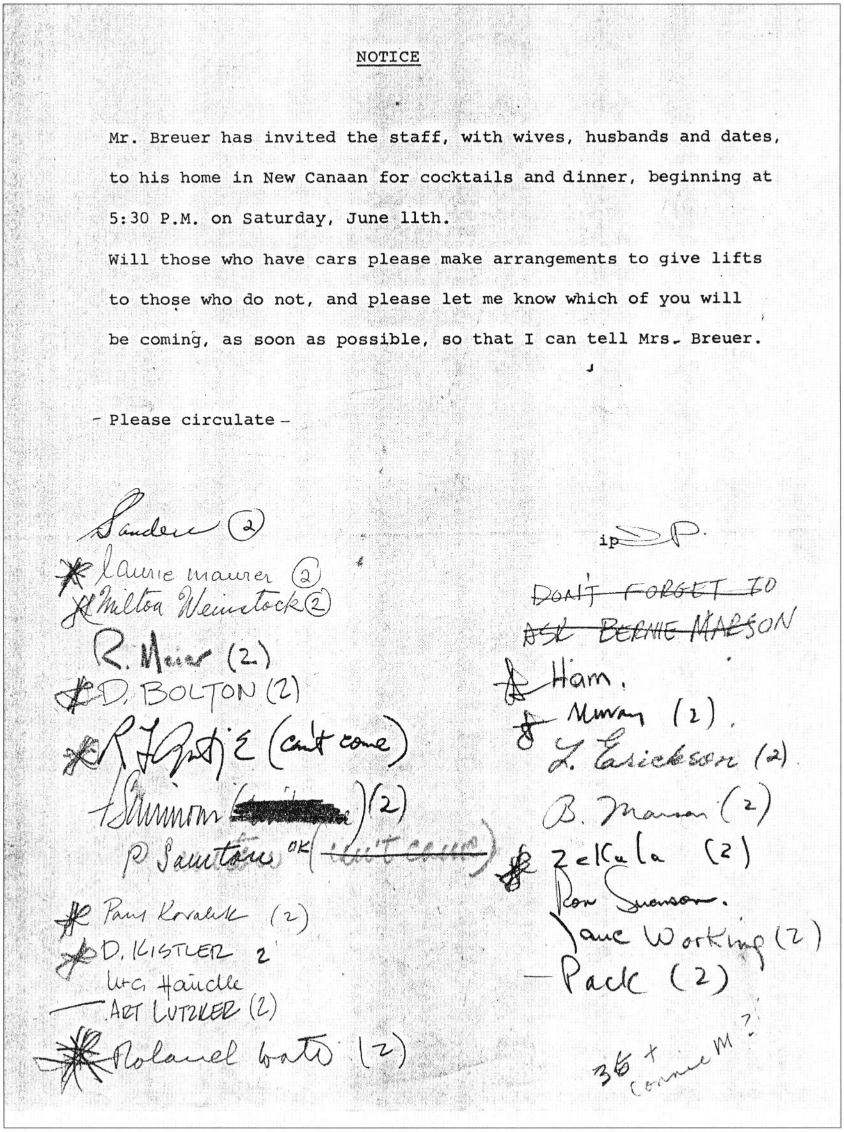

NOTICE

Mr. Breuer has invited the staff, with wives, husbands and dates,
to his home in New Canaan for cocktails and dinner, beginning at
5:30 P.M. on Saturday, June 11th.

Will those who have cars please make arrangements to give lifts
to those who do not, and please let me know which of you will
be coming, as soon as possible, so that I can tell Mrs. Breuer.

- Please circulate -

Office party invitation, June 11, 1960. Important office announcements were made by sending around a memo for all to sign.

which was a rare specimen of modern architecture in its day and very much an object of curiosity: "We would no sooner be settled down on the porch on a Sunday afternoon with the *Times* than I would hear the crunch of gravel on the driveway and knew that architecture students were slowly moving in." The couple was much too hospitable, and Lajkó much too appreciative of the interest, to turn such uninvited visitors away. So it was a bit like living in a fish bowl.

The second house was quite visible from West Road, even though its location, like Philip Johnson's nearby Glass House, was on the outskirts of a suburban town and had to be sought out by the interested. Herb Beckhard and his wife, Ellie, house-sat for the Breuers while Lajkó and Connie were living in Paris and would see the eager faces of architects pressed to the glass of the bedroom "looking at us in bed!"

Members of the office were among those who most longed for a visit, and the Breuers would host an office party at least once a year during nice weather. Older hands, and those young people to whom Breuer took a particular liking, would be favored by special invitations to dinner and, occasionally, weekend invitations to Wellfleet. All these precious moments gave us the chance to see Breuer in a more relaxed mood than was possible on an average day at the office. Families could mix—this included Connie, Tom, and a great shaggy poodle named Cairo—and the interior of the home was completely open to curious eyes. The Breuers' bathroom contained an enormous blowup of one of Lucien Clergue's most voluptuous nudes, which was a bit shocking on first acquaintance. Elsewhere were original Saul Steinberg cartoons of Tom as a cowboy, exquisite Klees, and classic modern furniture upholstered in sumptuous fabrics. Stan Abercrombie liked the idea that "Breuer served his homemade goulash in the same inexpensive blue-and-brown bowls" that Stan had bought at Azuma, an inexpensive housewares chain in New York, and created a "studiedly homey" atmosphere.

Caroline Smith, Lajkó, and Rufus Stillman at an office party in New Canaan.

83

*The UNESCO
Headquarters in
Paris. The assembly
hall's folded concrete
plates are in stark
contrast to the glassy
facade of the secre-
tariat and Miró's
tiled wall.*

In 1957 Herb was the first associate to become deeply involved in overseas work, starting with a huge, rambling stone house for a Swiss lawyer, Willi Staehelin, in Feldmeilin, near Zurich. Staehelin was later to become known for helping Stalin's daughter to defect from the Soviet Union—she used his name on her phony passport. Staehelin had a collection of eight or ten large sculptures by Henry Moore, and the grounds of the house functioned as a museum for their display. He may have run into Lajkó in connection with UNESCO, which was just being completed. Swiss architect friends of mine have later noted that they marveled, at the time, at how Breuer was able to get permission to build a flat-roofed modern house in such a prominent location when all the other sites near Zurich were under the control of the Heimatschütz, a body of legislation whose mission is to keep Switzerland "Swiss" and tends to call for cuckoo-clock residential architecture. Undoubtedly this was a result of Staehelin's power as a local lawyer and Lajkó's fame as an architect.

After turning over the execution drawings to the Swiss associate architect on the job, Eberhard Eidenbenz, Herb took on two commissions in Venezuela: El Recreo, a twenty-two-acre urban center project for downtown Caracas; and a resort development on the beach in Tanaguarena. These were each very large projects that fired up the enthusiasm of both Lajkó and Herb and involved frequent travel, the production of many beautiful drawings, and eventually, the decision to open an office in Caracas with Herb, Ellie, and their five- and three-year-old daughters in residence starting in mid-1959. A year after the new office opened, the Venezuelan economy was in shambles, the projects were canceled, and Herb and his family returned.

Lajkó's celebrity in the Netherlands, with De Bijenkorf and the U.S. Embassy in The Hague nearing completion, led to his selection in 1957 as the designer of a new headquarters building for Van Leer's Vatenfabrieken in Amstelveen right next to Schipol Airport. The board of this manufacturer of oil drums included Johnny van der Wal, one of Holland's most energetic business leaders, who also served on the board of De Bijenkorf and was president of KLM Royal Dutch Airlines. He became a close friend, sailing partner, client, and booster of Lajkó's reputation in Europe. Herb and Joe Neski worked on successive projects for Van Leer with Paul Weidlinger, who was serving for the first time as our structural consultant.

The final elegant glass-walled box was H-shaped in plan and used a dramatic folded plate structure to cover the central wing. Since it is cloudy in Holland much of the time, Lajkó thought he could get away with natural ventilation through the windows, as was the Dutch custom. Nevertheless he did mount a beautiful second layer of heat-absorbent glass panels in front of the floor-to-ceiling curtain wall to control much of the solar heat gain. It proved to be one of the most photogenic of Lajkó's many experiments in exterior

85

*The Van Leer head-
quarters building.
Its heat-absorbent
glass sunshades
created dazzling
double images of
the passing clouds.*

sun-shielding devices, but its efficacy in keeping the people inside cool in the summertime was severely questioned. Our American mechanical engineer wanted to introduce air-conditioning and be done with it. A furious argument flared up between the engineer and Breuer in which the engineer brandished his doctorate as proof positive of his position. Lajkó countered with his Harvard doctorate and would not be moved. (That it was an honorary doctorate was beside the point.)

Since Breuer frequently held conceptual discussions about structure with Paul in private and in Hungarian, it was usually **Matt Lévy,** a young associate in the Weidlinger firm, with whom the rest of us worked in developing the structural details. Lajkó had expressed a desire that a second-floor bridge required by the Van Leer program be executed with particular elegance. It was Matt who suggested a search for the nautical hardware that permitted the suspension of the bridge on stainless-steel cable capped with "swaged" fittings—bulbous forks and eyes that become a wrought end to the cable—which immediately entered Breuer's vocabulary of tension details.

In the United States, Saint John's Abbey, with strong support from the Vatican, had had sufficient success at fund-raising to allow drawings for its new church to start. The project had evolved in Lajkó's mind since its original design and submission in 1954, and there were many subtle changes made in the church and its bell banner by the time they were re-presented for approval in 1957. Shortly thereafter Breuer approached Val after the Michelsons returned from a vacation trip to Europe and asked whether he would be willing to move out to Minnesota as clerk o' the works to observe construction of the church. With his wife's agreement, Val accepted the assignment and, under Ham's direction, was put in charge of the working-drawing team. It was after the Atlas Cement Company had convinced Lajkó to allow it to make a new model of the abbey church for institutional advertising that it was discovered that the beautifully curved legs of the bell banner didn't

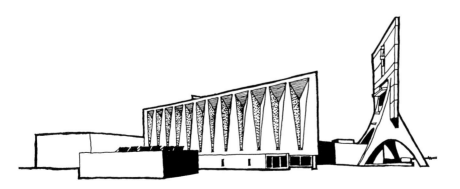

Chapter house, church, and banner at Saint John's Abbey (after Shin Koyama). The ensemble creates a surprising skyline when seen from the surrounding countryside.

look as wonderful in three dimensions as they had in the two-dimensional front and side elevations. The edges of the legs described a sinuous S-curve in space, and Val was asked to correct the situation. His hazy memory of calculus and the more recent mathematical training of our two British staff members, Allen Cunningham and John Meunier, succeeded in redefining the curves after considerable hand calculation (in those pre-computer days). According to Ham, Val would also often be deep in Smoley's Tables searching for the coordinates that would define the subtle curve that Lajkó had sketched intuitively for the side walls of the church.

Another benefit of the Atlas advertising campaign was that it attracted the interest of a brilliant engineer named Ted Hoffmeyer who lived in Minneapolis but was commuting in his own plane to a tiresome high-rise construction site in Los Angeles. Ted had worked with Albert Kahn during the Depression on the great steel city of Kuznetsk in Siberia and had helped construct eight military airfields in Alaska during World War II with the U.S. Army Corps of Engineers. He was so inspired by the challenge of building the church that he convinced Pete McGough, the head of McGough Construction in Minneapolis, to begin negotiations with the abbey and to hire him as superintendent in the field.

At the time of the master plan, the structural engineers for the project were Farkas and Barron with Pier Luigi Nervi as a consultant. Before the project resumed, Breuer had had a falling-out with his old Hungarian friend Nick Farkas over the late delivery of drawings and had appointed new structural engineers—Wiesenfeld, Hayward and Leon, a partnership of three young men who had left a larger firm and rented our Thirty-seventh Street brownstone when we moved out. Lajkó particularly liked working with Jim Leon, their imaginative Greek designer. From 1954 on, Jim served as Breuer's principal structural engineer.

The abbey church was an enormous challenge; it used much of Lajkó's creative energy and most of Ham's time for several years of design. In addition to the main structural shell, they had to design thirty different altars for the monks' worship, a baptismal font, seating, and confessionals, all during a time of major changes in the Catholic liturgy. The exterior was rigorously made of granite and concrete, and the interior prominently displayed both of these together with dark-stained oak and a waxed red-brick floor. Lajkó had originally planned to paint the interior folded walls in white and to gild the undulating roof structure. After the forms had been stripped and the concrete found to be clean and crisp, Val suggested that it be left untouched and Breuer agreed. I revisited the abbey in 1996 on a frigid Sunday morning and attended mass in the church. The sun was pouring through the yellow and orange glass of the cupola and bathing the adjacent concrete in golden light. It reminded me of the dappled colors of stained glass I had photographed on the cold interior stone of Chartres many years before, and I

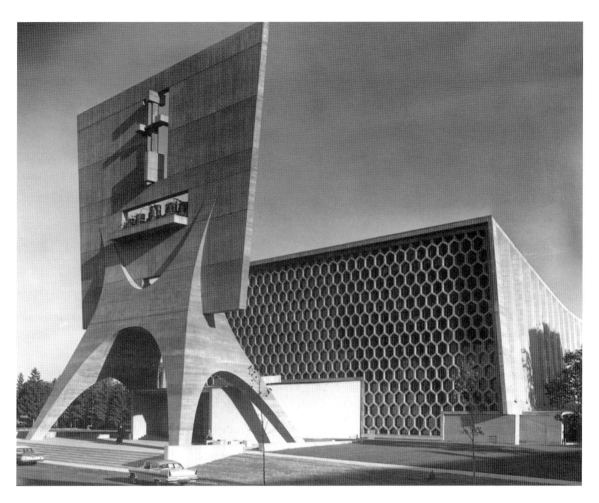

Saint John's Abbey church and bell banner. I. M. Pei says this would be one of the most famous works of modern architec- *ture if it weren't on the rolling plains of Minnesota, far away from the East Coast critical establishment.*

felt no regret about the absence of gilding except to wonder what it really would have looked like.

The interior was shaped for the music of Gregorian chant, reinforced by a great organ designed by Walter Holtkamp, America's best-known builder of modern organs, whose pipes and boxes are grouped into visually stunning compositions of shining silver and rich wood. The monks decided that their organ was so beautiful they feared it would distract visually from the monastic choir and the holy office. A tapestry with enough acoustic "transparency" to allow clear passage of the music was to be designed in front of the organ, and a temporary screen of rich red-orange fabric was put in place for the consecration ceremonies. The tapestry is still there and, while a bit dusty, does much to unify the view toward the altar. When the full choir swept into the *Gloria,* at the service of consecration, Walter Holtkamp declared, "This is the happiest moment of my life." The abbey church stands today as a major monument of modern architecture.

One important design element of the interior was the stained glass that was to fill the deep hexagonal concrete grid that Lajkó chose to stretch across the entire north-facing entry facade. He had intended to have this commission awarded to his friend Josef Albers, who had already designed the calm, understated window in the abbot's chapel. The community, however, had another idea, that of using a Polish artist named Bronislaw Bak, who had taught at the university. When Ham and Breuer realized that this alternative was being taken seriously, it was almost too late to turn it around, although they tried mightily. The community did agree to a paid competition, under pressure from Lajkó, but then chose the submission of the local artist. The abbot tried to explain that the community had not initially understood the depth of Breuer's feelings in the matter. Apparently Albers had put the fathers off with professorial lectures on the virtues of using a light-diffusing prismatic glass, while Bak was humility itself with his offer to train the local populace in the making of his colored glass.

At one point in the controversy, Frank Kacmarcik wrote Lajkó a strange letter in which he reported that members of the community were calling Albers an "atheistic Jew" and asked for clarification. Breuer wrote back that he had spoken to Albers and confirmed his understanding that he was a non-practicing Catholic; it did no good. It is interesting to wonder what those same monks might have said if they had realized that, despite his humanistic Protestantism, Breuer had been born to Jewish parents. This fact came to light in 1981, just before Breuer's death, in the course of research that Christopher Wilk had conducted using Lajkó's own papers at Syracuse while preparing his catalog for the Museum of Modern Art exhibition of Breuer's furniture and interiors. It was a complete surprise to his partners as well as to many old friends. Later, Abbot Baldwin Dworschak told me that the religion of Breuer's family wouldn't have mattered, and that they had never asked.

Rambusch Studios, an old family-owned manufacturer of liturgical arts and craft pieces—lighting, fonts, stained glass, altar rails, and the like—had become acquainted with Breuer through its work at Saint John's Abbey. Nancy Rambusch, the wife of the president of the firm, was headmistress of the Whitby School, a small Montessori school in Greenwich, Connecticut, that served the children of many Catholic families in the wealthy suburban community. Notable on the board was George Skakel, who controlled Great Lakes Carbon Corporation and whose sister, Ethel, had married Bobby Kennedy. Nancy Rambusch had served an intensive apprenticeship studying the work of Maria Montessori, the visionary Italian educator who perfected her theories of hands-on teaching while working with poor and retarded children in the slums of Rome earlier in the century. Nancy convinced her board of the need for a new school building and nominated Breuer, who was approved as architect. I was named associate in charge and learned a lot about the Montessorian theories while observing them in practice in Greenwich. Lajkó and I worked out a scheme for the new school that was made up of four one-story buildings defining a central courtyard. Each was covered by a folded-plate concrete structure that spanned from one outside wall to the other in order to permit maximum freedom for rearrangement of the interiors in accordance with the needs of a very experimental course of preschool and elementary education.

The design was presented in a spiral-bound book with a cover I'd based on the primary shapes and colors that were an integral part of the school's curriculum. Once approved, the working drawings were swiftly prepared and went out for bid. Then came disaster. Whether because of a saturated building market or because the local suburban builders were used to building wood-frame houses rather than long-span concrete structures, the prices came in above the budget and the project was canceled. The board was furious and sued Breuer to recover the fees he had been paid. Lajkó got equally angry and filed a claim in arbitration for the fees that were still owed him. Our agreement was clear on the two points at issue: disputes had to be settled by arbitration, and the architect, while doing his best to control costs, was not responsible for the vagaries of the building market, especially when the contract spelled out no obligation to guarantee a budget.

A panel was selected by the American Arbitration Association (AAA), and a one-day hearing was set. George Skakel was to be the principal witness for the school's board, and I was to give testimony for our firm. Nancy Rambusch made a factual presentation of our working relationship and was visibly uncomfortable in doing so, especially when she admitted that the budget had never been stressed as a major issue. While I was a little intimidated by the bombastic declarations of Skakel, I knew I was on firm legal ground in supporting our case. The panel awarded us 100 percent of our claim, much to the surprise of our lawyer, who had warned that arbitrators usually ended up splitting the difference. Breuer was so satisfied with the outcome, and the process, that he frequently served on AAA panels himself in later years and urged the rest of us to do so.

In 1959 my wife Barbara and I paid periodic visits to a property we had recently bought in Bedford, New York, and since it was only about twenty minutes away by car from New Canaan, we often dropped in to visit Connie and Lajkó. Lajkó was a good cook of a very specialized menu that always included goulash or chicken paprikás. It was topped off by very dense black coffee, brewed in a long-handled open copper pot, and apple strudel from Mrs. Herbst's bakery.

Connie had hoped to adopt a child to join their natural son for quite some time, but the Breuers were considered "elderly" by the adoption services of the era. With the help of Abbot Baldwin of Saint John's, who used his contacts at Maria Laach in Germany, and legal arrangements by Willi Staehelin, a cute three-year-old was adopted and quickly began to perfect her Connecticut accent. We were visiting one Sunday a year or so after her arrival, and Francesca (or "Cesca" for short, like Breuer's mother) took us in hand to show us around "her house." At one point she turned to Barbara to ask, "And when is *your* little girl coming from Germany?" (Barbara became pregnant shortly thereafter.)

The Brookhaven National Laboratory stands on the site of an old army base on Long Island known as Camp Upton. It conducted research for the Atomic Energy Commission and is staffed by an association of American universities. In the late 1950s the Physics Department had a new building constructed but the result was unsatisfactory. The regulations of the federal government dictated that the design and construction of buildings at Brookhaven had to be under the control of the General Services Administration (GSA), with very little input from the "user." The Chemistry Department, and specifically its chairman, Richard (Dick) Dodson, was determined to do better when its turn came for a new building. The scientists tried to preempt the role of the GSA by awarding a "program study" out of departmental funds to an architect of their own choosing. It was their hope that, when successfully completed, the study would lead to the commission for the design of the building. The department interviewed several architects in 1960 and selected Breuer, a rather surprising choice for a group of atomic chemists considering that our office had little experience in designing laboratories.

I was assigned to work on the programming. I quickly discovered that the chemists, especially Dick Dodson and his building committee, chaired by Jacob (Jake) Biegeleisen, were a very cultured lot, who cared deeply about architecture and the design process. We developed a cruciform, three-story scheme for the laboratory, and although it had to be kept very diagrammatic in its presentation since it was only a "program," we all had a good idea of what it would look like as a piece of architecture. The laboratory wings were based on an idea of Dodson's that eventually developed into one of the seminal schemes for postwar laboratory layout.

Prewar laboratories were adjacent to large pipe and duct shafts that carried all of the fluids and gases to the research equipment and lab furniture. As the need for additional services grew, including ways to deliver exotic new gases and to get rid of an extraordinary volume of exhaust air containing radioactive waste products, these duct shafts became overcrowded. Service workers were constantly interrupting delicate research as they came and went, opening access panels in the shaftways and wheeling in new gas tanks.

Dick had the idea that all this activity could be conducted inside a "service corridor" that would run along one side of all the laboratories. Technicians could circulate within these corridors and accomplish most of their hookups without even having to enter the labs. A second line of laboratories could be ranged along the other side of the service corridor, and a deep, efficient building plan would result. The laboratory wall that faced the service corridor in this scheme had previously been the source of natural light via windows, but we felt that if the partitions on the opposite side—facing the pedestrian corridor—were fully glazed, we could "borrow" light from the windows of the office walls beyond. The offices were even to be interrupted from time to time by informal, open lounge alcoves whose windows would serve the corridor and the labs beyond with direct natural light and views to the outside. Our client was pleased with the plan that resulted, and we even began discussing its setting in the midst of the industrial chimneys and utilitarian structures that dominated the site.

One of my last visits to the lab was scheduled for a Monday morning in early October 1960. I had stayed over at my wife's family home on Fire Island after a fall weekend at the beach, which I remember very vividly since we were awakened in the middle of the night and told that we were to be evacuated in the face of a hurricane that had suddenly picked up speed off Cape Hatteras. The meeting at Brookhaven was rescheduled, but the Chemistry Department's elaborate stratagem came almost to naught.

The GSA saw through the chemists' plot, and although we were interviewed along with other architects, the government chose a safe New York firm with plenty of laboratory experience for the building design. On the strength of that experience, however, Breuer received many more laboratory commissions, three of which utilized Dick Dodson's "service corridor" scheme. I met Dick some years later and asked him how things had worked out. He said he had handed our program book to the new architects with the statement that it fully represented their needs and wishes. The architects presented a schematic design a few months later that bore no resemblance to the plan we had arranged. Dick told them that they had not listened carefully and sent them back to their drafting boards. Eventually they came back with a building that looked nothing like what Lajkó would have designed but that functions to the chemists' satisfaction exactly the way we had jointly laid it out.

In the summer of 1960 I finished the working drawings of the house Barbara and I had been slowly designing. It was frankly derived from the Breuer residential vocabulary that I spoke every day at the office. The house was entered from the uphill side, had its principal rooms upstairs surrounded by balconies, and included a view of a mill pond in the woods. There were bedrooms for children below from which they would have direct access onto the lawn with its sandbox and play equipment. (My first daughter, Alexandra, or Alex, was born in late October of the same year.) I showed the finished drawings to Lajkó, not without a certain trepidation, and he admired them. He predicted that, even though he knew of my limited building budget, I would probably find that the dining room was a little tight. Indeed, as we lived in the house and gradually enlarged it, the dining room was one of the first expansions.

As Brookhaven came to a close in 1961, Rufus Stillman delivered another of his commissions for the Torrington Manufacturing Company, this time in Rochester, Indiana, and it was my turn to work for the company. We ultimately designed and built thirteen factory/administration buildings for Torin—as the corporation was eventually renamed—throughout the United States and in Australia, England, Belgium, and Canada. After Indiana, I worked on the Machine Division in Torrington, Connecticut, and at Swindon in Britain. Herb worked with Lajkó and Rufus on the lion's share of these assignments in Connecticut, Canada, and Australia, and Ham was partner in charge for Belgium. The basic plan for most of these assembly plants was more or less identical: a high-bay manufacturing floor at the back with a two-story office wing formed by a mezzanine across the front. Over time the basic scheme was clothed in many different skins, usually reflecting the current stage of Lajkó's thinking about sun control for the windows and the materials appropriate to the local building economy. Torin Indiana was never published, and all I remember about it today was that we bracketed vertical sunscreens above and in front of the office windows. The sunscreens were made of an industrial hexagonal aluminum grating that did the job and looked very handsome.

In 1959 Peter Ustinov had recently come to prominence as an actor and author of some of the funniest comedies to be seen in the movies and in the theater. He was so successful that he had hired Willi Staehelin as his tax

*The Gatje house.
By 1975 the house
had been enlarged
three times (as shown
in this photo) and
daughters Marianna
and Margot had
joined the family.*

lawyer. Willi's financial advice was to live in Switzerland, and his architectural advice was to hire Breuer. Ustinov had decided that he would not only settle in Switzerland but would give up the glamorous life of a movie star to devote himself to his writing and to his new wife, a French-Canadian actress. With Staehelin's help he found a spectacular piece of land on Lake Geneva in Vevey, just down the street from Charlie Chaplin and others seeking the same tax haven.

Breuer's conception was as brilliant as the site that inspired it. He proposed putting two hyperbolic paraboloid concrete shells side by side and supporting them at the three points where they approached the ground by faceted buttresses. The resultant roof, which covered the main living and dining areas, had a central gable peak in the middle of one side, with sharply sloping shed rooflines at each end and a V-shaped "butterfly" roof touching its pier at the center of the other side. All this framed the undulating alpine horizon that surrounded the house. Flat-roofed bedroom wings were tucked in under the shells at three points, and the composition was completed by a swimming pool located slightly downhill.

One of **Laurie Maurer's** first assignments had been to work with me on the Ustinov house. She bought a metric scale that was triangular in section and displayed six of the system's variations of 1:100, 1:200, and so on. Breuer had been trained to use a flat metric scale that showed only two of these scales, and completely familiar with the system, he could do the conversions in his head. Every time he needed a scale at Laurie's board, or at anyone else's, he invariably picked up the triangular prism in the wrong position and spent frustrated minutes searching for the 1:100 basic scale. He once threw one of these scales onto the floor in an exasperated fury and eventually banned them from the office.

The house went out for bid and the price was on the high side. Before serious negotiations with the builders could begin, however, troubles had developed in the Ustinov marriage. The project was abandoned, the land was sold, and Ustinov returned to his life as a movie star. The actor refers to the planning process in his autobiography as one involving a "small chalet."

Although the Ustinov house was not built for its original client, it was given another chance in 1968. Breuer was approached by a wealthy Filipino businessman, José Soriano—a director of the San Miguel Brewery in Manila—who asked for a house design for a piece of land he had just purchased in Greenwich, Connecticut. The site sloped down toward a panoramic view of Long Island Sound. Lajkó was by this time deeply involved in large, important institutional projects, and he had already announced within the office that he was no longer interested in designing houses. He gave Soriano a list of five or six talented Breuer alumni and suggested that any one of them would be eager for the commission and able to do a good job. Soriano was disappointed but dutifully went off to interview

every architect on the list. In two weeks he was back to announce that not one of them would do and to ask Breuer again to take on the commission. Lajkó said to himself, and later told us, "If this man wants a Breuer house so much, and since the sites and programs sound similar, maybe he'll build the Ustinov house." He showed Soriano the drawings of the Vevey house, and Soriano enthusiastically agreed to go ahead with the design.

The Saier house (after Yves Guillemaut). As planned for its predecessor, the soaring shells transfer their weight through X-shaped bronze brackets to three buttresses.

Of course the detailed program of bedrooms was different, the dimensions and contours of the site would require other adaptations of the scheme, and the drawings, which were in the metric system, would have to be carefully converted to feet and inches. **Tician Papachristou,** who had joined the firm in 1965, was put in charge of the transformation. Again the drawings were put out for bids, and again they came in very high. The residential builders of Greenwich were scared by an unfamiliar concrete structure, and the commercial builders didn't want to be bothered with a house, however grand. So the drawings were put back on the shelf and a different beautiful house was designed for Soriano in wood frame and rubblestone, which he built and lived in with great satisfaction. It was, after all, exactly what he had been looking for in the first place. (In 1998, when the Sorianos moved down to New York City, the house was bought by its new next-door neighbor, Leona Helmsley, and torn down because it "spoiled her view.")

Some years later, in 1973, Knoll International, the much expanded furniture manufacturer and distributor that had been founded by Breuer's friends Hans and Florence Knoll, had just bought out Dino Gavina in Milan and incorporated his line of Breuer furniture into theirs. The firm mounted an exhibition in their Paris showroom on the Boulevard St. Germain to celebrate the reintroduction of many of Breuer's most famous chairs to the French market. To put the furniture in context, they asked **Mario Jossa,** then the director of our Paris office, to suggest photographs and drawings of Breuer buildings that might be hung on the showroom walls. Among those selected was a perspective sketch of the Ustinov house.

Louis Saier, a wealthy Algerian wine merchant, strolled into the Knoll showroom one day and his eye was taken by the Ustinov sketch. Upon

The Saier house. This noble descendant of the Ustinov residence was finally built looking out at the Atlantic Ocean above Deauville.

inquiry he was referred to Mario, who told him about the project and that it had never been built. Saier announced that he had a spectacular site above Deauville, with a panoramic view of the distant Atlantic Ocean, and that he was now determined to build that house on that site. Mario tried to dissuade him, pointing out that it was a very expensive project that had proven too much for both Ustinov and Soriano. Saier assured Mario that he had enough money and asked him to consult Breuer. Mario remembers the transatlantic phone call vividly: "Lajkó, are you sitting down?" "Sure. What is news?" "I have a man in the office who wants to build the Ustinov House." "Mario, we've been through all that—I don't want to get involved." "Lajkó, I think he's serious and it would be terrific to see it built." "Mario, if you want to take this on in your own time, okay, but keep me out of it."

Mario did just that. Meeting with Saier on the weekends they revised the program and the drawings to suit his family and site. This time, there was no bid. Saier had good friends in the construction industry and he negotiated directly with one of the great national builders. The contractor hired a French engineer to completely redesign the structure, which relied on the edge beams for strength as well as stiffness rather than on the H.P. shells. They reached agreement on price and their best concrete foreman was assigned to the job. The house was finished in 1975, and first published in *L'Oeil,* an elegant magazine devoted to the arts founded by Georges and Rosamund Bernier. The house remains one of a kind.

IBM World Trade, the international arm of the IBM Corporation, was spreading its message of computer technology and good design throughout Europe and elsewhere in the early 1960s. Instrumental in establishing those design standards was El Noyes, thanks to his wartime friendship with Thomas Watson Jr. El served the company as adviser, sometime architect, and product designer of most of its typewriters and computers from the early 1950s on. The head of World Trade was Arthur Watson, the younger brother of Tom Jr., and he had his headquarters on New York's United Nations Plaza. IBM France, a wholly owned subsidiary of World Trade, was headquartered on the Place Vendôme in Paris and had gradually been buying up real estate in the neighborhood for its corporate activities. These holdings were somewhat redundant since, under French law, the management of IBM France had to be fully staffed by French citizens—even though most of them performed duties all day that had to be approved each evening with a telephone call to their counterparts in New York. The president of IBM France was an elegant nobleman, Baron de Waldner, and even he would at times chafe under the collar of World Trade's control. Research finally outgrew its facilities, which were located in converted nineteenth-century townhouses. IBM asked for permission to build a new, large research facility on the outskirts of Paris. President Charles de Gaulle had decided in 1960, like Napoleon and others before him, that France was being weakened by the increasing concentration of industry and commerce in Paris and determined to do something about it. He refused IBM's request, along with many others of the time, but offered help in relocating to the provinces. El Noyes had been consulted on the choice of site, and IBM had narrowed it down to two possibilities when he suggested that perhaps the architect should participate in the final vote. He recommended Breuer.

The first hint I had of the job was a discussion of some contractual details that were being worked out with IBM's powerful Wall Street lawyers and World Trade's project manager, Ralph Mork. It is a tribute to Lajkó's strength as a businessman that he was absolutely unfazed in dealing directly, and without counsel, with these captains of industry. He negotiated a fee structure that was unprecedented at IBM, and years later, when I tried to cite it as a model for further work with the company, IBM's newly formed Real Estate and Construction Division (RECD) laughed and said that its lawyers of that time had "given away the store."

Breuer went on the site tour and helped choose a beautiful piece of arid hillside a half hour north of the Nice airport in La Gaude. It lay on one flank of the Var River in the shadow of great buttes with a distant view of the Alpes-Maritimes. He swore that he had seen this very land when cycling down the opposite shore of the Var with Herbert Bayer in the late 1920s and had said then, "One day, I'll build something over there." The company had concentrated its site search on the Côte d'Azur because a poll of its Paris researchers had asked the question, "If you couldn't live in Paris, where would you like to live?," and the Mediterranean coast won. When the La Gaude Research Center opened a few years later an unprecedented 85 percent of the research staff moved with it from Paris.

When Breuer saw the site again on that visit, it was still largely uninhabited, with only a few old stone villages hugging the bases of the great rocky crags. Lajkó loved to stay at La Colombe d'Or in St. Paul on site visits, where he would occasionally run into Simone Signoret and Yves Montand. Although I met regularly with the World Trade staff as associate in charge in New York, Lajkó kept the traveling to himself, and I didn't get to La Gaude until I moved to France in 1964, shortly after the building opened.

The original program called for seventy-five-thousand square feet of laboratories and offices; French code and custom dictated that interior workspace should have natural daylight. This meant that, in contrast to the deep laboratory wings of, for example, Brookhaven, La Gaude could use only forty feet between its outside windows, and this resulted in relatively narrow, elegant wings. IBM wanted a low building—three levels at most—to reduce the need for elevator use, and this led to long corridors radiating from a central stair core. It seemed like another ideal use of the Y-shape plan that had worked well at UNESCO. Breuer's argument in its favor was that it

cut the length of the corridors, introduced interior variety with curving paths, and avoided immediate cross-views into the windows of wings otherwise separated by only ninety degrees. His real reason, of course, was that it looked good: a building with "welcoming arms" and many attractive concave surfaces across which the sun could play its delightful tricks.

To sheathe this curving Y shape, and protect it from the strong Mediterranean sun, Breuer came up with one of his more important inventions, a deep, modeled concrete facade that could be both load-bearing and sun-shielding. Within its systematic internal hollows—vertical and horizontal—mechanical systems such as ducts and pipework, electrical cables and heating elements, could be distributed. This kind of facade can be thought of as folded or pleated in two directions and as functioning in much the same way as the inclined planes of UNESCO and Saint John's—as purposeful and visually interesting elements of construction.

For many years, modern architects had gloried in their discovery that the structural skeleton of a building, whether of wood, steel, or concrete, did not have to coincide with the skin of the building, which was there to

IBM La Gaude. This construction photo, which shows the fantastic landscape of the area, was on the cover of the corporation's annual report.

101

keep the weather out, among other reasons. This had led to the use of taut exterior skins and window walls that tried to be, and looked, as light as possible. It made economic sense, but the real impulse derived from an aesthetic feeling that the separation of structure from enclosure was more honest and elegant. The results took two forms: the expression of the column-and-beam system as a grid in the plane of the facade with openings filled by windows and spandrels; and a pulling back of the columns from the facade and into the room behind while cantilevering only a slice of the floor system forward to support the facade. Mies and his followers did pioneering work following the former approach, while Le Corbusier developed the latter. Modern architects of the time, Breuer included, had tried their hands at just about every variation on the theme of expressing the separation of structure, systems, and enclosure. While many architects revel in freestanding columns inside offices and corridors, Lajkó hated them and considered them an imposition on his clients.

Structure and skin had not always been separate. Masonry buildings were typically built with walls thick enough to keep the weather out and the heat in, and strong enough to support themselves and the roof and floor systems that were framed into them. They were usually deep enough to allow chases to be cut out of their mass for drains, electric wires, radiators, and pipes. But multistory, load-bearing masonry structures reached their limit with Chicago's Monadnock Block in 1891 and its six- and seven-feet-thick ground-floor walls.

Aside from load-bearing masonry, the other traditional all-purpose wall was the "balloon frame" of the typical American house, which Breuer found when he came to New England. Although only five or six inches thick, this outer skin had developed from the techniques of ship-building. The timber, boards, and plywood sheathing that went into its "sandwich" supported both compressive and tensile forces when fastened together with nails, screws, and other devices. It was able to do all the work of keeping the weather out and supporting itself, and it still had enough voids left over within its thickness to house ducts, wires, insulation, plumbing pipes, and so on. A wood-stud wall was naturally limited in the amount of weight it could support, and it was not inherently fire-proof, but the idea was there. It remained only to find a new material, or a way of using an old material, that would have all these qualities in sufficient quantity to suit the needs of institutional building. Breuer knew that whatever this turned out to be would look "heavy" rather than "light," but at some point he clearly decided that this was fine—in fact, preferable—as a means of expressing his instincts as a sculptor rather than as a painter. Perhaps it was the rock outcroppings of the Var River valley, or the traditional stone villages, but something caused Breuer to turn on a dime and come up with a deep, heavy facade for IBM La Gaude.

Having digested the company's program of maximum flexibility in the layout of interior partitions, and knowing that the relatively narrow wings could be spanned from outside wall to outside wall, Lajkó sketched for me a pattern of horizontal and vertical folds that were to be the structure of that outside wall as well as the enclosure for all the utilities that the laboratories required. These pipes, wires, and ducts would be fed in toward the interior from the outside wall rather than outward from interior shafts, which would have defeated the desired flexibility. By the time these multidirectional concrete "pleats" had been made strong enough and deep enough to do all this work, the entire wall system projected out past the window plane by over three feet, more than enough to shade the windows from sunlight at almost any angle. The frequency of the vertical fins was set by an IBM planning module of six feet, and the three-dimensional grid that resulted is made up

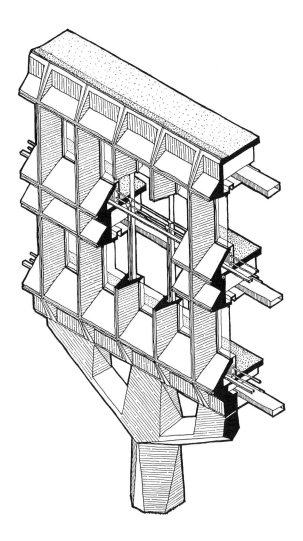

IBM La Gaude facade in section. This demonstrates its utility in providing folds for the passage of pipes while simultaneously supporting the upper floors above the tree columns below.

103

of triangular fins that are only six inches wide at their face. The pockets of space, seen from all angles because of the curves in the facade, are small-scale echoes of the larger concavity defined by the shape of the building itself and form a texture that catches both the light and one's interest.

Breuer was to use this type of deep facade with increasing frequency and to all sorts of purposes in the years to come, but La Gaude was the first and the best. The shaped wall was not originally designed to be precast of concrete units, although that proved to be the economical way to build it. The drawings and specs for La Gaude (in English, with our French associate architects, father and son Pierre and Michel Laugier, responsible for all the translations) left it to the option of the contractor as to whether the facade should be made of premolded pieces of concrete or cast in place with reusable flexible molds, as Lajkó had seen his friend I. M. Pei do at the Kips Bay Housing project in New York. The mild, arid climate and unpolluted air of the Côte d'Azur were also uniquely suitable for concrete that was exposed to the weather, which otherwise is known to attack it with freeze-thaw cycles that cause spalling of the surface unless the material is specially treated. And the bright, hot sun showed off the building's folded surface in a way that the gray days of more northern sites could rarely equal.

The hillside site was steeply sloping and made up of broken rock that was not ideal for building foundations. Breuer came up with his second improvisation, that of supporting the two levels devoted to laboratories and offices on massive columns of variable height that would touch the ground only every forty-two feet along the outside edge of the building. In this way, excavation costs would be minimized and the beautiful rugged land form would run uninterrupted under the huge building above. With all the vertical loads being supported by the perimeter wall above, Lajkó proposed gathering them onto the "branches" of columns that he envisaged as a sort of "tree." They became the prototype of a long series of similarly branched columns designed to pick up loads with highly visible drama.

His original sketch on the back of the proverbial envelope showed the column with a sinuous, curved outline coming to a series of points on which the building was to rest. (The pointed shapes were to recur years later in Lajkó's brass candlesticks.) By the time I had worked this over with our structural engineers, the column had changed its character dramatically and looked strong enough to support a building. Some critics have said that the columns look strong enough to support a building several times as high. The length of the building and the slope of the land resulted in a difference in height between the shortest and the tallest columns. They varied from twelve to twenty-two feet. They are all the same shape and appear to be more or less buried in the turbulent landscape. The shortest columns branch out from a stubby shaft that is Romanesque in its proportions, while the tallest have an elegance associated with the Ionic. Viewed together, they cre-

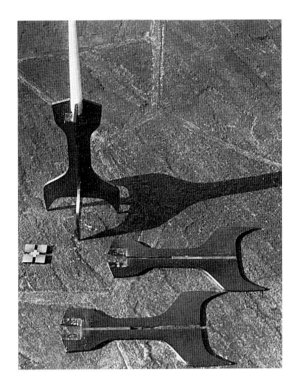

Breuer's interlocking candlesticks. Their pointed arms recall Lajkó's first sketch for the La Gaude tree column.

ate a looping colonnade that seems to be marching to mysterious music. There is something archaic about the building that Lajkó more than once referred to as being inspired by the ruins of a far-off civilization.

It is difficult to interrupt a repetitive facade such as La Gaude's with a major entry, and our instinct was to bring people into the building at the ground level, between the columns, as Lajkó later did at his headquarters for the Department of Housing and Urban Development in Washington, D.C. However, IBM insisted on having its staff, and particularly its visitors, come to one point of control at the main floor above. Lajkó didn't fight it (he rarely fought his clients) and decided to make a feature of the long triangular approach ramp and an appropriate entry "accident" in the otherwise unbroken facade. Critics have pointed to it as the one weak point in an otherwise powerful composition. But Breuer never sought pretty perfection and welcomed most opportunities for quirky incidents as giving to his architecture something of the improvised quality that he prized so in the native designs of old Europe and North Africa.

The design was developed and readied for presentation a bare three months after the start of contract negotiations. It consisted of a very detailed model and about ten large sheets of rendered ink drawings that were shown in a spiral-bound, plastic-covered presentation book. It was one of our best, with air-brushed blue sky behind the elevations and surfaces in section

105

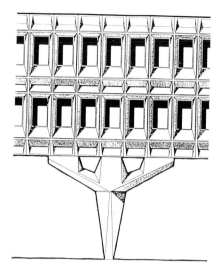

IBM La Gaude. This facade detail was shown on the cover of our presentation book to IBM.

pochéd in red-orange. The cover spelled out "IBM France" in my own variant of Paul Rand's great corporate logo and featured a large-scale rendered portion of the repetitive facade and the column that supported it. Because of the curves in the facade, and the constant changes in the angle of view, the elevations had been laborious to draw and render with shadows. Dick Meier worked long and hard on many of those drawings and received praise for their high quality. I held on to the presentation book until the mid-1990s when the Centre Georges Pompidou in Paris asked whether we had any original Breuer documents to include in a show they were mounting of IBM's many beautiful buildings in Europe. I offered the presentation book as one of the few documents not already given to the Breuer archives in Syracuse and Washington, D.C. Displayed in the exhibition, it is now in the permanent architectural collection of the Pompidou.

The design and model had already been shown to and approved by Ralph Mork and El Noyes on behalf of IBM when Lajkó and I set off to make a presentation to Arthur Watson in his office at U.N. Plaza in April 1960. The mounted drawings had been delivered early in the morning along with the model, and each sat under wraps on easel and table in Watson's office. We were sitting in the waiting area outside the chairman's office when his previous meeting ended. Three dark-suited corporate executives filed out with grim faces and were waiting for the elevator right next to my chair when I overheard one of them mutter between clenched teeth something like "Okay, Billy-boy, if that's the way it has to be, but I'm not going down without dragging others along with me . . ." I remember saying to myself and later to Lajkó that we were probably walking into the remnants of a firestorm that could have an effect on our meeting.

If so, it was a beneficial effect. Maybe Watson enjoyed getting things off his chest. In any case, the presentation went extremely well and Ralph Mork told us afterward he couldn't remember a better one. During the discussion, after receiving approval and congratulations, Breuer asked Watson what provisions should be made for eventual expansion of the 75,000-square-foot facility and he was told to provide for the possibility of a doubling, but no more, since the company had rules against concentrating more than 150,000 square feet at any one laboratory site. The building was in fact doubled in size while we were preparing the working drawings during the subsequent year—the Y became an H, and in the years that followed, we returned to the site as architects for three more major expansions while IBM bought up the neighborhood.

Lajkó's vision for the principal spaces of the interior was luxurious and featured extensive use of a dark North African hardwood resembling ebony. Laurie Maurer was responsible for much of the interior detailing, and we both remember the delight with which she drew up the dark wood push plates for the glass doors to the conference room. They were to be built up of thin laminations that defined a surprising hyperbolic paraboloid as their surface. The drawing took a day or so to work out; I was sad to see on a later visit that the final shape had simply been approximated as a folded plane.

The doubled project was bid in the following spring and awarded to a very good old-line French contractor, Dumez et Thorrand. The company was experienced in concrete construction and elected to precast the facade panels on site in an open-air factory built just for that purpose—another bene-

Breuer and his associate architect, Pierre Laugier, at La Gaude.

107

fit of the mild Mediterranean climate. Breuer arranged for his teen-aged son Tom and one of his New Canaan high-school classmates to work at the job site for the summer as common laborers. When Lajkó made his first site visit later in August he reported several surprises.

First, our working drawings, which had been labeled in English, with space systematically left for a French translation by our associate architects, were being used with no such translations (our associates found it to be unnecessary and pocketed the translation fee); instead, all the workers—French, Portuguese, Italian, and North African—were speaking an IBM patois of mispronounced American architectural terms that everyone had quickly learned and had no trouble deciphering. Second, Tom and his friend were bronzed giants who had been promoted to assistant chiefs of the concrete batching plant.

The decision as to how much water should be mixed with how much cement and gravel to make sound concrete is a very serious one and subject in the United States to all sorts of rules of the American Concrete Institute, interpreted by experienced foremen. After he had recovered his composure, Lajkó asked his son what measures he took to control the water-cement ratio. Tom reached down into the damp mix and rubbed it between his fingers while he explained that it had to "feel right" and that he had been carefully coached by the old chief. Breuer asked no more questions and the concrete has weathered reasonably well in the intervening thirty years.

The beautiful colored photograph of the laboratory under construction was chosen for the cover of the IBM Annual Report in 1962, and both Watson brothers have lavished the project with praise since its construction. The French government named it a Monument of French Modern Architecture several years later and thus protected it from any exterior renovation. The most significant honor for me came in the course of a taxi ride up Madison Avenue past the Whitney Museum with Lajkó in the late 1960s. He said, "I know most people think the Whitney is my most successful building, but my personal favorite is La Gaude."

James Marston Fitch had been the editor of *Architectural Record* for many years and knew and published much of Breuer's early American work. In 1960 he was a professor at the School of Architecture of Columbia University and was organizing a series of symposiums dedicated to the work of what he considered to be the four giants of modern architecture: Frank Lloyd Wright, Mies van der Rohe, Le Corbusier, and Walter Gropius. Each was to give a talk at Columbia and receive an honorary doctorate. Fitch called Breuer and asked if he would participate in the panel discussing and honoring Gropius. He was shocked to learn that Lajkó refused to participate in the program unless *his* name was added to the list of honorees, increasing the number to five. It is one of the very few instances I know of in which

*IBM La Gaude.
My daughter is at
the foot of its tallest
column. Raggedy Ann
is thirty centimeters
high, Alexandra is
one meter tall, and
the column measures
seven meters.*

Breuer spoke and acted directly on the issue of his fame and place in history. His name had been fifth out of six "20th Century Form Givers" as listed by *Time* in July 1956 (after Jim's four and ahead of Richard Neutra). None of Breuer's ardent fans would try to insert him into the sacred trio of Wright, Mies, and Corb, but I suspect it was Fitch's inclusion of Gropius that rankled Breuer, despite the debt he must have felt toward his old mentor.

Lajkó did see himself as an extraordinary figure, however, and this was reflected in his business card. Breuer had never carried one and at some point, when introductory cards were flying around a European conference table, someone must have mentioned that he should have a card. So he designed one. It was relatively small, square, and simply said "Marcel Breuer" along its upper edge. No title, no address, no telephone number. He was by that time a historical figure.

The church at Saint John's Abbey was under construction in 1960. Negotiations with McGough Construction of Minneapolis had been successful, and Ted Hoffmeyer had signed on as its superintendent. Val Michelson was in place as our clerk o' the works and had developed a very good working relationship with Ted. Val was busy checking shop drawings and working out in detail the complex geometry of the formwork for the bell banner that stood in front of the church.

Ham was making regular visits to the field, as was Jim Leon for Wiesenfeld, Hayward and Leon, the structural engineers. At some point in the middle of things, the relationship between Jim and Ted Hoffmeyer began to sour, and letters were sent to the architects protesting Jim's "attitude" in the field. This came as a surprise to the rest of us, since Jim was normally easygoing and friendly. Hindsight suggests that the tension may have begun early in the job when Ted had questioned the amount and position of steel reinforcing in the thin folded concrete plates of the church roof. This had come up in a job meeting but Lajkó had such confidence in Leon that he brushed the objections aside as of no consequence, although Ted's interference must have annoyed Jim.

The process proposed by McGough for the placing of the concrete was called Gunall and involved the projection, via huge hoses, of a very dry mixture of the concrete components against the surface of the formwork. Lajkó remained skeptical, in part because of personal experience with the similar sounding Gunnite that is used in quite different fashion for concrete swimming pools. After hearing the favorable results of full-scale testing conducted by Val and Ted, Breuer finally and reluctantly removed his objections with what the then thirty-six-year-old Val remembers as, "Well, okay. It's your responsibility . . ."

By the middle of the year the folded structure of the church had been erected and cured, and the wooden formwork against which the concrete

*The Saint John's
banner under
construction. Pete
McGough is in the
center of the group
of three on the left;
Val Michelson,
Jim Leon, Ham,
and Lajkó are
on the right.*

had been placed was being removed. The steel "shoring" (temporary support columns) had been sold to the Cold Springs Granite Company and was already off site. Inspection of the broad roof planes showed that the concrete was visually extremely well done, the pattern of its form boards giving it life and scale. Occasional fine cracks began to appear and were routinely reported back to New York. As concrete cures, it has to shrink. Fine cracks are not unexpected and would have been totally invisible from the floor of the church. The problem that began to develop had to do with the frequency and the pattern of the cracks, which ran parallel to one another at forty-five degrees and other angles radial to the span of the folded plates. This suggested an excessive shear stress—"shear" being the ability of any structural material to resist internal sliding of its own particles against one another. At Val's suggestion, plaster patches, or "telltales," were applied across some of the cracks to see if they were widening or had stabilized. The plaster itself cracked, and it began to be clear that something was very wrong. Telephone calls to Jim Leon led to recomputation on his part, and without acknowledging any defect in his design, he began to suggest a series of corrective measures that might be taken.

Val went to see the abbot, made some remarks about the risks that Abbot Suger had undertaken when he ordered construction of the first Gothic vaults in the twelfth century, and ordered all workmen out from under the shell of the church. He called New York but Breuer was in Europe; when Ham found him, Lajkó's first reaction was "It's the Gunall!" Then he asked that photographs and diagrams of the cracking be sent immediately to Pier Luigi Nervi in Rome. In fact, when Breuer telephoned, Nervi was able to diagnose the problem even before receiving the data based on his own personal experience, and that of Europe generally, with folded plate structures. He was sure that the American engineers had credited 25 percent of the shear force to the concrete itself, which is appropriate with horizontal slabs but not inclined ones. In the legal inquiry that resulted, it was shown that Jim's design had followed the code of the American Concrete Institute for concrete slabs and that folded plates were simply not covered by code. All of the American engineers questioned said they would have done the same thing at the time.

I was not directly involved in any of these discussions, which were carried on behind closed doors between Lajkó, Ham, and Jim in New York and Val and Ted in the field. But the air of tension in the office was palpable and everyone knew that something was up. At some point, Lajkó's sorely strained confidence in Jim Leon snapped and he called in Paul Weidlinger for an urgent consultation.

Paul was in the office a few hours later and spent a good part of the night reviewing the calculations that Jim supplied to him. He reported his initial conclusions the next day: there was no danger of immediate collapse, provided that the shoring was promptly replaced; and there was not enough steel in the concrete roof plates. The abbot was kept informed of every development; John Alexander, president of Cold Springs Granite, was the only outsider with a "need to know," since the company was asked for, and quickly returned, the steel shoring. Various insurance companies got embroiled in determining who was at fault and who should pay for the repairs. The task of redesign was a complex one: to keep the costs low enough to avoid bankrupting anyone while avoiding a ruinous end to Jim's professional career.

Paul, working with Jim, devised an ingenious method of repair that involved blowing another layer of new concrete against the inside planes of the triangular tubes that spanned the church. This new concrete would bond itself to the existing concrete with the help of specially installed anchors that were drilled into the structure and contained new, needed reinforcing. Prior to beginning the repairs, the method was tested for two months in the field on full-size simulated slab sandwiches with reinforced layers of "shotcrete" and anchorage as proposed. Repeated load tests could not separate the component slabs and the repairs went ahead.

With the client's agreement, no word of the problem was ever made public and the engineer's insurance company paid for the cost of the repairs. I learned only recently that Breuer carried no professional liability insurance himself at the time and could easily have been financially ruined if anyone had found him liable for his engineer's errors of calculation. Needless to say, our firm was fully insured after these events.

The church stands today, well over thirty years later, strong and proud as if nothing had ever happened. Lajkó once told Bernie Marson that his principal regret was that he would be unable to work with Jim Leon ever again. Weidlinger Associates became our structural engineer of choice from that time on, and Paul's young associate, Matt Lévy, who did much of the crisis legwork on the church redesign, became the Breuer office's close friend.

I recently asked Paul Weidlinger how he would compare the conceptual error with more recently publicized structural problems such as those encountered at Citicorp in New York and John Hancock in Boston. He assured me that they were in no way comparable. He considered Saint John's to have been a minor, albeit potentially very serious, error of calculation rather than conception—the sort of "there but for the grace of God" mistake that could occur, unfortunately, in any professional office despite the most careful controls. He did add that all concerned were very lucky to have discovered the problem in time to repair it elegantly and silently.

I happened to be in Lajkó's office one day in early 1960 when he received a telephone call from **Eric Boissonnas** an old New Canaan friend calling from Paris. He had me wait while he took the call and mentioned to me briefly after-

113

Eric and Rémi
Boissonnas at Flaine.

ward the possibility of a new ski town at Flaine, in the Haute-Savoie region of
France. It seemed like a long shot, and in any case Breuer understood that he
was being asked only to be the master planner of architectural work that
would be produced locally by others. He reminisced briefly about his project
for a hotel in Obergurgl, Austria, just before World War II, when he was apparently a very good skier, and we went on to other matters.

The valley Eric Boissonnas had briefly described to Lajkó over the telephone measures about two miles wide by four miles long and nestles in the
French Alps about an hour and a half's drive south and east of Geneva. Its
floor is at an altitude of about one mile above sea level. The mountains that
surround it rise another 3,500 feet or so and create a bowl shape with steep
cliffs to the north and broad, sunny slopes to the south. It was vacant in the
1950s except for some shepherds' huts and one shelter for overland hikers,
called Fédération. The land was owned by about three hundred French farm-
ing families, some of whom still drove sheep up to summer pastures, but
during the winter, snows blocked the only path up from the nearby towns
of Arâches-les-Carroz.

Gérard Chervaz, an architect who taught at the University of Geneva,
and René Martens, who ran a small company that made yogurt, were skiing
buddies who occasionally rented a light plane to take them for spring skiing
on the slopes of Mont Blanc. Flying up from Geneva in the mid-1950s, they
often crossed right over Flaine and wondered why such a conveniently
located valley had not been developed for skiing, at the time a booming
business in Europe. They researched the matter and in 1958 secured an
option on the valley's development from the local French authorities. They

114

soon found that their banking contacts in Switzerland were not interested in investing in France and began to look elsewhere. Their search finally led them to **Rémi Boissonnas,** a banker in Paris, who called his brother in Connecticut, knowing that Eric had decided to leave his wife's family's company, Schlumberger, and was looking for something to do. Involvement in the project led to Sylvie and Eric's return to France and would occupy most of their energies, and money, for thirty years.

Eric was a scientist/musician with business experience. Sylvie, like her sister Dominique de Menil, was a patron of the arts and a collector with impeccable taste. The couple had hired Philip Johnson to design a house in New Canaan, which wrapped around Eric's pipe organ, quite close to Johnson's own Glass House and to the Breuers. Philip later designed another spectacular house for them in Cap Bénat overlooking the Mediterranean, but he was irked when he heard that they had given the Flaine commission to Lajkó. Sylvie has said that he complained, "Breuer, I suppose, is good for big things whereas I'm only good for little things . . ."

By the time Eric took over the reins at Flaine in 1959, the design group already included several local architects expert in the layout of ski trails and alpine planning. Eric added a very progressive firm of economic planners headed by **Max Stern,** about whom he had read in *Le Monde,* and Max led him to an eccentric French structural engineer, **Jean Barets,** who was trying to market a system of prefabricated concrete parts for building construction.

Barets's approach appealed to Eric's intellectual side, and they soon developed a scenario involving precasting the building pieces in the Arve River valley below Flaine, where water and transport were readily available, and carrying the pieces by overhead télépherique to the building site. Barets argued that Eric could thereby gain crucial time and save interest on his investment while the road was improved and extended past Arâches-les-Carroz, over the pass, and into the valley.

The firm Eric founded to develop Flaine and to own its buildings was located in Paris—the Société d'Etudes de Participation et de Développement (SEPAD). In order to buy land and plan the surroundings, he needed a quasi-public corporation—the Société d'Aménagement Arve et Giffre (SAG)—which he named after the two rivers bordering Flaine. It was directed on a day-to-day basis by a brilliant and experienced civil engineer named **Frédéric Berlottier.** All of these people, and the work they had done, were unknown to me and, with the exception of Sylvie and Eric, to Lajkó in 1960.

*Marcel Breuer in his
office, 1960.*

New York:
1960–1963

By the time of an associates' luncheon several weeks after we received the phone call from Boissonnas, Lajkó had received some maps locating the valley of Flaine and an outline of the program, and had signed a two-page agreement for work on a cost-plus basis that was to last for twenty years. We briefly discussed the assignment of an associate-in-charge. Herb Beckhard was the logical choice, having just come back from Caracas with little else in the way of major projects in New York.

Paul Koralek had left a résumé a few weeks earlier that mentioned his fluent French. He was hired to digest the enormous written program that had started to arrive from France, and he continued with the project for the balance of the year. He worked under Herb's supervision but had direct access to Breuer—a tribute to the immediate rapport that sprang up between the two men. They developed a series of trial-and-error schemes for the layout of Flaine as a resort town based on the environmental studies of Laurent Chappis, a member of Eric's original design team who looked at the valley first in terms of exposure to the sun, viability of ski trails, and risk of avalanche. As the only one who had waded through the French texts, Paul felt honor-bound to speak up for the functional pros and cons of building placement as opposed to the sculptural effects that seemed to be driving Breuer's search for a solution. The very large contour model of the valley, built up of hundreds of layers of thin cork, became an object of wonder in the drafting room. It measured six by four feet and rose about two feet above its base. Pushpins defined alternate routes for the road snaking down from the pass above, and small wooden blocks were moved around daily by Lajkó

Fred Berlottier with Lajkó at a master-plan discussion in Annecy.

as he searched for the form of a town that could be created at the base of the awesome cliffs.

Lajkó first visited Flaine Valley by helicopter with the Boissonnas brothers in the spring of 1960. Rémi Boissonnas remembers meeting him for the first time as he landed in the midst of the northern slope: "Breuer got out of the helicopter, waddled over to a nearby rock, and sat down. After fifteen minutes, during which he looked carefully but said hardly a word, he indicated that he was satisfied and asked to be taken to the other side of the valley. There he got out, waddled to another rock, surveyed the scene, and that was it. I remember noting that he was a very good listener." According to Eric, Lajkó's principal remark was "We must not spoil the site."

Lajkó returned to New York and continued his own personal evaluation of the site. Several months later, Eric's design team appeared in New York, and its three French architects presented their preliminary sketches of a site plan. Lajkó listened attentively to the presentations, and when he spoke eventually in critique, his remarks were totally practical in nature rather than the aesthetic evaluation that the French had been expecting. He pointed to contours that would cause a road to drop suddenly by ten feet, a plateau that was not wide enough for the depth of a useful building, and the interruption of a ski trail by a road crossing. Rémi says that the French architects were totally deflated and that he was embarrassed for them by the time Breuer rose tentatively and modestly to show the sketches on which he and Paul had been working. They showed a greater familiarity with the actual site, gained through a careful study of documents and the model, than that of the local people who had been walking and skiing the valley for months.

Sylvie Boissonnas said of Lajkó, "He had such strength, and he made good sense, too."

Members of the design team—architects, planners, and client—would come to New York every other month for a few days of discussions, and on alternate months Lajkó would attend meetings in Paris with his latest scheme. The topography of the mountain terrain was so complex that the working model, which had changed by the time of each meeting, was an indispensable aid with which to picture the logical route for an approach road and to find areas flat enough to be adapted as building sites.

During a lull in the Flaine job, Paul Koralek worked with Ham Smith on the presentation of our entry to a developers competition for Charles Center in Baltimore. Our sponsor was the Ferry family, for whom Lajkó had also worked at Vassar College and the Bryn Mawr School. The project boasted two spectacular five-armed tree columns at its base. According to Paul, great care was lavished on these huge sculptural objects at the sloping ground level while the stories above were treated as being almost unimportant—not an entirely unreasonable response to the way the average pedestrian experiences an office building. One of the other competitors was Mies van der Rohe—who eventually won—and the drafting crew was excited to be in such exalted company, although Breuer shrugged it off.

By the end of 1960 Koralek had agreed to move to France to participate as Lajkó's representative in a Flaine planning office run by the design team. But when he won the Dublin Library competition, on which he had worked after hours with two classmates, he decided that his career required his return to his home in London. It was clear to Lajkó that Flaine would somehow have to be restaffed.

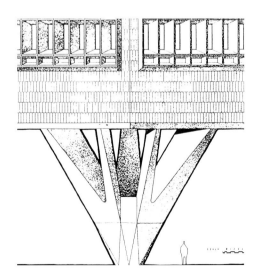

The Charles Center project. There were to be two of these tree columns at the base of the tall office structure where there was a sharp drop in the site.

The matter came up at the next associates' luncheon in early 1961. Herb was less than enthusiastic about the prospect of taking over the project directly without Paul and his knowledge of French. After the dashed hopes of Herb's Caracas adventure, Flaine seemed just one more pipe dream. In addition, a brand-new building commission for a temple in Short Hills, New Jersey, had just been offered to Breuer, and Herb preferred to be in the running to head up its design crew—a decision that Lajkó usually made on the basis of each associate's work load. Although he expressed a general opposition to switching horses in midstream, Breuer had no strong feelings in the matter, and he suggested, as he occasionally did, that in the absence of any overriding reason one way or the other we should decide by the flip of a coin—a very "American" way. Herb won the toss and chose Temple B'nai Jeshurun. I was assigned to take over Flaine.

Lajkó and Herb designed a very handsome, large synagogue, and a big crew produced the working drawings under Herb's direction. It included Dick Meier, whose parents were members of the congregation. He worked for many weeks on the design of the menorah and in developing a method for gilding ceramic tile—a typical Breuer juxtaposition of noble and common materials—which was to be used at the bema of the temple.

Unfortunately all this work came to naught when the 1961 bids turned out to be high and the congregation decided to abandon the project. Its cancellation came as a particular surprise since the congregation was a wealthy one and their representatives had not been particularly demanding about budget restrictions. Apparently several factors worked against us: the client's representative with whom we had been dealing got sick; he was replaced by a new man who felt he had to assert his own authority at a time when the stock market took a sudden nosedive and fund-raising pledges became hard to redeem. It didn't help that most good contractors were busy working on the upcoming New York World's Fair.

Breuer sued the congregation for the unpaid balance of our fees. The matter went to arbitration, and once again, Lajkó's confidence in the method of dispute resolution was supported when we got a full award rather than the usual fifty-fifty split. The congregation eventually built a smaller project with the Gruzen Partnership as architects that cost more than the bids on Breuer's design.

Herb's energies were quickly absorbed by a new assignment, the design of a Catholic parish church in Muskegon, Michigan—Saint Francis de Sales. After having brain-stormed with Paul Weidlinger on a variety of structural possibilities, Lajkó came into the office with a sketch of his choice, which was based upon side walls in the shape of hyperbolic paraboloids. They initially met at a point, then at a line, and were finally resolved in a tilted trape-

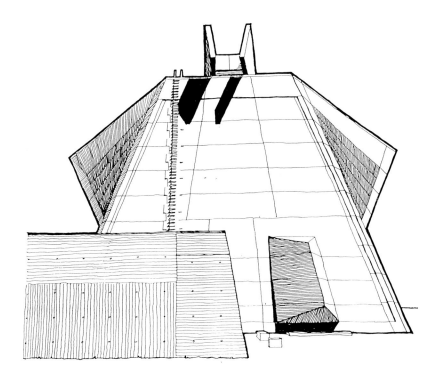

Saint Francis de Sales (after Bill Hedrich). The rear facade was more complex and intriguing than the front.

zoid supported by twisted "bents" that Herb developed from the initial framing plan proposed by Matt Lévy. The church, in terms of both exterior and interior, is pure sculpture and one of Breuer's most confident and convincing designs.

The problem was how to build such an unusual structure within the limited budget of the church. A Chicago contractor named Mike Lombard—a devoted Catholic whose two daughters were nuns—was consulted early in the proceedings, and an ingenious method of pouring the warped surfaces in eight-foot-high sections was worked out. This most striking monument to architectural and engineering ingenuity in a small town in Michigan would never have existed but for a miraculous coincidence of dedicated collaborators coming together at just the right time.

To help in drawing up the initial ink presentation for Muskegon, Herb interviewed and Lajkó hired a young Cuban expatriate, **Guillermo Carreras.** His first stop in New York in 1961 had been the Breuer office, where he arrived without drawings or résumé and was told by fellow Cornell alumni Dick Meier and Tom Simmons that there were no openings. Thanks to his banker father's friend David Rockefeller, one of Skidmore, Owings & Merrill's principal clients, he spent a year with SOM and, after briefly considering a return to Cornell for his master's degree, ended up back at

121

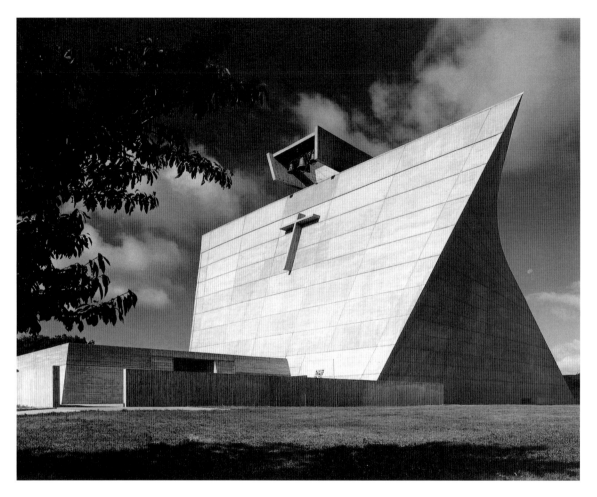

*Saint Francis de
Sales. The form of this
powerful building
derives from its sup-
porting hyperbolic
paraboloid side walls.*

Breuer's. He found the new office much more to his liking, although his father was sure he'd offended Rockefeller by leaving SOM. At his first meeting, Lajkó greeted him with, "Those are very nice drawings. Do you like to work here? By the way, we're having a little party for the staff . . ."

Breuer had been invited in 1961 to visit Pakistan in connection with a master-planning job for a new capital city to be called Islamabad—perhaps the country's answer to Le Corbusier's work at Chandighar in India. It was a fantastic commission, but Breuer was leery of doing work so far from home. It may be that Connie didn't like him traveling so much or that he had heard horror stories from other architects about not getting paid. In any case, he could not resolve a contractual issue with the Pakistani government and refused the commission. The problem had to do with the arbitration of potential disputes, which the government wanted to refer to its supreme court. Breuer held out for the International Chamber of Commerce, assuming that the Pakistani court might be biased. The meetings broke up in acrimony: "You mean to suggest, Mr. Breuer, that a Pakistani supreme-court justice would not be fair?!" Many times later Lajkó wondered out loud whether he should have given in to secure such an exceptional job.

On the way back from Pakistan, Lajkó and Ham Smith, who had accompanied him, had planned a layover in Athens. Ham had the joy of roaming the Acropolis with Breuer, who was admiring and unstinting in his praise of the superimposition of that marble marvel on its rocky base. When Ham mentioned that he had never visited the hill towns of Italy, Lajkó made him change his plane ticket at once and take a detour on his way home. According to Ham, his later discussion of the black-and-white-striped marble of the Orvieto Cathedral influenced Breuer's decision to use black-and-white striated marble-faced panels for the facade of the addition to the Cleveland Museum, which the two were later to design together.

In taking over Flaine, I plunged into the correspondence and drawings that had been produced in a year of work with Paul Koralek. There were eight volumes of commercial program data, all in French, and I understood very little of the language. Paul said I was not to worry, since Lajkó had waved it all aside in order to concentrate on the three-dimensional problem of fitting building shapes into the hollows of the valley. In fact, Paul was rather surprised to find one of the preeminent "functionalists" of the modern school making formal compositions independent of their eventual use. Were these blocks of buildings that formed streets and squares to be used for hotels, apartment houses, or shops? Lajkó didn't seem to care at that point. It was also a surprise for me since every other project I'd ever worked on with him had begun with a rigorous analysis of the program, its areas, and its interrelationships.

His reliance upon sculptural instinct rather than fickle programming was based upon his experience and proved to be correct. In the years that were to follow, many of the components changed their role not once but several times in response to the realities of a wild real-estate market. He saw that the first problems to be solved were how to get vehicles into the town without crossing the paths of pedestrians and skiers, and how to relate building forms in an unobtrusive way to the overwhelming physical drama of the bare stone cliffs that lined the northern face of the valley. The use of the buildings would come later. The first master plans were more theoretical than practical since Breuer knew little of how a winter resort worked; for example, the original skating rink was a dramatic circle, but people don't skate in circles. In fact, Lajkó, and the rest of us, had no idea what we were getting into.

I approached our first design meeting in New York with excitement and some trepidation. How would this august body of French professionals accept a new lieutenant who spoke no French and had a lot to learn in catching up with their deliberations? As I met and got to know them, my fears subsided and I realized that the best evidence of Eric Boissonnas' genius lay in the high quality of the people he had chosen to work with him and the decency and fairness with which he presided over their deliberations. It was a project that occupied the rest of his business life, and while it gave him and Sylvie many problems, it was ultimately a source of great satisfaction.

The geometry involved in creating alpine roads is challenging, since the rates of ascent and descent must be strictly limited in percentage terms

Eric Boissonnas, Gérard Chervaz, René Martens, Breuer, and Max Stern on the slopes of Flaine, 1960.

Flaine, 1961.
The alpine shelter,
Fédération, was still
standing at the start
of construction.

and must periodically provide a space wide enough to include the partial circle of a hairpin turn. Throughout 1960, Fred Berlottier, the chief engineer and technical director, had traced the route of the new road from Arâches-les-Carroz over the pass and down to the first set of cliffs. To keep the costs under control he tried to minimize blasting and the need for bridges.

Construction had just started when the first snow fell in October 1960. Plans were stymied at that point, however, by the natural terrain and the need to avoid crossing certain of the ski trails with the road. When I joined the team, it was on its third or fourth variant of the master plan, which was based on bringing cars eastward along the base of the cliffs to the north and then descending south and west on a spiraling bridge that would provide a dramatic but expensive entry to town. There were other objections to the scheme besides its cost, and we faced a figurative and literal impasse. All our drawings were derived from complex topographic maps that had not been surveyed in the field, because of the difficulty of access, but were generated by remarkable aerial stereographic techniques that were nevertheless limited in accuracy. There was one point on the map just west of the future town where the contour lines, which join points of common elevation, all came together in a big black mess that had been assumed to indicate a tall or even overhanging cliff. It threatened to become the absolute obstacle.

Fred Berlottier was not convinced and, after worrying about it for months, asked for a helicopter reconnaissance to look at the location close up. As the helicopter hovered in front of the cliff, Fred could see that there was just barely room for one last narrow hairpin turn, and the problem was solved. Driving in today, no one is the wiser, but I always slow down for that last turn, remembering the drama of Fred's discovery.

The guidelines that had been established at the outset and were to influence what was eventually built included: no parking in town (drivers get a ticket if their cars stand longer than ten minutes before returning to a parking field); short walking distances for those carrying skis (hence, a con-centration of relatively high buildings rather than the customary widely scat-tered chalets—a practice Lajkó used to call "smearing houses like butter all over the landscape"); minimal air pollution and avoidance of tearing through frozen roadways to access underground utilities (which led to a gas-fired central heating plant that gave off only water vapor—Breuer's wood-burning fireplaces create the only smoke in town—and a network of utility tunnels that distributed high-pressure hot water for heating to all the buildings and allowed a maintenance worker to stand erect inside when making repairs to the plumbing). These rules were tough to abide by and required a client who was willing to invest for the long haul, but Eric was just that. The goal was a clean town with white snow where children could run anywhere and friends would pass each other at central meetingplaces rather than wave from within cars. It seemed like something worth trying to achieve.

The basic building blocks of the town were to be hotels with varying degrees of luxury (although few ski hotels try to compete with their city cousins). They were measured by the standards of the Credit Hôtelier from five stars (deluxe) to a modest two stars (even our two-star hotels were eventually reclassified as three stars because of all the nice features we built into them). Each hotel was to be paired with and directly connected to an apartment house so that co-op owners could use the hotel restaurants and turn their apartment keys over to the hotel staff for service while the own-ers were away and subletting.

The final master plan of 1961 (it was to continue through many more revisions as experience and governments dictated changes) called for a five-story luxury hotel and apartment house along the north side of the central square, a comfortable pair of four-story buildings defining the western edge, and a modest pair to the south of only two stories so as not to spoil the view of the valley from the north. The buildings formed a U that was open to the eastern slopes and had a skating rink at its center, tucked into a rock out-cropping that had been the site of an old shelter for mountain hikers. Immediately surrounding the central pedestrian space at the town's center (a *place* in French, and a *piazza* in the drafting room) were to be shops, offices, cafés, and restaurants that would give Flaine the animation and the life of a real town. It was a European composition and one that Lajkó took to his heart.

Early on in the planning and design process, two of the local architects, Denys Pradelle and Laurent Chappis, began to tangle with Lajkó. He tried for a while to respect their local experience, but when they began to insist that only steeply sloping roofs could be used in the Alps, it was clear that we had a problem. It had been Eric's democratic idea that Flaine would contain buildings by a whole variety of architects whose relationship would somehow be made coherent under Lajkó's guidance. The theory never had to be put to the test since, once the master plan was resolved and approved, Pradelle and Chappis quietly withdrew from the design team, sensing that their ideas would never prevail over those of Lajkó as long as he had the total support of Eric Boissonnas.

There did remain the formality of getting the general council of SAG, the quasi-public body that controlled the land, to approve Breuer as the only architect of Flaine. A majority of its members were local politicians, and Eric feared that there might be some opposition on behalf of local, or at least French, architects who were in effect being shunted aside. The night before Eric was to go to Annecy to defend his decision, he found a pocket edition of a French encyclopedia by the bed of his young son when he stopped by to bid him good night. Leafing through it, he came upon the entry for "architecture" and found a roster of great architects of the past and a list of five great modern architects; Breuer was one. In mentioning this in the next day's meeting, he observed that among the five there was not a single French architect. Someone on the council, thinking that perhaps the encyclopedia's author was prejudiced against the French, asked about the previous centuries. In the seventeenth was Mansart, in the eighteenth was Gabriel, and in the nineteenth were Eiffel and Haussmann, although neither of these last were architects. Finally, a council member said, "All right, if, thanks to Mr. Breuer, Flaine becomes as well known as the Eiffel Tower, we'll have to accept him."

Guided by the commercial program of our planners, we began tentative sketches of what the buildings might look like. The technicians suggested a palette of exterior materials that began with concrete, both poured-in-place and prefabricated in the river valley below. This was to be combined with a local stone ranging in color from dark gray to sandy beige and an imported wood from Cameroon in French West Africa—doussié—that looked and acted like teak, due to its natural oils, and required minimum exterior treatment and upkeep. We were imposing a visual discipline similar to the natural homogeneity of the old villages of Europe. The pedestrian center would be embellished with flags, awnings, signs, umbrellas, and placards of every conceivable color, but the body of each building was to be very restrained in hue and appearance.

We had originally been encouraged by Jean Barets to be very free with our designs ("Anything is possible with precasting"), but after the first set of hotel plans, with their varying room sizes, had been submitted for discussion, he changed his tune ("We must be reasonable"). We were led through an exercise of standardization that would allow the maximum reuse of repetitive forms and a resulting economy in costs. It turned out to be remarkably easy and productive since the largest bedroom was to be about fourteen feet wide and the smallest about three-quarters of that, or ten feet. That meant that a pair of large bedrooms could be faced with four facade units while the small pair used three, provided that the central panel was blank or designed to accept the end of a partition.

Then it came time to establish exactly what the dimensions were to be. The luxury hotel, which was then called "A," was initially to have parking underneath the building between the poured concrete columns that supported it. The standard width for European parking stalls at that time was two and a half meters (about eight feet two inches), and the width of the columns necessary to support the seven floors above (five floors of bedrooms, a ground floor or rez-de-chaussée, and a penthouse) was forty centimeters (sixteen inches). Three cars at "2m50" (as it was written) plus one column at forty centimeters added up to "7m90"—just right for a pair of large hotel rooms. Of course, to the mathematically inclined (which included me, as the party responsible for the preparation of drawings), 7m90 was awfully close to a nice round eight meters, and considering that we were then going to divide this into halves and quarters, four and two meters seemed terribly logical. Eric Boissonnas had another logic in mind, that of absolute cost. He pointed out that eight meters was almost exactly 1.3 percent longer than 7m90 and that, rather than extend the length of each of the buildings, he would prefer that the draftsmen master the arithmetic.

And so it was that the basic planning module of Flaine for almost twenty years was 1m975, or "one ninety seven five!," as we used to shout across the drafting room. This measure, which is exactly 77 3/4 inches, was then occasionally divided into 98.75 centimeters, making a mockery of the beautiful metric system. A final ironic twist to this cautionary tale was provided by history. Construction was halted for a while on Hôtel A, and when work began again with a new program, it had grown two stories in height, adding ten centimeters to the required column width. In the meantime, however, parking under the buildings had been prohibited, so that we never had to go to eight meters after all. We took the ten centimeters out of the space between the columns and stayed with 7m90. Eric was right, of course—I can still do the mathematics in my sleep—but he was wrong about the size. All the rooms at Flaine are too small, but that had more to do with the times, economics, and our shared Calvinism.

Eric and his financial advisers had figured out that in the inflationary 1960s money could be saved by swift negotiations, rather than by traditional bidding, and we were under great time pressure to complete designs and drawings on or ahead of schedule. He had to invest ten million dollars in the access road and would be partially compensated by the government only after five hundred beds were available in hotels or apartments at Flaine—an arrangement that was obviously meant to preclude having the state pay for roads to nowhere if the developer was to go bankrupt. This put a premium on opening two hotels and an apartment house as soon as possible. It also led to an overall program based on ten thousand beds and a schedule that called for the completion of the town in ten years.

The pace of production picked up, and we met once a month for a week at a time, alternately in Paris and New York. Lajkó was always in attendance in New York, although he sometimes avoided the meetings to tend to other projects, while I was pretty much imprisoned with ten or more experts around the table. Initially everyone spoke English, but gradually the pressures of the project led to internal discussions in French, which I had either to begin to understand or risk being taken advantage of. My knowledge of the technical jargon grew quickly, but I was hopelessly lost when the same friendly figures conducted colloquial discussions at lunchtime. Lajkó's knowledge of French had never grown much past what he had learned in Paris in the 1920s, and his favorite ploy when stumped was to select an English word and give it a French pronunciation—which often worked.

In honor of his twelve years in the United States, and his choice of an American architect, Eric decreed that not only was Breuer to be referred to as Lajkó but that everyone on the design team was to go by first name or nickname. This succeeded remarkably well considering how contrary it was to normal French usage. Rémi told me years later, "I never had any problem calling you 'Bob'—after all, you were American—but for me Laurenti was never 'André.' Why, I never even went to school with him."

The rhythm of meetings imposed a rigorous discipline on the large drafting-room crew that was by now working on the project. Included were Peter Samton, **Jeff Vandeberg,** Guillermo Carreras, Allen Cunningham, and **Paul Willen**. Peter produced many of the early rendered elevations and perspectives that Lajkó used to sell his ideas. Breuer seemed to prefer his loose, conceptual style to the more polished professional renderings that were standard at the time. Jeff reminded me years later that I had suggested he be fired as a "goof-off" at some tense moment in the drafting schedule. Murray Emslie intervened, Breuer said he was to be "given to Herb," and Jeff went on to become a productive member of another crew. Jeff thought at the time, and perhaps still does, that, since he was the only Dutchman on staff, I was annoyed at his spreading the translation of my last name.

Guillermo worked on the team for two years. He was in charge of the detailed design of the first-stage buildings before he left in mid-1963 to join Peter Samton and Mario Romanach at the Gruzen firm designing buildings for the upcoming New York World's Fair. Allen came on board in late 1962 and soon proved to be the most responsible member of the group—thoroughly immersed in the sweep and complexity of the project, and immensely respected by Breuer. Paul Willen joined us late and briefly. He knew he had "arrived" when he was given the job of folding and filing all the hundreds of record prints of Flaine drawings that we accumulated in the New York office. With this special knowledge, he assumed he would avoid being laid off.

All-day meetings of the Flaine design team would be followed by hasty discussions over the drafting boards and frequent all-night work to change the drawings for the next day's meeting. If I were leaving for a week in Paris, many drawings had to be finished, printed, and folded in the French manner at the last minute while the taxi was waiting downstairs. Lajkó usually came along but would go off to Holland, Switzerland, or Belgium to look after other projects once the essential decisions had been made. We always stayed at the Hôtel Pont-Royal, which was just around the corner from the office of the SEPAD. It was Lajkó's favorite, since he had first discovered it in the 1920s, and was frequented by writers and movie stars.

Another ritual of the meetings in Paris was lunch. In New York we could only offer our clients a Third Avenue deli, but lunch in Paris was invariably at the Restaurant du Mont Blanc of Charles Allard on a little square behind the church of Saint Clothilde. It was an easy walk from the rue de Villersexel, and we would sometimes be twelve or fifteen in single or double file as we strode through the narrow streets of the seventh arrondissement. Eric insisted on everything being first-class and even paid for Lajkó to travel in the front of the plane, although there was one embarrassing flight when Breuer found his thrifty clients flying in the back.

Jean Barets convinced Eric that "fast track" bidding could surmount his time problem. This is a technique designed to select a contractor based on incomplete contract documents in order to get the contractor mobilized and underway while the documents are being finished. The time saved translates into savings in the escalation of costs in inflationary periods; the downside is a relatively restricted period of time during which the contractor is working on a cost-plus basis before a firm fixed-price bid is agreed to.

Our drawings for the first four or five buildings were fairly well advanced, but Lajkó was leery of using this procedure before the final details had been worked out. He preferred to see the specifications written and the architectural drawings coordinated with the structural and mechanical demands of our engineers, Barets's firm COFEBA—which were slow in coming and had already forced us into many last-minute revisions. Nevertheless he went along with the proposal, deferring to the French experts who were the responsible parties.

A solicitation for fast-track proposals was launched in early 1963, and

A detail of the Hôtel Le Flaine. All the essential materials of the ski town—board-form concrete, rubble-stone, wood, and pre-cast concrete—were to be seen in its first building.

one of the great national builders, Boussiron, was chosen based on its unit prices and fine reputation. Activity in the field really began to heat up as excavation began at the building site while construction of the precasting plant was completed in the river valley below.

We had designed three hotels, of which "A" was to be the most luxurious. Its facade was determined by Lajkó's desire to break away from the typical hotel plan in which closets were placed adjacent to the corridor by the bathroom: "Why not put it next to the window?" Why not, indeed? So I worked out a pattern whereby the closet block on one floor protected the

131

balcony of the floor below. It was a three-dimensional checkerboard with many ins and outs and resultant shadows. The problem lay in precasting its forms; the idea was set aside when the first bids came in and the future of Hôtel A was put on hold.

Hôtel B was more straightforward except for the fact that the land available for its foundations was cut short by a cliff that tumbled down to the valley floor below. Breuer decided to push the building out into the air over the cliff by means of an audacious concrete cantilever. I gulped silently when he first proposed the idea, since it seemed such an extravagant gesture, but its image, jutting out over its cliff, became a symbol of the resort that was published on the cover of innumerable international magazines. Sylvie remembers that Lajkó always liked to surprise people and catch them slightly off guard. It was certainly true that in the drafting room Lajkó felt free to make wild suggestions that the rest of us would only rarely have dared to offer and frequently tried to discourage.

The facade of Hôtel B was made up of what was to become a typical mixture of Flaine facade panels—windows with and without balconies and the famous inverted pyramid that Eric adopted as a trademark. It was nothing more than Lajkó's way of making a blank concrete panel look interesting under sunlight. (Hôtel B was soon to be renamed the Grand Hôtel Le Flaine after its sale to the Provenaz family, who ran the Grand Hôtel d'Albion in Aix-les-Bains.)

Hôtel C was renamed the Gradins Gris after its gray concrete steps and contained one of the most handsome of the many cast-concrete fireplaces with which we enlivened each of the hotel lounges.

Two apartment houses and a group of shops completed the first stage of construction for which Boussiron was under contract. Once we had completed all the documents for each, the contractor had agreed to turn the unit prices and cost-plus billing procedures into lump sums with which the SEPAD could budget and begin to plan for future construction.

I visited the site with Lajkó and others a number of times as the extraordinary project began. On one of the first of my visits, I shared the open steel back of a dump truck with René Martens, one of the original discoverers of Flaine, as we bounced along the provisional gravel road into the valley. We talked about the past, and he explained that at one time or another he had held three different passports as his family tried to keep him from conscription during World War I. One of them was American since he had gone to school briefly in the United States. My request for further details narrowed it down to New York, then to Brooklyn, and eventually to P.S. 152—the very same grammar school I had attended many years later.

By the summer of 1963 the cables had been stretched from the valley floor to the top of the Grandes-Platières, although the only vehicle that could ride them was an open box big enough for six people. It normally

Breuer with his golfing cane, André Laurenti, and me, Flaine, 1963.

took the workers up to the site of the upper lift station, then under construction. It was a thrilling ride, which would be duplicated in a proper gondola many times in subsequent years.

The valley of Flaine in its virgin state was truly remarkable. Bright sun and cool breezes were characteristic throughout the entire summer, and from a vantage point alongside the old stone hut, Fédération, at its center, with only the ashes in the fireplace to hint that anyone had ever been there in a hundred years, the valley was awesome. There were fields of moss and wildflowers, evidence of mountain goats and rabbits, wind song in the tall black pines, and gray rocks everywhere. The air was so clear that distances shrank, and it was hard to keep dimensions in mind no matter how familiar the survey maps. Rémi Boissonnas always kept this vision of Flaine and its first generation of pioneers as his ideal and regretted years later, in the full flower of its commercial success, that we had to share it with "all these people."

My first impressions of its wild beauty returned when I visited Flaine years later in summer with two of my daughters. We took the gondola to the summit of the Grandes-Platières and stepped out onto the crest that they had seen only as a broad snow field. Now the wind-worn mountaintop showed itself to be sliced by wide, deep crevasses that made even walking dangerous, and the taming of the valley for which we had been responsible during twenty years of construction could almost be forgotten.

One wintry evening the design team arrived at the Hôtel Croix de Savoie, at the far side of Arâches-les-Carroz where the new road began, and found that

Lunch in the workers canteen at Flaine, 1963. Sylvie Boissonnas and Christian Boucher are in the foreground; Breuer, Aliette Texier Laurenti, and I are in the background.

the power lines were down. Dinner was prepared over a coal stove and served by candlelight. With the snow beginning to fall heavily, we spent the night in the metal Quonset huts that had been built as the workers camp just above Flaine. When we awoke the next day, we were surrounded by three feet of new-fallen snow, and Eric announced that the morning's work session would be delayed until after lunch so that we could all go skiing.

As the pace of construction picked up, Eric began to get nervous about the time lost in sending drawings and messages back and forth between Paris and New York and asked Lajkó to consider again the idea of opening an office in Paris. Toward the end of the summer of 1963, Breuer asked me what I would think about moving to Paris and I put the question to Barbara that night in Bedford. Within a week my family began the preparations that were to see us move out of our home just after the new year and into a great adventure.

Establishing a new office had its complexities, and Lajkó decided that I should spend most of the month of November in Paris making the arrangements. Our economic planners, the Bureau d'Etudes de Réalisations Urbaines (BERU), owned a full floor in a new office building by the Parc des Expositions, southwest of the city center; and they had more space than they needed at that moment. Thanks to its president, Max Stern, we were offered temporary space there. I advertised in the *Figaro* for a secretary and draftsmen/designers and had hired three employees just before returning home for Thanksgiving. Drafting tables, desks, chairs, and file cabinets were ordered for January delivery, and my new friends at the BERU were extremely helpful in making us feel very much at home.

Lajkó came over to join me during the third week, and he approved of the arrangements I'd made. We dined with the Boissonnas family one night, and on the next he introduced me to his favorite nightclub—Le Crazy-Horse Saloon ("saloooon," as he pronounced it with glee). We stood at the bar and enjoyed the raucous show, although I was initially inhibited by all that female flesh while standing at the elbow of my fatherly mentor. The next night we were on the Right Bank for an opening of an exhibition of Alexander Calder's new "stabiles" (as opposed to his more familiar "mobiles") at the Maeght Gallery, where we met quite a number of Breuer's old friends. As seven o'clock approached, Lajkó's stomach was rumbling, and after making arrangements to breakfast the next morning with Leo Lionni, Calder, and one or two other friends, we headed off by taxi to his favorite Hungarian restaurant, Le Paprika. It was a festive evening highlighted by the appearance of a cimbalom player who had just defected from the French concert tour of the Hungarian National Orchestra. He played complex arrangements of old gypsy tunes that astonished me and reduced Breuer to tears of happiness.

The following morning, I was downstairs ahead of Lajkó and asked the concierge for my copy of the *Herald Tribune*, which he handed over, folded in quarters. I noticed a headline in the lower left-hand quadrant that spoke of "President" Johnson and said to myself, "The *Trib* is getting sloppy when they can't get the vice president's title right." Then I opened the paper to the shrieking headlines of Kennedy's assassination and shared the shocking news with Breuer a moment later. The report had hit the Maeght the night before, just moments after we had left, but I marveled that it had been possible for us to move around Paris oblivious to such horror. Once before I had seen world-shaking news for the first time in a newspaper headline—the dropping of the atomic bomb in the *Los Angeles Times* in Deep Springs, California—since the remote mountain location cut off radio transmission during the day. I never thought it could happen again.

Breuer and his friends huddled over breakfast as we explored the same dire possibilities that troubled the rest of the world that morning, but we were so far away from home that the conversation was edged in terror. I was only able to reach my family by phone a day later in Atlanta where they were visiting friends, and I joined a vast throng of expatriates to hear Ambassador Charles Bohlin speak at the American Cathedral that Sunday. I was invited to the home of French friends for dinner that night and my host suggested we watch the evening news to catch footage of some of the funeral preparations. At seven o'clock the screen went black with the startling announcement that late-breaking news of the assassination of Kennedy's assassin was awaited; the ground seemed to tremble in uncertainty. I have rarely been so glad to head home as I was a few days later, when I arrived just in time for Thanksgiving.

The Paris Office: 1964–1966

Marcel Breuer at Flaine, 1964.

My family sailed aboard the *France* in early January, and the first days in Paris were exciting, complicated, and didn't leave much time for productive work at the office. My new bilingual secretary, Solange Gaches, was in charge of the telephone and arranging for the delivery of office furniture, but it was a few days before a drafting staff began to assemble.

Allen Cunningham had been fully occupied with Flaine for a year or more, and he and his family were due to follow us to Europe in early March 1964. Lajkó had offered him an associateship—enthusiastically supported by the rest of us—but although he agreed to move to Paris, he was unwilling to make the ten-year (and perhaps permanent) commitment that Breuer wanted. Along with the Cunningham family, the Paris office also welcomed Guillermo Carreras and his wife and children. Although he had left the office six months earlier to follow his mentor, Mario Romanach, to the Gruzen office to work on the Spanish and American Express Pavilions for the New York World's Fair, he was offered the job captaincy of a new French commission by Breuer, which proved irresistible.

Meantime, the supposedly routine issuance of my residency permit (*carte de séjour*) was taking much more time than Cabinet Rougier, the expediter we had hired, had predicted, and I made repeated visits on short notice to the central police station on the Ile de la Cité, each time appearing with that "one more" document that had not been requested the previous time. The *carte* was a necessary prelude to all sorts of other business—opening bank accounts, getting a work permit—so the delay became a big deal. When the paperwork was finally complete I was amused

137

to read its explanatory, conspiratorial preface, which, loosely translated, said: "Mr. Gatje, having entered the country in the guise of a tourist, desires to have his status regularized . . ."

In Paris I established relations with two accountants, Guy Warnod (for our taxes) and a Monsieur Pert (for the books), and a lawyer, Jack Hutchins of Cabinet Archibald, and they served the office for years to come. Jack was an American who had settled in Paris with his wife, Alice, after his service at the Nuremberg trials and had handled Lajkó's affairs at UNESCO.

In the 1960s there was a small scholarship organization in New York called Atlantique that was devoted to the exchange of French and American architects. Some years before, its executive director, Annie Garrigue, a school friend of my wife's, had arranged for a job in the Breuer office in New York for Jean-Paul Kozlowski, a Polish-born, Parisian-trained architect. He was living with his wife in Paris when we arrived. We became friends with another Atlantique alumnus, Jean-Pierre Chevalier, who introduced me to one of his classmates from the Ecole des Beaux-Arts, **Eric Cercler.** I hired Eric as one of our first French employees along with **Daniel Chiquet,** a professional draftsman who was working toward his degree in architecture. Once Allen Cunningham was settled, we had the beginnings of an office. Drawings were unrolled and the design principles of Marcel Breuer in general and Flaine in particular were explained to the newcomers.

In coming to France I knew that I would be dealing with a different language, but I was totally unprepared for the legal differences of the Napoleonic Code, which would govern the practice and responsibilities of architects in constantly surprising ways.

Even the tools of the trade were different. In New York we made working drawings in pencil on soft-surfaced tracing paper. It required care and rubber erasers to keep the drawings from smudging during their life of continual change. Lettering was done by hand, and an ability to letter neatly in pencil was a matter of pride, and something I demanded.

In France the paper was hard and brittle. Drawings were laid out casually in pencil to be overlaid carefully in ink. Errors were corrected by scratching with a razor blade. Scribbled notes were replaced eventually with mechanical ink lettering using plastic templates. And worst of all, although a graduate architect was expected to lay out details and compose facades in pencil, it was up to a draftsman to translate the architect's grand designs into legible drawings. Eric Cercler was aghast at the idea that we were all expected to draft our own drawings and could never understand that I actually found pleasure in organizing and producing a fine graphic document.

If I had been more experienced, I might have decided that it was easier and better for us, as Americans, to adapt to the local traditions; instead, I insisted, with Lajkó's agreement, that we were an American office and we would run it our way. Everyone who flew over to Paris, including Breuer, usually carried a supply of drafting materials from New York to provide items that were not available on the Parisian market. Rolls of sketching trace were yellow in New York and white in Paris; erasers were pink and soft in the United States and green and hard in France; and so on. We did convince the French that our "parallel edges" were an improvement on T-squares and drafting machines, but we kept running out of the braided cable that made the edges work. In the years that have followed, thanks to exchange studies and work patterns, I've seen other offices in Paris begin to draw in pencil while some in New York have adopted ink. Today, computer-aided drafting (CAD) has in many cases made hand work a thing of the past.

Practicing architecture at "long distance," as Lajkó used to describe it, had its difficulties but also its advantages. The principal advantage in being in New York in those days was that our Flaine clients and engineers could not expect constant, daily attention and their questions and comments tended to be saved up for our monthly meetings. Once we were close at hand, the temptation to organize meetings for discussion and coordination proved irresistible, and COFEBA even put one of its engineers to work in our office. The pressure to complete our sets of coordinated documents was very real, and as we began to feel at home, the productivity of our drafting staff improved dramatically. By February 1964 we had eleven people at work on the boards. Lajkó paid us a first visit early that month, but once he had sampled the pace and detail of the coordination meetings, he moved on to other appointments in Europe. Soon the snows at Flaine would melt, and Boussiron, the general contractor, was anxious to be at work as soon as the ground began to thaw.

The Gatjes and the Sterns in the Forêt de Fontainebleau. The two families play boules as Lajkó looks on.

I found that being in Paris finally put us in a position to understand the enormous undertaking Eric Boissonnas had begun and the terrible difficulties that he was having in carrying it through. While we had been in New York, despite our monthly meetings in the early 1960s, Eric had chosen to keep me, and Lajkó, largely in the dark about the local political problems he had encountered. It may be that he reasoned that we could not possibly understand them (probably true) or that we were better left alone to do our architecture. In any case, once I was in place in France it was impossible not to hear stories, rumors, and facts (although it was sometimes difficult to tell one from the other) about our so-called friends in Annecy and Arâches-les-Carroz.

Improving the road up from Magland, through the villages en route and up to the start of our road, required the aid of the national government, the purchase of land, and the cooperation of the local municipalities. Our road, which the SAG was to build, descended from a pass called Pierre Carrée to the valley floor. For a time all was going well and land could be bought at the going rate. Then Gaz de France, which had to buy land by a specific date for the gas pipeline that was to fuel Flaine, began to bid at higher prices. Before long, land speculation on the part of the farmers, who should have felt some loyalty to the development that was going to enrich them in other ways, was rampant. There were 170 families involved, embroiled in centuries of friendships and feuds. If one farmer agreed to sell, it might cause a neighbor to renege on a previous agreement. This ballet went on for months. To try to calm the waters, Eric brought in an "expropriation judge" to set the land prices, but it was too late and the judge was literally run out of town by pitchfork. It was only when Eric threatened to close down the ski lifts in les Carroz, which he had bought in the meantime in order to modernize them, that the locals saw the wisdom of an orderly acquisition of land by Flaine.

As the building season of spring 1964 approached, the SEPAD was under severe financial pressure, and important low-interest loans that had been promised by FNAFU, a development arm of the national government, were months overdue. No one spoke openly of a crisis to come, but tensions were rising and there was a risk that all our efforts to rush drawings for the first four buildings through to completion might have been wasted. Writing in his own book about Flaine, Eric Boissonnas quotes a highly placed French official summing up the situation: "Flaine is something like a planetary space program whose launching is controlled by the way that cows are milked in Arâches."

France in the 1960s was far ahead of most other countries in terms of an enlightened national policy for urban planning and the construction of low-cost housing. One of the experts in the field was our planning consultant at Flaine—the BERU—in the person of Max Stern. The firm was already involved in the planning of several large projects that went by the acronym

*Flaine, 1964.
Eric Boissonnas,
Breuer, Jacqueline
Westerkamp, Gatje,
Pierre Lamy, and
Rémi Boissonnas
stand at the end
of the construction
road.*

ZUP (*zone à urbaniser en priorité*, or priority planning zone) and were usually under the control of very distinguished architects, including foreigners such as Oscar Niemeyer from Brazil. The ZUP program was an attempt on the part of the national government to stimulate local initiatives in the planning of extensions to or within existing cities and awarded a considerable subsidy, provided that the local city or town followed strict rules, chose good architects, and received approval of the final site plan from the appropriate ministries in Paris. The program worked well and several years later Lajkó spoke of his happy experience to a dinner partner, New York's Governor Nelson Rockefeller. I wrote a brief description of the process for Breuer in the late 1960s for transmission to Rockefeller, which may well have helped in the formulation of New York's successful planning program, the Urban Design Council (UDC).

Max knew of the plans of the city of Bayonne, a medium-sized city in southwestern France near the Atlantic coast and north of the more famous Biarritz, to launch a ZUP to develop and control a large area of land just across the Adour River from the center of town. Centuries ago, it had been the Jewish quarter, and the city had just acquired it by expropriation from several old landholding families. The program specified a resident population of fifteen thousand people in low- to medium-cost housing—so-called "HLMs" (*habitation à loyer modéré*, or housing at moderate rental)—and was a major undertaking for Bayonne. The BERU had already been named as programmer and commercial planner for the project, and Max Stern nominated Breuer as architect, noting that he was just about to open an office in Paris. The commission came through just before I left New York and gave Lajkó a good excuse to ask Guillermo to return to the office. The two had a drink together, and Breuer offered him the chance to join our new Paris office and to work on the ZUP as project manager. Guillermo made the move to Paris in February 1964.

The scheme developed for Bayonne consisted of an undulating line of twelve-story apartment houses riding the crest of the hill that was the northern boundary of the project and from which, at least from the upper stories, one could see the ocean. At the foot of this wall of buildings was a traditional town square surrounded by shops and four-story residential blocks, with other neighborhoods located along a parabolic ring road that gradually sloped down the hill to the plain alongside the river. It was drawn up after Guillermo's arrival in Paris and was ready for presentation toward the end of the month. Through subsequent years of refinement and use it has remained essentially true to the initial conception.

Guillermo stayed in our guest room for a month or so. When it came time for the presentation in Bayonne most of us had dinner together before going to the Gare d'Austerlitz for the ten o'clock overnight sleeper to Bayonne. Breuer and I joined Max, who was accompanied by Guy de Ponçins and Jean-Pierre Portefait from BERU. Guillermo had previous dinner plans with some old Cuban friends but promised to meet us at the station. We were all lounging around the train gate as the hour for departure approached and no one knew where Guillermo was. I called home and my wife told me that he had left hours before. Finally we had to board without the project manager and without any drawings.

Guillermo reached the train station just before eleven o'clock—he had misread the departure time on his ticket—and was crushed when he realized what had happened. He thought of driving all night but didn't have his driver's license. He returned to our apartment where he and Barbara considered all his options. He had learned that there was an early morning train to Bayonne and returned to the station at six o'clock after a sleepless night. Before boarding, he called the apartment one last time where Barbara had since received a message from Max in Bayonne suggesting a flight to nearby Pau.

We arrived in Bayonne at half past six and were driven out to the elegant hotel in the countryside that Max had booked for the entire party, arranging for it to be open out-of-season: the Larraldia Country Club. The club was a recent renovation of the eighteenth-century Château Larraldia and was renamed to attract the jet set to its swimming pool, golf course, and beautiful woodland setting. The outdoor sports facilities were of no use in February, but after the bumpy train ride, we welcomed the chance for a few added hours of sleep in huge old beds, of which Lajkó had the best—a four-poster in a grand chamber with a private fireplace.

We met Dr. Henri Grênet, the mayor, and members of his city council for an elegant lunch at the city hall. As we were about to start dessert, the mayor's chauffeur, who had been sent to Pau to pick up our project manager, returned empty-handed and assured us that he had waited until the last person was off the plane. We decided to start the meeting with Lajkó explaining his original thoughts in narrative form and Max doing the translating.

Dr. Grênet was the principal surgeon of Bayonne and represented the city in the National Assembly in Paris. Jokes were told of his arrival at afternoon meetings of the city council while wiping the blood from his hands on his surgical smock. His face showed a prominent scar—a souvenir of turning over his Alfa Romeo on the way north to Paris in the wee hours of the morning en route to the National Assembly. He proved to be an excellent, perceptive client.

His chief aide for our project was the city engineer, M. Ferrère, a native of the nearby Basque region who always wore a beret and spoke his French with *r*s that rolled off his tongue like the purr of a motorcycle. He took Breuer to the best hat shop in Bayonne to buy him a beret that Lajkó wore on and off for the rest of his life. The only other notable member of the client group, M. Forcade, the head of the local HLM society, ran the largest Renault dealership in the region. He was to be a real thorn in our side.

Just as we were about to give up all hope of proceeding with the presentation, a dusty taxicab roared up and out stumbled a bedraggled Guillermo, who had been picked up at Pau by the wrong chauffeur. While he was sent off to compose himself, the rest of us tacked up the drawings and Lajkó conducted a successful showing of his preliminary site plan, which was met with an enthusiasm that continued through the next day of detailed discussions.

Our first dinner in Bayonne had been quite elegant and was served in a private dining room at the Larraldia with a roaring fire next to a long baronial oak table. We were indeed the only guests in residence. For the next night, in celebration of a very successful set of meetings, Max had outdone himself. There was, and is, in Biarritz a famous stylish restaurant, the Café de Paris, which was also closed for the season but reopened just for our banquet with the mayor and the city council. Our dinner that evening was one of the best I can remember. Lajkó was the center of attention and managed a spirited conversation with Dr. Grênet at his side; Max helped out with translation when necessary. The evening was capped by cognac and cigars, and when Guillermo saw that he was being offered an H. Uppmann Monte Christo from Havana, which had been unavailable in the United States since Castro's takeover, he had tears of gratitude in his eyes.

Work on the Bayonne ZUP proceeded more or less steadily in the Paris office for the next two years while Guillermo was there and continued well after we had both returned to New York. Guillermo endeared himself to the city administration with his easy charm and rapid progress in their language. There was only one early, momentary setback when he inadvertently threw in a word from the gutter while making a presentation to the city council.

Once we got involved in creating actual building types, Lajkó's ingenuity proved invaluable. The legislation that controlled the design of HLM apartments was extremely literal and complex. France's wartime experience with power outages, elevator failures, and inadequate natural ventilation imposed specific requirements on all apartments that contained more than one bedroom. Each such apartment had to have "through ventilation" with windows on at least two different facades; kitchens were required to have windows and an adjacent drying room for laundry exposed to outside breezes; bathrooms were to be ventilated by interconnected systems of chimneys, permitting natural draft, rather than by electric ventilating fans that might break down.

Breuer responded with ideas he had first proposed in the early 1920s (but never used) for "skip-floor" plans and apartments served by corridor elevators on every third floor. Since the French government was subsidizing the construction of these low-cost apartments, the strict rules limited the size of each apartment type. The contractors, in bidding for the right to build them, were accepting a fixed price and only competing with one another on the standards of finish and fittings. The architect had very little room in which to maneuver, and the three-dimensional jigsaw puzzle that Breuer proposed provided duplex apartments of considerable beauty and utility, considering all the rules that had to be obeyed.

The concrete forming method adopted by the builder when construction finally began in 1966 was equally ingenious in adapting an industrialized technique called "tunnel forming" to the complex interior shapes required. Metal tunnels were built side by side on the ceiling slab of the apartment below; after the concrete had been poured around and between them, they were collapsed inwardly and re-erected on the next floor. Precast-concrete facade panels provided deep shade for the un-air-conditioned apartments. Their pattern reflected the different room arrangements on each floor. Some had corridors, while others crossed over or under the corridor that served them. It was one of Lajkó's most subtle and complex checkerboards.

French chimneys, which look picturesque on the sloping roofs of sixth-floor seventeenth-century garrets, made for an odd-looking rooftop forest of tall spindly stacks on our flat roofs. We decided to mask their bizarre profile somewhat by using a high parapet all around the roof perimeter, with just enough openings to allow the natural draft to work. We were not the first to propose this solution, but each exception had to be argued before the insurance authorities in Paris who controlled much of the architecture of France.

The ZUP de Bayonne. By expressing the internal arrangement of skip-floor apartments on the facades, Breuer created patterns of great depth and complexity.

I found a sympathetic bureaucrat who understood exactly what we wanted to do and why it would improve the looks of our buildings. Still, he resisted, with crystal-clear Gallic logic: "If I let you do this, soon everyone will do it and the problem of the ugly chimneys will become less severe. Our organization believes the better way is to change the law and permit artificial ventilation with low fan housings on the roof. We need the ugly buildings to convince the legislators to change the law." When I asked how long this battle had been going on, he admitted to fifteen years and shrugged as he approved our plans. The law was changed the next year.

Lajkó visited the Paris office about once a month, prompted by the need for regular meetings at Bayonne and others in or about Flaine. They became a pleasant routine, and we saw more of him than we would have in a typical week in New York. On one visit I went with Breuer to the inaugural celebration of an installation at the Musée des Arts Décoratifs of the dining room that he had designed many years earlier for the Kandinskys in Paris. Madame Kandinsky was moving to a smaller apartment and had given the furniture to the Louvre. We had dinner with the painter's widow, who had remained a close friend of Lajkó's over the years, but it was difficult for me to follow the chatter, which tended to drift free-form from German to French, with a little English thrown in. Sylvie and Eric had once invited Madame Kandinsky to dine with Lajkó, who found her sad and bitter. Lajkó tried to cheer her up: "Oh, Nina, don't you remember all the fun we used to have in the cafés?" She would regularly call the Paris office to find out when Breuer would be in town next, and years later, a new secretary was scolded by the imperious lady for not recognizing her name and its importance in art history.

In early April 1964 the rumblings of Flaine's political problems became louder, and I was called in for the first in a series of complicated meetings with the general contractor, Boussiron. In addition to the other financial pressures weighing on Eric Boissonnas, Boussiron was trying to wriggle out of its agreement. Chosen from a very short list of reputable contractors with the right banking connections, they had agreed to begin work on the project on a cost-plus basis. They were to be reimbursed for their actual costs plus a profit rather than being held to a fixed-price bid. They were, however, obligated to turn the unit prices into building-by-building lump sums as soon as the documents were ready, and that moment had come. Boussiron, in the meantime, had discovered the comfort of working on cost-plus and was dragging its heels, claiming that it had not foreseen all the difficulties of building in a remote alpine valley.

In a way, each party to the dispute that erupted had a hidden agenda. Boussiron was having financial difficulties that had nothing to do with Flaine and was looking to the Boissonnas family to bail it out. Eric was worried that the promised government loans might never come through, and he was beginning to think that an enforced pause in the program of building might not be such a bad idea. It almost seemed as if Lajkó and I were the only ones who wanted the argument resolved in the interests of not seeing this beautiful project abandoned. Breuer was incredulous when I wrote him of my first fears, and when he came over in the end of April he told Eric, "In all my years as an architect, if I have learned any one thing it is *never fire the builder!*" Eric replied, "Lajkó, *you* know I can't fire the builder. *I* know I can't fire the builder. My problem is that *the builder* knows I can't fire the builder, and that is going to lead to blackmail." So he fired the builder.

A lawyer specialized in building matters was called in, and his first advice to Eric was to fire the whole building team—everyone who had gotten him into this awful mess. Eric knew that Lajkó had opposed the advice of COFEBA in embarking on the premature fast-track system and refused to let us go, but he did dismiss Jean Barets and some of the other technicians. The next few months were devoted to legal wrangling over the terms under which Eric's development company, the SEPAD, would take title to everything in and around Flaine Valley. Foundations, buildings, precasting plant— all were to be eventually mothballed. Boussiron would not budge, and we had many a long and turbulent meeting, all orchestrated by the lawyer. My French was not up to following most of the shouting, but I had an occasional role to play. This usually involved standing up on cue from Rémi, slamming shut my attaché case, and joining our side in marching out of the room while someone stayed behind to avoid an absolute breakdown in negotiations. Eventually, Boussiron gave in, canceled the contract, and abandoned its claim to an indemnity. Rémi told Boussiron they had tried to "harness Flaine to a white elephant."

The lack of the title *architecte* made it impossible for Breuer to personally assume the responsibilities and the potential liabilities of his practice in France. He had associated with Bernard Zehrfuss for UNESCO, the Laugiers in Nice for IBM France, and temporarily, COFEBA for Flaine. When it came to public clients such as the city of Bayonne, and even the SAG, the title was required. Normally it was reserved for graduates of the Ecole des Beaux-Arts who were awarded diplomas by the government, giving them the exclusive right to use the initials DPLG after their name. Graduates of "lesser" schools in France, such as the Ecole Spéciale in Paris (which in the 1960s actually offered a better education in architecture than the Beaux-Arts), could call themselves architects and join the Ordre des Architectes Français (French Order of Architects), but they always lacked the DPLG, which helped in getting work, especially from the government.

I used to get into arguments with my French friends over what I saw as the sorry state of French architectural education, and everyone tended to agree that the Beaux-Arts was behind the times. Even the government that ran it had such lack of confidence in its graduates that it gave more and more authority to engineers, who were better trained at their schools, also run by the government.

Then, to cap it all off, the national insurance companies, who had to pay for the liability claims lodged against architects, decided to band together in self-protection. They formed nationwide control bureaus that had to approve an architect's plans before they could be used as a basis for the umbrella coverage required by the client for a project of any size. This may have avoided many building errors, but it also had a stultifying effect on the inventiveness of French architects. If there were no precedents, no examiner at the Bureau de Contrôle was likely to approve a detail. Without the approval there was no insurance, and without the insurance no client could afford to proceed. At the same time, architects were required to carry their own liability insurance, which would be incorporated into the overall "umbrella" written for the project. Under the Napoleonic Code, an architect is responsible for his or her errors for ten years. The Ordre des Architectes Français had formed its own insurance company to write ten-year insurance, but only for its members. It was possible to obtain similar coverage from Lloyds of London, but the cost was prohibitive. Since America had, and still has, no reciprocal agreement with France regarding the licensing of French architects in the United States, the French government was not about to make it easy for Americans to practice in France.

The contract for the ZUP de Bayonne contained a clause limiting Lajkó's activities to master planning until he could call himself an architect for the buildings that he hoped to design. In addition, Eric Boissonnas knew that sooner or later the SAG would want its architect to be so titled, if only for local political effect. In the fall of 1963 Eric had offered to intervene with friends in the government on Breuer's behalf, and André Malraux, the minister of culture at the time, agreed to help Lajkó get into the Ordre. Problems arose when it was discovered that whatever paper Breuer had received on graduation from the Bauhaus had never been given equivalency to a French diploma. His years of teaching at the Harvard Graduate School of Design didn't count either. Finally, after months of wrangling, an escape clause was found in the legislation, granting the title of *architecte* to established "men of art whose ability to build had been adequately demonstrated." Lajkó was admitted to the Ordre des Architectes Français on June 1, 1964, almost exactly a year after Malraux had intervened.

Up to that time we had been using the New York letterhead of Marcel Breuer and Associates with an overprint of our Paris address and telephone number. We now became "Marcel Breuer Architecte." Of course, I was not able to call myself *architecte* at the time and I hid behind the invented title *directeur des études* (something like design director). Since none of the New York associates were French architects, we could never use the firm name "Marcel Breuer and Associates," and all the firm's business had to be channeled through Breuer personally—taxes, real estate, and the like. When Lajkó eventually retired, the rules had been simplified, and with my Cornell diploma I applied for, and received, the title of *architecte* in 1976. It took me exactly a year, without the help of Malraux. In this way, we could continue to have a partner at the head of the Paris office.

It came time for me to formally join the partnership in June 1964, a year after my "elders"—Murray, Herb, and Ham. My signature on the documents that had arrived from New York was witnessed by the U.S. consul, and the document was secured in blue ribbon under a wad of hot red wax embossed with the seal of the ambassador.

In July of the same year the termination agreement with Boussiron had been reached, the shutdown of the job site at Flaine had begun, and COFEBA had been dismissed. To replace the engineers, Eric retained another

Flaine, 1964. The design team inspects precast parts at Magland in the Arve River valley.

engineering firm (BET, or Bureau d'Etudes Techniques) with the confusingly similar name of COTEBA, a much bigger office that was a part of the great banking syndicate of Campenon-Bernard. The significance of all this back-stage maneuvering was not clear to me at the time, and even today I only dimly recognize useful connections to Eric's family and key people in the Protestant financial world. During this period, my chief contact in the Catholic banking community would tell me confidentially of rumors on the street that Eric was almost ruined by his reverses at Flaine. I chose not to believe the stories, and they proved to be untrue, but they were indicative of the fact that vultures were circling.

The principal with whom we dealt at COTEBA was Yves Tayssier, an elegant and high-energy professional. We developed a strong mutual respect for one another, although we were never exactly friends, as is often the case with architects and engineers. The firm took great care in studying the dossier of Flaine and was able to build on all that we had been doing with COFEBA in a very constructive manner. Lajkó was skeptical about the larger and more demanding organization at COTEBA. He always preferred to deal with consultants who showed him a certain deference, and Tayssier's initial attitude was that we should consider ourselves lucky that he had come along. It took about a year for Breuer's guard to drop a bit, and by the time the project got moving again he and Tayssier were acting like old friends.

During a family vacation to Italy that September, I received a message at our hotel in Taormina asking me to call Breuer in New York the next morning at nine o'clock Taormina time. This seemed very odd since that would be three in the morning in New York. (It turned out to be his secretary's mistake. He'd meant New York time.) I made the call. Once he'd shaken himself awake, Lajkó announced that Murray Emslie was leaving the partnership. No explanation was offered, and I was too shocked to ask for one. Murray was a very conscientious and loyal individual. His insistence on serving as a juror, rather than requesting the statutory six postponements, used to drive Breuer crazy. This time, he had apparently scheduled a vacation with his wife and given Lajkó plenty of notice, which was forgotten when it conflicted with some last-minute business in the office. When Breuer asked him to postpone the trip, Murray refused and Lajkó apparently said something like, "If you don't turn up Monday, don't ever turn up."

It all happened so quickly and was so uncharacteristic of our senior partner that shock and confusion reigned. Murray was gone in a few days and joined Dick Meier's office shortly thereafter. Lajkó knew he would have to find an office administrator to replace Murray and asked his friend I. M. Pei for advice. Pei had just designed the Boulder, Colorado, headquarters of the National Center for Atmospheric Research (NCAR) and had a great deal of respect for a local Greek-American architect, Tician Papachristou, who had been acting as the owner's representative at NCAR. Pei recommended him to Breuer and Tician joined the firm a few months later.

Toward the end of summer, my excellent secretary, Solange, left to have a baby, and before I could advertise for a replacement, Max Stern had recommended an old friend, **Yolande Roche** (I always called her Madame Roche), who had just returned to her native France after many years in the United States and was looking for a job.

In October Lajkó came over with a new commission for the Paris office that was welcomed as something to fill the gap left by the slowdown at Flaine. It was another small assembly plant for his old friend Rufus Stillman, now president of the renamed Torin Corporation. The British affiliate was located in the Cotswold district west of London and had just bought property in an industrial estate at Swindon.

The program for Torin UKD (United Kingdom Division) was almost identical to the plant I had helped to design for Rochester, Indiana, and another Ham had produced for Nivelles in Belgium. The buildings didn't look alike—they were quite different in facade treatment—but the interior layout and overall size were more or less the same. I had nominated my old Architectural Association friend Geoff Spyer as associate architect, and we both joined Breuer at the Belgian plant to familiarize ourselves with the European operation. Nivelles was a strong architectural composition in heavily modeled precast concrete made by Schokbeton. The company employed a process then unique to the Low Countries in which a very dry mixture of concrete was densely distributed throughout the form by violent vibrations. Lajkó was enchanted by the process almost as much as by its results.

When it came to building in Britain, however, the economy dictated a light steel frame, and the building that we eventually produced, while neat and clean, lacked the architectural power of Nivelles. Allen Cunningham ran the job in the Paris office, and what was thought to be a very simple assignment turned into a nightmare. Rufus had no plans to provide anything more than the vending-machine snacks that were typical in all his other assembly plants, and the drawings were finished before his local manager was able to convince him that he would have a strike on his hands if he deprived the workers of their one good hot meal of the day. We had to make major revisions to provide a full cafeteria. The firm of Henry Hope and Sons was well known in America as a producer of high-quality steel window frames, and we welcomed the services of the parent company in Britain as mechanical engineers. They promptly embarrassed themselves with the service they provided. Finally, we hit a sharp upturn in the building market and the bids came in high, which cost us more time in making simplifications.

Probably the sorriest moment in that ill-fated job came during one of Lajkó's visits to Paris. Allen and I had not been able to resolve a design difference, so we left it to Breuer. It had to do with an opening in a wall that was to be either a floor-to-roof slit (my idea) or a hole (Allen's); it seems totally inconsequential in retrospect. We presented two sketches to Breuer, and he said he marginally preferred Allen's proposal but would leave it up to me as partner in charge to make the final decision.

After he had moved on, I said to Allen something like, "Well, lad, since it's my call, we'll go with the slit." He told me later that he was deeply offended by "lad," which I had meant to be flip but not demeaning, and shocked that I would pull rank, even though I had been given the authority to do so. I learned some important lessons in the process, but it was years before Allen and I returned to the easy, friendly terms of what had been a very positive personal and professional relationship up to that moment.

Madame Roche knew that we were looking for office quarters of our own, especially since business at BERU was picking up and the company was beginning to make noises about needing our space. She checked the real-estate section in *Le Figaro* every morning and reported a possibility to me in mid-November. It was not the best neighborhood, but the space offered seemed adequate and the price was right. I called for an appointment to see it and took a cab over at the end of the afternoon.

Rue Chapon is in the third arrondissement, one of the oldest quarters in Paris; it is called "Sentier" after the many light manufacturing plants in the area. We always said we were in the Marais (named after the salt marshes that had been there before it was settled), but Madame Roche has subsequently corrected my geography. Rue Chapon is two blocks long. It starts at the rue du Temple, crosses the rue Beaubourg, and then—becoming narrower and narrower—turns into a cobbled walk across the rue St. Martin before ending at a gateway onto the sidewalk of the boulevard de Sébastopol. In 1964, long before the Centre Georges Pompidou had been built and gentrified the area with its attendant galleries and chic restaurants, this was the garment district of Paris. There were a few old *hôtels particuliers*—grand family homes that had been fixed up as museums and held summer theater performances in their courtyards—but they were several blocks away. This was seedy, with the narrow street lined by wholesale shops selling jeans, bolts of fabric, underwear, trimmings, all manner of items from French West Africa and the Far East. Above the shops were three or four floors of walk-up apartments, which had windows that gave onto the street and the cobblestoned courtyards within.

When I arrived at number 48 it was dark, and a cold drizzle had soaked the entire neighborhood. The real-estate agent met me just inside a pair of big, flaking green doors that gave access to the courtyard for the parking of the owners' tiny cars and vans. Pedestrians used a smaller doorway cut through the right-hand door that opened with a buzz and a click and was never locked. Access to the upper floors was via an open wooden staircase in each corner of the court. At the rear of the ground floor was a warehouse for boxes of raincoats. The right-hand wooden stairway was cracked and leaned inward as it climbed past the toilets at the intermediate landings; the hall light always threatened to go out without leaving enough time to reach the second floor. The agent remarked that the co-op owners had just appropriated money to refurbish the stairways; although they were painted the next year, they never received the promised carpeting.

Inside the door at the first floor (actually the second level) was a scene out of Dickens. There were four large rooms, once a modest apartment with windows to the street and court. Now each was lined and filled with rough wooden shelves made from packing crates that grazed the relatively low ceiling. The shelves were stuffed with French comic books, and three or four workers selected and packed the books for mailing around France. A pot-bellied stove in a hole in the wall between the two principal rooms didn't offer much heat—everyone was working in a coat and wore gloves that were cut off at the fingers. One bare bulb in the center of each space gave the whole scene an eerie air. It took me about twenty minutes to be able to imagine using the space as an office, but the asking price was attractive and the layout was not bad. I told the agent that we were interested and asked for a week to consider it.

When Allen and Guillermo arrived at the office the next morning I sent them off right away for a second and third opinion and they took the metro to check on its accessibility. They returned a few hours later, smiling and shaking their heads uncertainly. The sun had come out and they agreed that the interior space could be transformed into a light and pleasant workplace. But the neighborhood! They had been propositioned by prostitutes three times in the short walk from metro Etienne-Marcel. The great wholesale market at nearby Les Halles was still functioning in those days, and the workers got off at about nine in the morning after a full night of work. The bars and the women who catered to these men were quite busy as the rest of the Parisian workforce was arriving to start the day. The markets were gradually being moved to Rungis, near Orly Airport, and the street trade steadily decreased while we were in residence, but the neighborhood never completely lost its character.

I called Lajkó in New York about our find, and he was definitely interested. He asked only that I check with the Boissonnas family and make sure that they would come to meetings held at such an address. Eric assured me that it was a classic location for architects and artists, and he even joined me on a further inspection trip a few days later. **André Laurenti,** who acted as my professional adviser three afternoons a week, had his own office only two blocks away on the rue de Montmorency and spoke of the joys of the neighborhood and the fair asking price. So we made the deal, and on his next trip Breuer was enthusiastic about his "real" Parisian office. He always preferred it to the anonymous space we occupied in midtown Manhattan.

The comic-book publishers moved out just before Christmas and we were involved in renovations until the following Easter.

Once the shelving was removed, we could inspect the space we had bought. It dated back to at least the sixteenth century, and the wooden floors showed their age. The masonry walls were covered with cracked plaster, and the ceiling in the entry had a disconcerting sag in the middle. As co-op owners of the space we were responsible for adding what we needed—a central heating system, new electrical circuitry and lighting, and a toilet for staff and visitors.

A good part of André's practice involved the renovation of old space in Paris, and since he worked only two blocks away, he took over all the dealings with the builders and the inspection of the work as it progressed. We laid new heating pipes and electrical cable, scraped the floors, and repaired the french windows. Before replastering the walls and ceilings, we had to do something about that central sag, despite the agent's assurance that it hadn't moved in a hundred years. Once the ceiling had been taken down, we looked aghast at what might at any moment have been a disaster. The main hand-hewn beam that crossed the space had been notched at one side to receive a cross-member that would have framed the hearth of a now long-gone fireplace during the building's residential days. This was normal and would have presented no problem except that a century or so later someone else had come along to frame the hearth of another fireplace on the other side of the beam and, unaware of the first cut, had made a notch nearly opposite. The notch was so deep that there was little wood left in the main beam. Perhaps three inches remained of what had been a twelve-inch-wide beam, and it had dropped about six inches at this point of weakness. We had to wonder what was holding it up except habit.

We eventually slid the shallowest steel I-beam we could find under the old wood one very carefully and inserted some gentle wedges between them. The ceiling was replastered, and the dropped beam that resulted from all these gyrations was just high enough for me to walk underneath. It served to hide a line of lights that illuminated a large photo-mural we installed just behind the receptionist's desk.

We had one setback just before we were due to move in. One of the plumbers left a hot torch on some oily rags as he left work for the day. The fire didn't spread far before it was detected, but an area around two of the street windows had to be braced until the insurance company agreed with our repair plan. The arched opening between the entry and the adjacent room, which had housed the pot-bellied stove, was closed down to an arched window for verbal communication between the two spaces, and we always kept a bouquet of bright flowers there next to the receptionist.

Finally, just after Easter 1965 we said goodbye to the BERU at Parc des Expositions and loaded everything into a big moving van. When parked outside 48 rue Chapon, it completely blocked the narrow, one-way street. I didn't know what we were going to do about that as the movers began the process of unloading and carrying all our furniture and file cabinets up two winding flights of stairs. It probably lasted only an hour or two, but the screeching horns and shouted curses that echoed up from the street below still resound in my memory.

After we had been in the office for several years we realized that the street came to a grinding halt every time any truck had to stop for a delivery; our holdup had simply been a little longer than usual. The noises on the street picked up with the arrival of spring as more kids were playing outside and we opened the windows for ventilation. We even had an accordionist who came by once a month or so.

Outfitting the new space after the furniture had been moved was relatively simple. The walls and ceiling were glossy white, the doors and carpet were charcoal gray, exposed pipes ran everywhere, and there wasn't a straight wall or flat floor to be found. Lajkó loved it. He did suggest some dark cork for a few walls as a tackboard, and I roamed all over Paris before finding exactly the right two-by-four-foot panels in a warehouse devoted to commercial refrigeration equipment. The final touch was an enameled plaque to go beside the great dark green doorway on the street. It read "MARCEL BREUER ARCHITECTE" in blue letters on a white field. It took six weeks to have made but lasted until we moved the office to Montparnasse many years later; by then it had accumulated a few rusty dings and looked as if it had been in place for centuries. We really felt like Parisians.

As 1964 drew to a close, Eric Boissonnas had put much of his financial house in order. He invited Barbara and me on a largely ceremonial visit to Flaine to inspect the job site, which had finally been taken over from Boussiron. We met Eric and Sylvie, Rémi, Fred Berlottier, and Gérard Chervaz at the precasting plant at Magland under low-lying clouds that hid the tops of the mountains lining the Arve Valley. In contrast to the bustle of my last visit, everything was dead still. Tall piles of gray precast concrete pieces were neatly stacked and cataloged with painted numbers. Fresh snow had left most of them wet and dark. We boarded a special open bin about ten feet square that was transported by cables that normally carried building material. After a jerky start, we rode over pylons that jutted out from the mountain face at an almost perpendicular angle. The swirling fog suddenly gave way to brilliant sunshine above a solid cloud bank. The truck that was waiting for us, and the valley beyond, could be clearly seen way down below.

We had a pleasant lunch in the workers barracks—there were a few left over as site guardians—and then drove down into the heart of the valley where, again, all was silence. Tall cranes had been folded in half and seemed to have their heads bowed in sadness. Great holes in the rock, parts of poured concrete walls with projecting spikes of reinforcing steel, each wrapped in

155

protective plastic, and a fleet of mothballed trucks—it was both grim and exhilarating. It was grim if this was the end of a great adventure; it was exhilarating if this could be taken as the Boissonnas' celebration of a boundary between past reverses and a new start. It was hard to know which was the case, and we all put up a brave front as we walked among the building sites. This was to have been the inaugural Christmas in the original time schedule of Flaine. Although I didn't know it at the time, Eric had just solved his loan problem by ignoring his French sources and going directly to an old friend who was president of the First National City Bank in New York. Another friend, Al Hayes, who also knew Lajkó, led the Federal Reserve Bank in New York and quickly approved the transfer of funds through the currency controls. Until all was settled, however, the Paris office needed more work.

Jack Freidin had left the New York office shortly after I joined it in the mid-1950s to establish an independent practice in real estate and interior design. In the early 1960s he had met the Sackler brothers, who ran the Purdue Frederick Company, in the course of renovating a Yonkers loft building for the company's New York affiliate, Bard Pharmaceuticals. **Mort Sackler** was looking for a French architect in connection with Purdue Frederick's joint venture in Bordeaux, which had outgrown its former office and production facility. In 1965 Jack recommended Breuer's Paris office and served as our programming consultant.

One page of an interoffice letter illustrating the long-distance design process between Lajkó and myself for Laboratoires Sarget.

I received a hasty briefing over the telephone just before I was to receive a visit from Georges Negrevergne, the president and chief executive officer of Laboratoires Sarget-Ambrine, the affiliate of Purdue Frederick. The gentleman who walked into our office a day or so later seemed completely bemused by the new situation in which he found himself. He had been running a family business all his life and had now been joined by a brash American owner who wanted to improve their corporate image with a new headquarters building. Sackler had suggested the world-famous Marcel Breuer as architect after meeting him in New York. With the agreement of Purdue Frederick's board, Lajkó and Mort had come to a general agreement; now it was up to Georges and me to make it work.

We danced around each other during the first interview, in which he expressed his personal preference for working with his long-time Bordeaux architect friend Paul Daurel. This didn't fill me with confidence about our long-term chances, but I did offer to work with Daurel as our local associate, an arrangement that eventually worked out very well for all concerned. Daurel was proud to be known among his professional friends as Marcel Breuer's co-architect; we had a loyal local voice to inform and help us through occasional political thickets.

The headquarters of Sarget-Ambrine was in an elegant limestone palace that had been a residence in downtown Bordeaux. Truck access for

48 RUE CHAPON PARIS 3 TELEPHONE 887-14-58

MARCEL BREUER ARCHITECTE

MARCEL BREUER F.A.I.A.   ARCHITECTE
ROBERT F. GATJE A.I.A. DIRECTEUR DES ETUDES
ANDRE LAURENTÍ ARCHITECTE D.P.L.G.

MARCEL BREUER
& ASSOCIATES
FEB 24 1966

2-24-66
Original mailed
to R. Gatje

BREUER	
BECKHARD	
GATJE	
SMITH	
PAPACHRISTOU	
FILE NO.	

22 February 1966

Mr. Marcel Breuer, Architect
635 Madison Avenue
NEW YORK, N.Y. 10022

Re: Sarget-Ambrine

Dear Lajko,

Your letter of 18 February received, its contents noted and in the process of digestion.

To take the simpler points, as you have, first :

1) A third floor over the factory presents no problems re stairs because the two "double unity" exit stairs which we provide have a theoretical capacity of 300 people and the present two floors contain only 100 employees. The structural aspects are, however, important since the present roof would have to support the same 1500 kgs live load as the other "floors" instead of simple roof loads. Columns throughout would change in dimension and foundations would increase in size. Bancon estimates the extra cost of such a change at 300,000 Frs. What I would shudder about would be the difficulty and danger in breaking apart the facade at the roof line, removing the railing piece (maybe we should just abandon it now anyway), and re-establishing continuity with the structure below in a system in which the major members and all connections are poured. To really try to make provision for that eventuality now would, I feel, involve us in considerable difficulty and expense at this stage, though it's very hard to put a price tag on it. This is why I suggested, and I believe you agreed, that even if we add to the lab by building up it should be done in the form of a penthouse, set back from the facade and perhaps with a structure that would be lighter both in appearance and in actuality.

[handwritten in margin: this means, we have to forget the whole idea. In any case, I would not consider it in the dwgs, and, if it is seriously requested after bidding, I would change dwgs etc. later, as an extra.]

[handwritten in left margin: I still agree with this, - what I don't see, is how you can set back the freezing cxt. walls, if the penthouse, so they are behind the parapet. However, all this is much later and I would not advise any provisions or complications now. Also no cost additions at all.]

2) Dining Terrace - OK

3) Bridge - I don't think I misunderstood him, I think he changed his mind. Anyway OK.

4) Office Extension - Again there's no real problem with the size

/...

Laboratoires Sarget. The three-dimensional logo in concrete can be seen along the road to the Bordeaux airport. It was removed recently when the building was sold.

the transport of even their limited production was becoming difficult. The new site was on Airport Road, soon to be renamed after John F. Kennedy, about a mile from the Bordeaux airport itself and convenient to long-haul highways. It was highly visible to traffic driving into town, and the move out of downtown congestion seemed to be welcomed by the company's growing staff. The operations of the old plant were so antiquated that the phone lines between its offices in Bordeaux and Paris were overloaded and unpredictable. There was one employee who did nothing but continually dial the company's Paris number. Whenever he connected, he would shout with joy, "I have Paris! Who needs to talk?"

The architectural scheme that developed featured a signature Breuer stand-alone three-story administrative wing forming a shallow curve. It was raised on shaped columns and was attached to the manufacturing/

158

laboratory block behind by an overhead bridge. The two-story pharmaceutical plant had an open well in its floor through which fork-lift operators delivered raw materials on pallets to the assembly line above. The finished products then filtered down through testing and packaging to the warehouse below and eventually to wrapping and shipping. The "gravity feed" had originated in Bard's Yonkers facility, which had been an old carpet plant. The assembly line, with its conveyers, pill-makers, and bottle-fillers, was in the center of the block surrounded by a visitors' corridor from which all this modern equipment could be shown off. The exterior precast-concrete wall was more intricately modeled than usual and was combined with a honey-colored limestone, the local building material of Bordeaux. Mort and Georges insisted on a reflecting pool to show off the administrative wing in full drama, but Lajkó resisted this element for a long time as "corny."

I suggested and designed a concrete sign structure for the roadside that had the corporate name in three-dimensional Egyptian letters. It was to become the company's logo. There was much discussion about its location, visibility from the road, and nighttime illumination. Happily, the name was shortened to Laboratoires Sarget before we cast the letters. The sign was so monumental that I thought we were building for the ages, but the business was later sold, perhaps due to the untimely death of Georges Negrevergne, and the sign removed. In the years before the sale, however, the plant grew to three times its length along the highway and improved in appearance with each extension. Allen was job captain for the original building, and Mario Jossa directed its growth from the Paris office after I had left.

By the time we moved to rue Chapon, MBA's staff had grown to include most of the people who were to dominate the activities of the office for the next several years. They were a disparate bunch, and it made Breuer proud to see that his name and presence in Paris could attract such an interesting group of architects. He enjoyed visiting our polyglot team as much as we looked forward to his more or less monthly trips. In addition to Allen, Guillermo, Eric Cercler, and Daniel Chiquet, our staff included two Frenchmen: Henri Bronchard, a resistance figure from northern France who became my administrative assistant, and Bernard Darroquy, who came from St. Jean-de-Luz to help us with Bayonne politics. There was also an American, John L. Sullivan, to whom I gave his first job after graduation from Cornell; a Brazilian, Claudio Cavalcanti, who came to us from the office of the great Oscar Niemeyer; and Andy Weunsche, who came from the Architectural Association in London.

Rue Chapon did not offer a great variety of restaurants, but the one that it did have was excellent. Chez Jean was laid out on two levels and had a traditional zinc bar with a small eating area on the ground floor. "Madame Jean" did all the cooking in the kitchen beyond, which was about as big as

*Andy Weunsche,
Claudio Cavalcanti,
Gatje, Eric Cercler,
John Sullivan, and
Guillermo Carreras
in the Paris office
drafting room.*

a large walk-in closet. A narrow winding wooden stair led to a dining mezzanine, and within a few months of our arrival, the restaurant had expanded to a third level. A nimble set of waitresses carried every meal up those stairs and every dirty dish down them. We used to arrive for lunch en masse—five or six at a time—at about one o'clock and had to wait for at least a half hour before being seated. This became annoying, especially as we saw the regulars—the plumber from across the street, the shopkeepers from down the block—ushered past us to waiting tables.

We delicately took up the matter with Monsieur Jean behind the bar and learned that most of his clientele had regular reservations; if we intended to dine there consistently he would happily give us a time slot. So from then on we had a large table waiting for us daily at half past one, and our napkins were even assigned cubbyholes in the rack downstairs. We were usually five or six, but if Lajkó was with us the party swelled to include every chair we could borrow from the neighbors. The food was good country cooking, inexpensive and based upon what was featured at the market that day. We felt very much at home in our neighborhood.

When Lajkó was in town, he dominated lunch with news from the New York office and memories of Paris in the 1920s. Otherwise discussions were rarely about architecture and frequently concerned art or politics. Our common language was French, but the regulars at nearby tables noted all the foreign accents. The Vietnam War was on, Johnson was running against Goldwater, and de Gaulle was up for re-election. John and Guillermo could

160

speak for the right wing; Andy, Allen, and Henri took strong positions on the left; the rest of us would slosh back and forth guided by liberal instinct or, in the case of Eric, a determined independence. I remember one particularly animated argument over dessert that involved two of the waitresses and the construction workers across the aisle. It had to do with the regularity of French verb formation.

Jane Yu, the head of interior design in the New York office, came through Paris in June and stayed at our apartment for several days before heading down to Italy to join Breuer's secretary, **Mary Farris.** Breuer was trying yet another cure for his bad back at a thermal spa near Vicenza and had invited the two of them to stop by and relieve his boredom. "It's so sad, surrounded by old people and my own dark thoughts," he remarked. He rented a convertible with which to show them the sights but must have been distracted. After driving straight through one of the pedestrian city squares as the locals scattered wildly with vocal and gestured objections, he found himself going up the down ramp of the Autostrada with the wind blowing his fringe of gray hair straight up over his forehead. Jane kept leaning over and hitting him: "Wrong way! Wrong way! Breuer, you're on the wrong side!"

I went to New York in July and received a once-in-a-lifetime tongue-lashing from Breuer over the excess time we were spending on Torin UKD. I was devastated to see that Lajkó had taken Rufus Stillman's side in our argument over why the project was moving so slowly and the fees rising so quickly. I appreciated the support that Herb gave me at the end of a turbulent partners' meeting convened just to chew me out. When I got back to Paris and explained the situation to Allen, we succeeded in cutting the number of working drawings we had planned, and the client stopped changing the program.

Back at the drafting boards, some of us were still working on future plans for Flaine, and we tried to keep au courant with its political prospects. By mid-1965 the problem of the road seemed to have been settled, but Flaine had still to acquire rights to ski on the 1,500 broad acres that faced north, across the valley from our building sites. In the eleventh century the nobleman who owned the mountain had given to his peasants the right to graze cattle on these slopes during the summer, but this right was not passed on through inheritance. It was available only to those who owned cattle and enough land to feed them in winter. Anyone selling land or moving away lost grazing rights. The original contracts had been kept in Milan, since the dukes of Savoy were then in control, but they had been destroyed by fire and only imperfectly replaced in the seventeenth century with documents now held in Annecy. This ancient form of "ownership" went by the name of "Albergataire" and was only known in certain alpine valleys. No one had been using the rights for years and title to the land was cloudy indeed.

161

The design team riding the work gondola to the Grandes Platières, Flaine, 1966.

Eric Boissonnas placed a notice in the local newspaper asking claimants to state their rights. Three thousand people responded. To cover administrative expenses, each respondent was asked to put up the very modest sum of five francs, and the number dropped to six hundred. To deal with the candidates who remained, Eric asked that they elect a president. He proposed a price that the president found to be fair; the assembly, however, rejected it, along with a half dozen proposals that followed. Finally, Eric made one last offer. He gave the president his price and said that, when all the signatures had been secured, he would double the sum. It worked.

Sometime in the autumn, faced with continuing legal and administrative problems, Eric Boissonnas realized it was time to play serious politics if he was ever to pursue his dream of developing Flaine. Wolves were circling and there were rumors that the Rothschilds were interested in taking over.

He began by contacting his cousin, Maurice Couve de Murville, who was then the French foreign minister. With a few words from the top, the bureaucracy began moving again, although it was not until the following spring that the minister of tourism finally took definitive action. The minister convened a meeting at the prefecture in Annecy composed of the mayors and town councils of the three communities involved. He wasted no words: "Gentlemen, in my role as minister of tourism I am frequently asked to intercede in disputes between Parisian promoters and the local citizenry. And I know that it is usually the moneymen from Paris who are squeezing the country folk. I am here today to tell you that I have studied the dossier of Flaine very carefully and I know that, in this case, the shoe is on the other foot. Monsieur Boissonnas is being treated most unfairly by your towns-people. I haven't much time but wanted you to know that we will give you twenty-four more hours within which to convince everyone that they must honor their solemn agreements. If the options are not ratified by that time, your towns will be expropriated and we will take care of matters from Paris. No questions." With that, he turned on his heel and left the room. Twenty-four hours later, everything was settled. Work was resumed on the road, and there was clear title ahead for construction.

There remained the matter of a collaboration with the Rothschilds to resolve. Eric had great admiration for the technical qualifications of the experts who were part of the Rothschild group: **Emile Allais,** the dean of French skiing; Denis Creissels, France's leading designer of ski lifts; and COTEBA. In order to maintain the possibility of working with them, he decided not to close the door on negotiations with the parent group. And his hand was immeasurably strengthened when someone passed to him the confidential report from Allais to the Rothschilds in which, after surveying the valley on snowshoe, he predicted, "Properly developed, I think Flaine ten years from now will be one of the greatest ski areas in the world."

Fatigued and under pressure from Rémi, Eric was on the verge of making a deal with the Rothschilds. Eric had chosen Henry Briffod, an old friend and loyal politician, to head the SAG, and the two brothers decided to explain the situation to him during lunch just before a general meeting of the board. The president listened with apparent agreement, but during the board meeting that followed, the old Socialist launched into a long, impassioned diatribe denouncing any association with a Rothschild. With this evidence of opposition within his own organization, Eric decided to disclaim any such intention and the threat passed. He did manage to retain the services of Allais and Creissels, who both became enthusiastic members of our design team.

I worked with Emile Allais very closely at times as we tried to respect the needs of his ski trails when they got near our buildings. In order to draw the trails and their contours, I had to know as much about their slopes as I did about Berlottier's roads. When describing a trail that he was sure was possible to build between the upper and middle plateaus, he gave me his rules regarding percentage of slope; after testing it at the drafting board, I tried to prove it to be a physical impossibility. "Well then," he said, "we'll just have to break my rules."

In anticipation of the relaunching of Flaine, Eric had hired a new public-relations and advertising firm in Paris called ICPA headed by a woman named Hugette Imber-Vier. One of its first assignments was to design a logo for Flaine. I was a little miffed by this, since we had been using the italic

*My final proposal
to Eric.*

lowercase letters in a box that I had designed years ago for our presentation drawings and had assumed their official status. Eric explained that they needed something much more "mode" than our disciplined letterform and predicted that Lajkó would also hit the roof when he told him that ICPA was suggesting colors for Flaine that were not red, yellow, and blue. (He was right, especially when they turned out to be magenta, chartreuse, and navy.) I asked to have a crack at the logo, and Eric said he would consider a mini-competition.

I sketched for many hours at home in the evening, plumbing the essence of those six letters and their relationship one to the other. Rarely have I enjoyed a pure design challenge as much. I submitted my version, but ICPA's was chosen as more commercial. Eric told me privately that he preferred the looks of mine and suggested that we use it on all our drawings, which we did. Lajkó later added his compliments but told me frankly that mine was illegible. He was probably right.

In early December Lajkó was on his way to a meeting with Max Stern and me in Bayonne, and some problems had arisen that I was anxious to see resolved before his arrival. Our fees for the design of the buildings at the ZUP were funded by the local HLM society rather than by the city itself, and we had to deal with the infamous Monsieur Forcade. Whether it was because a foreign architect had been forced on him or just because delay was part of the bureaucratic game, Forcade was simply not paying his bills. I had tried to explain by telephone to Breuer that Max had assured me that sooner or later the society had to pay; in fact, the French government had set up a special bank that gave low-interest loans to professionals who were waiting for other parts of the government to pay their fees. Breuer was a tough businessman, and he had become sufficiently Americanized that his last words to me by telephone were "Threaten to sue them!" When I told this to Max, he nearly fell over. I had a problem.

I turned to our secretary, Madame Roche, and we explored every aspect of the impasse. She offered to compose a letter. After reading it with satisfaction, I signed the letter and sent it off to the mayor. During our meetings the next week, it was evident to Max and me that the tensions had been relieved, and Lajkó wondered what all the fuss had been about. It was noted for the record that our bills had been approved for payment, and that was that. As we were leaving the final meeting, Dr. Grênet took me aside: "Monsieur Gatje, I just wanted to say a word about your letter of last week. When it arrived, we were approaching something of a breaking point, and I was concerned by what you might have to say. After reading your letter, I was greatly relieved and realized that, with it in hand, I would be able to bring everyone back together. But more to the point was the elegance of its composition. I passed the letter around the table to the members of my city council and said, 'How is it possible for an American to deal with such a difficult situation in *our* language with a subtlety and nuance that I know I could not possibly have employed?' I just wanted to congratulate you." I smiled appreciatively and passed the compliment on to Madame Roche.

Lajkó and I had decided that I should return to New York in the middle of the summer of 1966, since the pace of the Paris office remained slow compared to the explosion of commissions that Lajkó had received in New York. Flaine was still on hold, Bayonne was in Darroquy's hands, Eric Cercler could handle Sarget, and Torin UKD posed few remaining problems for Geoff Spyer in London. There were meetings with IBM France about the need for new buildings at La Gaude, but no one was prepared to make a commitment.

One of the last projects Guillermo and I worked on with Lajkó at Bayonne was a pair of water towers needed to maintain water pressure in the twelve-story apartment blocks we were building. These utilitarian structures dot the countryside in France, which has an approach to hydraulics that is different from that of most other countries. When they are well designed, they can become local monuments. For our ZUP it was decided that something special was required since the towers would be tall enough to read as a signal from afar. We gathered all the technical storage data from the city via COTEBA and explored the most economical forming and pouring methods then available for such a tall concrete structure.

As we fed the data to Breuer on one of his visits to Paris, we shared one of those magical moments of pure sculptural creation. The three of us were hunched over Guillermo's drawing board while Lajkó moved his soft black pencil and occasionally an eraser over the several sketches that had been produced for his consideration. The shapes that evolved looked like nothing so much as great wine goblets with a ribbed surface that was inspired, if not dictated, by the slip-form and post-tensioning techniques suggested by our engineers. There were to be two, side by side at heights of 150 and 235 feet. The final presentation drawing, with its complex ink-toned shadows playing across the curved and faceted shapes, became one of Breuer's favorites and

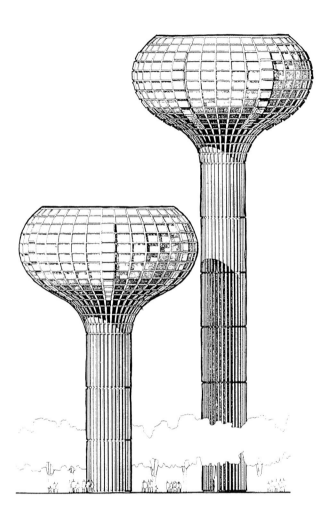

Breuer's proposal for the châteaux d'eau *(watertowers) at the ZUP de Bayonne.*

has been extensively published. Unfortunately, the construction price came in over the estimates and the project did not go forward. The hydraulic problem was eventually solved with low-lying pumps and reservoirs.

In the spring of 1966 we began to prepare for the changing of the guard in Paris. Guillermo Carreras returned to the United States in late March. He rejoined the New York office briefly but then moved on to a series of jobs that took him to Miami via Puerto Rico and Venezuela. When he spoke to Lajkó, Breuer knew something was up: "What's cooking? It's goulash, but it's not good goulash." Then he said, after Guillermo had explained his need to try something different, "You know, Guillermo, you're always leaving me."

166

Just before he returned to New York, Guillermo took a weekend trip to Amsterdam and reported to me on the following Monday a curious thing he had noted. Passing by the largest modern furniture shop in town he had seen a pair of cantilevered steel Breuer side chairs in the window with the attribution "Mart Stam." Since it was Sunday, he was not able to ask anyone about the error, but we decided together that I should write a mild letter of correction as head of Breuer's Paris office, which I did from a rather haughty and naive position, regarding the "chairs, that all the world knows were designed by Marcel Breuer." Several weeks later I got a letter from the store, which was also the manufacturer and distributor of the chair. The store "found it astonishing that, after all the years of litigation, the Breuer camp was still asserting authorship." I was, at that time, completely uninformed about the Breuer-Stam lawsuit, which was particularly sensitive in this case because Stam was Dutch. (Stam also apparently later claimed authorship of the great van Nelle Factory in Rotterdam designed by van der Vlugt and Brinckmann, for which he served only as job captain.) I casually mentioned the exchange of correspondence to Breuer during his next trip to Paris. He turned stony-faced as he said simply, "I don't want to talk about it."

My second daughter, Marianna, was born at the American Hospital in Neuilly in late May, just in time for some farewell picnics in the Chevreuse Valley out past Versailles with the Kozlowskis and Cunninghams and *their* newborns. I later told Marianna that we'd given her a priceless opening line—"You know, I was born in Paris . . ."—but she trumped that when she married a Frenchman.

Allen Cunningham was slated to return to England and a career in architecture and planning that led to a very prestigious post as the head of the London Polytechnic School of Architecture. I was to pass the director's baton to Eric Cercler, who certainly had the training, if not the personality, to run the office. Lajkó had chosen Mario Jossa, a young Italian-American architect, as his principal design representative in Paris. Mario had been working in New York while I was abroad and had come over from the Gruzen office at Guillermo's suggestion.

In a great irony of professional timing, Eric Boissonnas announced at the end of spring 1966 that he would recommence the building of Flaine, and a new contracting group began work that summer. Similarly, the negotiations with IBM became more active, and new design work began shortly after my return to New York. I remained the partner in charge of all the French work, and we did most of the design with Lajkó in New York. During the following years I was in France almost monthly, as Breuer began to weary of the travel, but the work I had initially been sent to do passed gradually to the hands of others, and I became a New York architect rather than an expatriate.

"The Taste of Space . . .

The New York office remained extremely busy while I was in Paris and perhaps presents the moment to reflect on the architecture we were practicing and were to further develop with Breuer. While the forms of every architect are personal, it was perfectly possible for each partner and many of the designers to follow and elaborate upon the precedents set by Breuer. Each of us contributed something new and different to the practice over twenty years—but our interpretation was close enough to that of the master that all the buildings for Flaine, IBM Boca Raton and La Gaude, Saint John's, and Torin are Breuer buildings despite the successive management by two or more of his partners.

Breuer did not have the time or inclination to make, or even review, every drawing that was required and every stone that was laid. Nevertheless, we did learn to speak his language and teach it to others. Any artist with a large and consistent body of work develops a recognizable vocabulary with which he or she forms what he or she wants to say. It becomes the mark whereby the artist's signature is instantly authenticated.

A painter is probably closest to the final shaping of the medium and need only fend off agent or gallery. The writer must resist some of the advice of a well-meaning editor to preserve the distinctive flavor of language that attracts readers. A dramatist or composer depends upon directors, conductors, and performers to deliver the message. The creator of a movie must deal with all of these individuals plus those controlling the expense of costly productions. Perfect or imperfect, the work of the artist is recognized, almost subliminally, by the turn of a phrase, the shape of a brushstroke, the

"The Juice of Stone"

mood of an orchestra. Whatever rivets our attention makes us want to come back for more.

Those of us who were born, rather than trained, with a liking for the shapes and colors Lajkó used were attracted to his side—either as students or as employees. We wanted to work in his "style" and didn't have to fight it. Those who were uncomfortable, or unconvinced, by the lead he offered soon left. In a firm as tightly controlled as his, there was no room for a loyal opposition or alternate camps. An architect was either "with us or against us."

Breuer had no time to study the details of a client's program, especially later in his career, and he relied on his team leader to analyze and present the program to him in graphic form. From that point on he tried to find an overriding idea that might inspire the particular building. This was an exercise in simplification, and although he might find some practical reason to "break out" a separate form, it was usually in a search for economy rather than for articulation for complexity's sake. His "decorative" sunshades and exterior stairs were gradually abandoned in favor of more monumental massing of sculptural columns and deep, purposeful facades. Where others try to break up their buildings, Breuer tried to simplify their envelope. Paul Rudolph told me that Breuer organized his buildings in order to channel his insights toward great architectural principles.

Stairs are potentially three-dimensional sculpture implying motion and direction. They are and promise to remain one of the few parts of a building's interior that is unlikely to be altered by others. Small wonder that they were such a source of delight to Breuer and his grateful clients. First, they present something of a three-dimensional puzzle to the draftsman. They must be arranged so that they fall within a range of ratios between the height, or "riser," of the step and its depth, the "tread"—ratios that have been codified over time and in law to represent comfort and safety for the user. Since the stair is frequently part of the escape route in case of fire, it should not be so steep or so shallow as to cause one to stumble or hesitate. Then, since the stair frequently continues to rise above itself, there must be room to pass under the flight above without the user banging his or her head, even when running or jumping.

Only after these basic requirements have been satisfied can an architect begin to study what it looks like. What are the surfaces of the step or even the mass itself made of? Is space provided for the toe of a climbing shoe by sloping the face of the step, undercutting it, or pulling the steps apart with a slot in between? How does the last step below a landing relate to the first step above? Does the handrail, which must protect the user from falling inward and provide a support at a constant height above the steps, move gracefully in space or have awkward kinks and interruptions? Is there a thoughtful relationship between the slopes of the stair and the horizontals of the side wall material and landings? (French subway designers created a relationship of step to wall that provides a continuous sloping slot down

The Gagarin residence. The concrete treads are cantilevered out from the rubblestone wall while the graceful handrail is supported by the treads.

which all discarded tickets and Gitanes can be driven by hosed water—an elegant trick that most architects know as the Paris Metro Detail.) Can anyone balance the appropriate safety concerns of an average adult against the possible high-jinks of a child out of control? And finally, does the stairway itself become a pleasant space through which to pass or is it just a utilitarian alternative to a slow elevator?

The main stair of the Whitney, which Breuer conceived and Hamilton Smith worked out in detail, is used by hundreds of admiring museum-goers each day: they take the elevator up and walk down. The elegant materials—bush-hammered concrete, green marble, bronze, and teak—combine with subtle adjustments in length of run and headroom required by the differing floor heights in the building to make it a magical place. When we were fighting to save the Whitney from its expansion plans, more than one architect went out of his way to say, "Whatever they do to the building, make sure they don't monkey with the great stair."

When Lajkó was working on UNESCO, he had to contend with a quirk of the Parisian fire code that required a separate outside stair to allow firemen to gain access to certain floors. This was usually a circular or spiral stair, since the geometric problems that cause difficulties for the public in an emergency did not apply to a fireman lugging a hose. Breuer piled up wedge-shaped pieces of precast concrete to create a decorative addition to the exterior of the building, and he was always looking for another use for this concept. He tried to accommodate it to the New York City Building Code and suggested it descend from the main floor of the Whitney to the sculpture court but couldn't get it approved. We finally used it very successfully on a grand sweeping stair for Mundipharma in Limburg, Germany.

Peasants and architects in Middle Europe have been embedding stone steps into the stonework of side walls for centuries. They are supported by the step below or, more audaciously, by nothing: they are simply cantilevered out from the wall itself. Lajkó surely had seen this done crudely in the farmland of Hungary, or elegantly in the Romanesque cathedrals of Italy. He designed many a concrete stair cantilevered out of rubblestone retaining walls for his early houses. The handrail slats were integrated with the steps in such a way that it was not immediately apparent whether the steps were holding up the handrail or vice versa. Breuer's cantilevered treads gradually got wider and grander until they began to feel springy underfoot and we had to have them structurally designed rather than developed empirically.

Sunshades were another subject of endless experimentation throughout Breuer's early domestic work and probably reached their peak of variety and ingenuity on the UNESCO building, where each facade of the Y-shaped plan faced the sun in a different direction and suggested a different solution. Lajkó was certainly trying to keep out annoying heat and sun glare. But he was also "decorating" the facades with three-dimensional objects that broke up the flat facades of modern architecture. Elsewhere he made them of wood, steel, aluminum, smoked glass, "subway" gratings—and more. Some were very beautiful, and most kept out at least some sun. And then suddenly, in the late 1950s, he gave them up. It may be that he hoped that the depth of his precast-concrete facades would accomplish the same purposes, or simply that his mechanical engineers told him they could cut the heat gain more effectively with air-conditioning and thermal glazing. He told us that he was tired of buildings with three or even four different facade treatments and preferred instead to search for unity in expression.

UNESCO (after Marcel Breuer). A stack of identical precast concrete stair treads was used to practical and decorative effect as an emergency fire access stair.

Wood siding as used in New England was a revelation to Breuer when he first arrived in the United States, and indeed, to this day, foreign visitors marvel at our traditional wood houses, which are rare except deep in the countryside of Europe. He wanted to build with the simplified cubist components that the modernists rendered in white stucco over masonry but found problems with stucco when it covered a flexible wood frame. It took some time to develop a suitable alternative in wood. The horizontal clapboard sheathing that was typical of New England could not be carried smoothly around a corner, as I. M. Pei pointed out to me. A vertical column or corner trim was required to cover the overlapping edges of the clapboard. Cedar shingles or shakes were too rustic for Lajkó's concept of clean geometric form. Then he noticed that many interiors used vertical wood siding as a finished material. The joints were prevented from opening up as the wood shrank in curing by a tongue-and-groove joint between the boards. Breuer reasoned that the vertical joints would guide the run-off of rain if used outside and that any water that got through could be stopped by tar paper, which was then coming into common use, between the sheathing and the exterior siding. He thus introduced a whole new material to domestic architecture.

As water-repellent treatments were developed, Breuer would leave the wood to age in its natural colors. There was hardly a "modern" house built for twenty years that did not feature vertical wood siding as a principal material. He eventually got a little tired of all the natural wood siding, particularly in the hands of his many followers, and used white-painted board-and-batten siding to great effect on several of his houses toward the end of the 1950s.

Mundipharma's main staircase. Lajkó finally got to build the monumental spiral stair that he had proposed for the Whitney after experimentation at UNESCO.

Colors Lajkó brought with him from Europe were the standard pure primaries of de Stijl and Mondrian—red, yellow, and blue—and he used them as panel accents under windows on a number of his early houses. The only other "colors" were the natural ones of wood and stone plus accent trim in black and white. There developed within the office, and among paint suppliers who wanted our business, a finely graded and very personal version of each color.

172

Red was always a red-orange, one that the industry frequently calls "poppy-red." Yellow, if used at all (it gradually dropped out of his palette), had to be as pure as possible. The slightest hint of gold or yellow-orange was derided as being too "sweet," and anything verging into chartreuse was unacceptable.

Blue was surely Breuer's favorite, probably because it went so well with the orange and ochre tones of natural wood and stone. But it was a very special color that the profession knew as "Breuer blue." Again, anything with a hint of green in it—turquoise, cerulean, or aqua—was too "sweet," and even cobalt was suspect unless it was mixed with some ultramarine. The best examples glowed with just a hint of purple, which the trade would today call "periwinkle."

Breuer was often quoted as saying that the greens of nature were too good to be competed with. Although he denied making the statement, Lajkó never used green except in its olive or bronze extremes.

White remained a puzzle, since his taste seemed to change constantly. It was always to be cut with some other combination of colors to become off-white, but it was never to approach ivory or cream. Yet I heard Lajkó angrily order large sections of "cool white" repainted because they had too much blue in them. It often seemed safest to use pure white, straight from the can, since all paint colors were dulled in the process of manufacture.

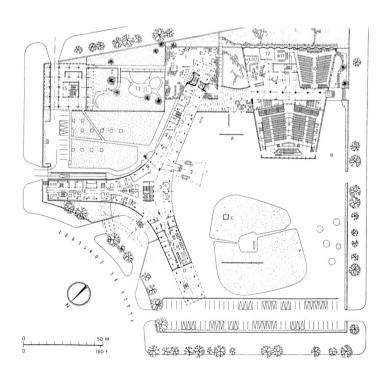

UNESCO. The free-form lawn area in front of the head-quarters buildings is a pure Breuer shape made up of arcs of varying radii and straight lines.

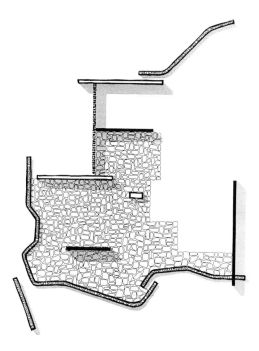

The Neumann house. This study for the masonry planes surrounding and defining the extraordinary house hung on Breuer's office wall for many years.

Black was black, except that it wasn't—as anyone familiar with the paintings of Ad Reinhardt knows. We erred on the side of warm rather than cool.

Gray came in all tones and values and was the color most often referred to Breuer for final judgment. A light, coolish gray was his favorite choice for carpeting, and charcoal gray worked well on his furnishings. Breuer resisted the beigelike grays, or "putty," that industry adopted as an all-purpose paint finish for cabinets and appliances.

Orange and all browns and tans were, Lajkó felt, fully represented in the natural colors of wood and stone that he used so freely. Purple never came up.

Shapes of a distinct sort were very much a part of Breuer's personal signature. We tried always to avoid L-shapes as being inherently "weak" and prone to break apart at the joint. This was true of pieces of stone, panels of concrete, or cutouts of wood. But even in the purely abstract shapes of paths, driveways, and site plans, L-shapes were not preferred. Breuer also detested the sinuous S-curve and the free-flowing, soft curves of landscape architects and highway engineers, however well attuned they were to the growing patterns of plant life and the speed of vehicles. This meant that as drafting instruments we used compasses and circle templates far more often than French curves. The ideal "free" forms were bounded by straight lines connected at their corners by rather tight circular curves, and we drew and

175

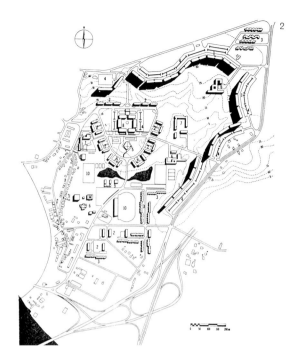

The ZUP de Bayonne. The one major S-curve in Lajkó's oeuvre was determined by the shape of the hill that it crowned.

built many driveways that way, even though owners later left tire marks in the grass beside the pavement. The original main parking lot at Flaine was a marvelous shape that would have worked for parking and looked great from above, but we had to scrap it for a more prosaic form when the realities of snow-plowing were brought to our attention. When Philip Johnson annotated his great glass house for its publication in *Architectural Review*, he pointed out the shape of his paths as being pure Breuer.

Precast panels recur frequently in the latter part of his career; Lajkó used them to wrap and support his buildings. He liked the heavy, sculptural possibilities presented by the product of the technique and considered it a sort of universal language that could be used repetitively wherever repetition was called for. Comparisons to the almost anonymous but effective facades of the rue de Rivoli, the Royal Crescent at Bath, and the Georgian squares of Bloomsbury have been made and may have been in his mind.

The advantage of concrete panels was that, from the mid-1960s to the 1970s, the precasting industries on both sides of the Atlantic were very active and inventive and there was real competition to keep costs quite low. Chemical additives and surface treatments added to the life of the finished product, and the freedom to shape its final form as window, sunshade, pipe chase, and stiffening rib proved to be irresistible.

The disadvantage was that after many years of experimentation Breuer's facades began to resemble one another and even within the office we could hear, "Oh no, not another one." I think the criticism was unjustified and believe that the development over time of Lajkó's variations on the theme provided a rich palette of interesting textures and useful devices that suited his purpose.

One of the principal drawbacks of precast concrete has been the lack of maintenance by owners who would never have left a brick or stone facade untouched for years. Part of this inattention derived from Breuer's own assurances about the virtually indestructible nature of the material. In practice, except in the pure alpine air of Flaine, many of the facades became dirty and stained with urban soot and today look rather grim. Most of them need only a cleaning job; others require careful patching.

Concrete is not without its problems, particularly if it is exposed to weather, which allows it to absorb moisture that later expands as it freezes, causing the gradual deterioration of the outer surface in a process of spalling, or peeling away. Nevertheless, there has been a great deal of research and experimentation on the use and placement of concrete both in the United States and internationally since World War II, and our office, particularly Ham, closely followed the latest developments in sealants, admixtures, formwork construction, and the like. I am sure that Breuer's specifications for structural and architectural concrete were among the most thorough and tested of any architectural office in the country.

I recently spent a couple of months in France and had the opportunity to revisit a number of our job sites—now thirty years old—as well as a number of other modern buildings of more recent vintage. Le Corbusier's Unité d'habitation in Marseilles is reported to be falling into slumlike conditions, whereas I found the similarly low-cost housing at the ZUP de Bayonne to be thriving. Some of the concrete had been painted and the signage of the stores had exploded beyond the bounds of our rigorous prescriptions, but the joy of the community and the glories of its landscape were palpable.

By contrast, the Bordeaux headquarters of Mort Sackler's French affiliate, Laboratoires Sarget, had been sold to a less interested German firm. The administration building is topped by an ungainly sign and the precast concrete is badly in need of cleaning. Once again, however, the surrounding greenery has grown to towering proportions and serves to dazzle those passing by on the way to the airport.

Modern architecture is getting a bad rap these days, based in part upon the current condition of some of its monuments. In my experience, however, every one that has been maintained by caring hands remains eloquent testimony to the vitality and worth of the movement.

Comparative drawings of eight buildings made at the same scale and rendered in the same fashion illustrate the rich variety of facade treatments that Lajkó developed over many years of experimentation. They also show family resemblances as well as progressive differences.

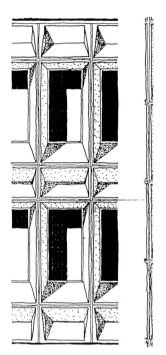

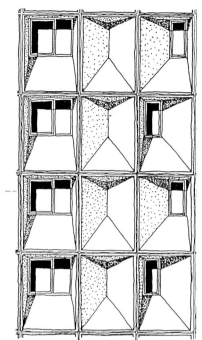

IBM La Gaude, 1960

This was Breuer's first deeply modeled facade in concrete, which, at the contractor's option, was precast. Each of its two laboratory floors was relatively high because of the depth of structure needed for long spans and the large amount of ductwork hidden in the hung ceilings. The facade is more than three feet deep and serves to shade the tall, narrow windows, spaced at six-foot intervals, from the harsh Mediterranean sun. The faceted panels above and below the windows enliven the appearance, reflect the horizontal "folds" that carry utilities, and bring the surface back to its starting plane both at the roof and at the top of the great columns below.

Flaine, 1962

Precasting was a precondition of the decision by Eric Boissonnas to use Jean Barets's patented facade system. The panel depth, just over eighteen inches, was set by the molds, and Breuer did everything possible to exploit the ins and outs required for windows. He modeled the blank panels that cover irregular wall endings and closets with the inverted, faceted prism that became the trademark of the resort. Since most of the floors were used for hotel rooms and apartments, the ceilings were relatively low and the structure, which spanned between the side walls, was relatively shallow. As a result, we squeezed four floors into the height of two of La Gaude's.

Department of Housing and Urban Development Headquarters, 1964

The floor-to-floor height of the offices at HUD was somewhere between that of La Gaude and that of Flaine, and Herb got three stories out of the same overall dimension. This facade bore the weight of the building and looks it. The government's standard planning module was five feet—not far from the six feet dictated by IBM at La Gaude. Breuer wanted something wider and chunkier and argued successfully for doubling it to ten feet. The sides of the window modules were very robust to start with and got thicker at the bottom and top of the building since they accommodated pipe chases that originated at both the roof and basement levels of the ten-story building.

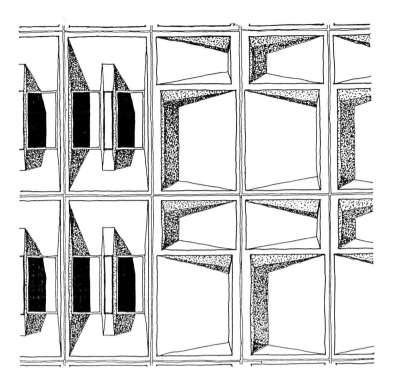

Yale, 1966

One facade of this engineering laboratory building had windows on a five-foot planning grid; the opposite facade was largely windowless. To animate this blank wall under the sunlight and, to some extent, in reflection of the scale of a nearby Gothic chapel, Lajkó and Ham began playing with faceted shapes. The sloping sides facilitated removal of the precast-concrete pieces from their metal formwork. The subtle changes from thick to thin and the reversal of slopes established a pattern that pleased us all and provided the inspiration for later experiments.

SUNY Buffalo Chemical Engineering Building, 1968

By the time I got to work on a laboratory building, I was able to incorporate some of the play of shapes that was used at Yale. We were working with a planning module at ten feet, and the justification of the rib above the window (if it needs one) is that a structural T was centered behind it.

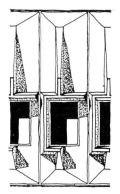

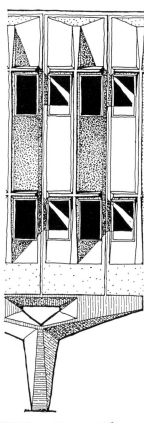

Torin Headquarters, 1966

This building is only one story tall and sits in a beautiful woodland setting. The "box" under the window was, according to Herb, inspired by the requirements of a heating and air-conditioning element under the sill. The box over the window is pure sculpture, and taken together they made of this "hollowed-out" window unit a thing of baroque splendor. By combining and editing two such elements, Breuer created a monumental T that stands in front of the headquarters as its logo.

Torin Nivelles, 1963

Ham had been working on an assembly plant in Belgium when the engineers of Schokbeton, which was to do the precasting, suggested projecting fins as sunshades and stiffeners on the tall factory panels. The beautiful, asymmetric positive patterns that resulted were startlingly different from the negative hollows with which we had become familiar.

IBM Boca Raton, 1967

When I was working on the three-story laboratory wings in Florida, the engineers suggested a number of economies that derived from the very advanced precast industry of the area. First, they proposed that one panel cover and support both of the upper two stories. Then they asked for a central rib in the middle of each eight-foot panel to stiffen it and to receive the load of long-span Ts arriving at each floor level. Without the window-shading canopies that we added, this panel would have looked remarkably like the many tilt-up factory panels in the neighborhood. With the intersecting ribs, they look somewhat like a doubled crusader's cross and, in the long curving lines of the Y-shaped buildings, play optical tricks under the hot Florida sun.

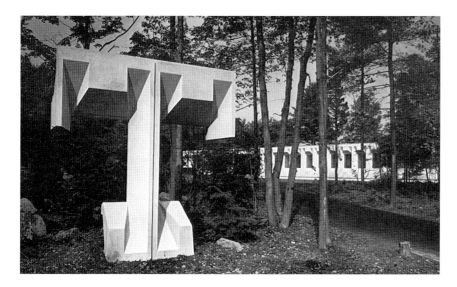

The Torin T. The logo was made up of parts from two facade panels of the headquarters building in the background.

There came a time in the late 1960s when the practice had grown so in size and substance that someone wondered if we shouldn't stop continually reinventing the wheel and settle on a catechism of standard office details that could be referred to by new draftsmen and -women as an introduction to our way of doing things. **Don Cromley** was assigned the job of pulling this material together—sliding windows, stair treads, copings; there seemed to be enough to fill a book. What he found, of course, was that there was no such thing as any one standard way of doing anything. Each solution differed slightly from its predecessor as we learned from experience and were prodded by Lajkó's constant search and invention.

In Kenneth Frampton's book *Studies in Tectonic Culture,* he discussed the 1851 writings of Gottfried Semper in which dwellings were divided "into four basic elements: (1) the earthwork, (2) the hearth, (3) the framework/roof, and (4) the lightweight enclosing membrane." I never heard Breuer refer to Semper, although in his dealings with Sigfried Giedion and his German-Swiss practice he may have been familiar with his theories. But unspoken and unacknowledged, Breuer practiced his profession in strict adherence to Semperian distinctions.

Earthwork is both the foundation that grows out of the ground and the masonry that is supported thereon and, in turn, at least appears to support itself. Stone, whether in slabs, drums, or Breuer's trademark "rubble," is clearly part of this category; brick and concrete block are other examples. The characteristic of masonry is that its strength lies in compression rather than tension: its units will support a lot of weight if pushed down upon but will fracture if pulled apart hard enough. (Poured or precast

181

concrete is not included since it is laced with reinforcing steel that gives it strength in tension.)

Making openings in masonry walls has always been one of architecture's greatest challenges. A slab of stone will span a relatively short distance and form a lintel over a door, window, or the space between columns, as in a Greek temple. For larger openings, the arch was invented, each element of which supports and is supported by the others (and at its base, does its own pushing). If a designer doesn't want to see a beam or lintel over an opening in a masonry wall, it is possible to hide it—with a steel angle built into and behind the face of a brick surface, for example—but many architects are uncomfortable with this lack of "expression" in structure. Frank Lloyd Wright once dismissed this concern by saying something to the effect of, "If anyone is so sensitive to structure as to feel the need for a lintel over an opening in a brick wall, he'll be able to imagine the steel lintel." Breuer, on the other hand, avoided punching holes in masonry walls unless there was a visible lintel or roof fascia to bridge the opening and therefore, like Mies before him, tended to use stone in planes, with openings above or alongside but never below the visually unsupported units of masonry. Ham Smith said Lajkó never punched a hole in a rubblestone wall, but there were exceptions—such as at the Hooper house in Baltimore, which still makes me uncomfortable. And there are lots of steel lintels to be seen over his stone fireplace openings, where Lajkó instinctively pulled the lower, horizontal leg of the angles forward of the face of the stone. He said it was to keep the smoke from staining the stones above, but it gave the lintels an obvious presence.

During the 1950s and 1960s, rubblestone was one of Breuer's favorite materials, both for residential work and for institutional projects such as New York University, Flaine, and Hunter College. He was very particular about the

The Hooper house. This appears to be the only instance in which Breuer let rubblestone go over an opening with no visible means of support. It makes a dramatic frame but is unconvincing masonry.

The second Stillman house. Lajkó used a lot of his signature rubblestone in the second house he designed for his old friend Rufus Stillman. In combination with the white forms above, it seems very Greek in inspiration.

way the stone was to be laid and insisted that if we were to expect the mason to do the job right, we had to draw it right. He lectured us so often that anyone who had been in the office a year or so could pass on the litany to the newcomers. Each stone was to be no larger than what one person could lift (approximately eight by sixteen inches, at a maximum) and no smaller than about four by four inches (anything smaller amounted to "chinking," and Breuer preferred to see the cement joint widen rather than to fill every hole with a sliver of stone). Most stones were to be laid with their main axis horizontal; they would appear prepared to receive additional weight. A vertical stone could appear at a corner, but diagonal setting was to be discouraged and any stone notched to form an L would be forcibly removed.

The surface was ideally cleft or flat; if the fieldstone had not been found that way, then the mason was to split it. Bulbous, rounded surfaces that protruded from the plane of the wall were to be avoided. Sharp corners were not in the nature of the fieldstones that Breuer loved; even if the stones had come from a quarry (as at NYU), the mason was expected to blunt the corners with a mallet before putting them in place. While the glory of a good rubblestone wall lies in the richness of its subtly varying colors, it was not preferred to place a strong reddish stone in, for instance, an otherwise tan or gray wall. The mortar was to be slightly recessed from the face of the stones and to maintain a continuous plane that flowed around and between the stones with its width varying from no more than two inches to no less than a half inch. Long continuous joints, whether vertical or horizontal, were to be avoided; swooping, sinuous curves were the worst. Once a joint had passed two or three stones it was to be interrupted by a stone that

183

would break its axis. Draftsmen and masons had to be trained but the walls were rarely built entirely according to the Breuer rules.

These guidelines didn't mean that every Breuer stone wall or fireplace looked like every other one. Differences in local color and source made for qualities as unique as the hand of the mason who was laying the stone. Walls at Flaine range from black to gray in color, while the New England houses are a symphony of earth tones. But in each case they look like a Breuer wall—even though Le Corbusier may have been the first to use rubblestone architecturally at his Pavillon Suisse.

Rubblestone is a great example of Semperian earthwork because it originates in the earth and shares its color. Breuer was perfectly content to have such a wall rise directly from the ground, since any rain-spattered dirt that might stain its surface would blend with the color of the stone. Brick or dressed stone were preferably laid on a base growing out of the concrete foundation to free it visually and literally from the dirt of the ground. If this was not possible, due to sloping ground, for instance, Breuer would call for a two-foot-wide strip of gravel at the base of the wall to absorb the rain and ease the grass-cutting. These methods of articulation between materials happened to look good, at least to our collective eye, but it's hard to say whether this was because they served a useful, practical purpose or because of their sculptural effect.

Jointing is a characteristic quality of any masonry material, and its pattern reflects its purpose and, frequently, its strength as well. If units of masonry are laid with a stacked vertical joint they don't look as if they will hold together very well, and they won't, unless they are tied back to some other structure. Brick, if used purely decoratively as a facing, often has stacked joints to emphasize that characteristic. If instead the minute vertical joints are offset in what is called a "running" bond, they appear to have greater integrity as a bearing wall, and they do. Breuer always preferred a running bond simply as pattern, and he would offset joints even in tile work, where strength was irrelevant. If we staggered the joints in a ceramic-tile wall, however, we usually let the vertical joints run through in order to make the decorative intent perfectly obvious.

For a floor of quarry tile, Breuer had another, very practical reason for offset joints. He had learned that quarry tile was extruded from a clay molding machine and cut to length. He reasoned—correctly—that the width of a "square" tile set by the machine was likely to be more dependable than the length controlled by the knife that cut it. If the tile wasn't exactly square, it was difficult to make sharp cross corners, and thus masons always asked that joints be wider than really necessary. Since Lajkó preferred seeing the joints in tilework kept to an absolute minimum (to prevent the buildup of dirt and mildew on the cement of the joint), he called for fine joints and recommended that the extruded side of the tile be used for the continuous

Hôtel Le Flaine. Non-load-bearing windows, balconies, and facade panels are stacked on the left to create a "fabric" of mullions and voids; Breuer instinctively staggered the joints of the end wall to imply the masonry's ability to bear load.

The Caesar cottage. The fireplace is of bush-hammered concrete; the opening is bridged by a projecting steel angle. The freestanding flues (usually hidden within the chimney) are of the same tile.

joints that had to line up. Staggered joints became so much of a part of his palette that we drew them instinctively and often forgot the rational process that lay behind them.

Many of the building corners at Flaine have joints between the precast-concrete panels that are stacked on one facade and staggered just around the corner. All the panels were supported in the same way—by tying them back to structural walls—so their literal strength in compression was not the issue. It seems to have been simply an architectural instinct that said that if the panels were largely window frames they were clearly a curtain wall and should be hung in a fashion that would make their non-bearing purpose clear, whereas a largely solid end wall should "read" visually as if it were doing some work in supporting itself.

The *hearth*, according to Semper (via Frampton), is an essential part of any dwelling, and I can't think of any of Lajkó's houses that didn't have at least one beautiful fireplace. Each was different and presented a continual challenge to his ingenuity. We made them of stone and brick, concrete and clay tile; sometimes they were part of a wall but more often they were free-

The Clark house.
The all-brick fireplace
features a projecting
lintel over the firebox.
The lintels supporting
the upper band of
brick are apparent
from below.

The House in the
Garden at MoMA.
The fireplace featured
a rare combination
of rubblestone and
brick.

187

standing as the sculptural symbol they certainly were. Every hotel at Flaine had a fireplace, as did several of the grander apartments. Breuer was very impressed by the "scientific" way that Americans built their fireplaces, and we were instructed to rigorously follow the proportions and dimensions listed on two pages of *Architectural Graphic Standards*, an industry bible that floated around the office in two tattered copies. As he departed from the norm of a single, shallow opening to explore the virtues of a double-sided "see-through" version or even a totally open, round hearth—as in Hôtel A at Flaine—Breuer was insistent that we check the aerodynamics of flue and draft with a consultant he trusted. Since his fireplaces had become such a trademark of his practice, it would have been very embarrassing to have one that billowed smoke into the room.

Whether it is the altar of a church, the proscenium of an auditorium, a CEO's conference room, or the circulation desk of a library or museum, every building that is custom-designed has its "hearth" (as opposed to a speculative office building, whose only fixed interior element is an elevator core). Lajkó didn't always succeed in maintaining control over the interiors of his buildings, which is astonishing considering that they were an early source of his fame, but he did fight hard to design those essential parts of the interior that would be seen by the public as characteristic of the architect's intent: at a minimum (and by contract), the lobby, cafeteria, meeting rooms, and monumental stairs. He seemed guided by the need to recognize the importance of every building's hearth.

The *framework/roof* or structural skeleton of any building becomes independently identifiable as columns and beams replace walls and slabs. Many architects feel a need to express the independent structure of a building as opposed to the earthwork on which its stands or the outer envelope that may protect it. The visible poles of a tent and the colonnades of Greek temples clearly illustrate this. There seem always to have been two warring impulses raging within the architectural world: the tendency to break apart and articulate the various parts of a building according to its purpose, and the desire to make it look all of a piece. The latter is characteristic of the great periods of masonry construction—Egyptian pyramids, Roman vaults, and the Romanesque, including its revivals.

In Breuer's long career his own preferences changed. His early infatuation with lightweight metal structures was expanded to include the daring use of wood. Gradually, however, a fondness for the sculptural unity he found in masonry and particularly concrete structures took over. He loved the idea that the same concrete that was folded over the UNESCO assembly hall and Saint John's Abbey or warped around Saint Francis de Sales in Muskegon was both structure and envelope. One disadvantage of moving his practice from Europe to the United States was that the relative cost of labor and materials was reversed: labor for building wooden formwork was cheap in Europe, while steel was frequently in short supply and often costly; in America, steel was plentiful but unionized construction workers were well paid. Breuer knew the economic logic, but even in America, he always preferred concrete as something he could mold and show with pride.

As for roofs, Breuer had an obvious aversion to the hips and gables of traditional architecture—he had learned the language of van Doesberg and de Stijl too early to give it up later. His houses were almost always capped with a single plane faced in one strong white band of fascia board. It might be bent or inclined in a butterfly or shed roof, but it rarely showed its graveled surface and never ended in a pediment. Breuer's larger, institutional buildings end with the horizontal line of a parapet or the narrow metal edge of a gravel stop. In relying upon interior drains and even arguing for the perfectly flat roofs made possible by improved roofing membranes, Breuer was avoiding the gutters and drainpipes of his European youth, and he missed the characteristic rooflines of a romantic past not one whit.

The *lightweight enclosing membrane* has been considered one of the principal characteristics of modern architecture, although it has existed throughout history in the skins and woven fabric of even the simplest shelters. Probably the most successful glass curtain wall is to be found surrounding the apse of Sainte Chapelle in Paris. Upon "discovering" its thin flying buttresses outside, Nikolaus Pevsner described its magic as being akin to the thrill of going backstage to see the stage braces that hold up the scenery.

It is the threads that make up the fabric of a curtain wall (though Breuer never used this terminology). Those "threads" might be the relatively heavy post and lintel of a precast concrete window frame, but their pattern was always to be respected and never broken for fear that the fabric might visually tear. When Breuer designed a glass curtain wall, he tried to make the threads of its fabric as thin as possible, as in his infamous sliding windows that attempted to do away with most of the frame surrounding the slider. For him, glass was a void that contributed to lightness and transparency. He fought the use of dark tinted glass, despite its heat-saving qualities, and never used reflective glass.

If Breuer had to pierce the fabric of one of his curtains, he made sure to reinforce the opening as he did in passing through the hexagonal stained-glass drapery of Saint John's; otherwise the curtain was either hung from the upper structure found at Armstrong Rubber and the HEW Headquarters in Washington or edged along its bottom with the hem of a heavy beam. Lajkó rarely explained what he was suggesting, and we rarely questioned it. His sympathy for Semperian principles, even if he had never encountered them, was a natural one.

The Department of Housing and Urban Development in Washington, D.C. This was Breuer's first building for the United States government.

The New York Office: 1964–1966

Back in New York, Breuer's American practice was flourishing as the architect's fame grew daily. Herb Beckhard was assigned to share in two important office-building commissions that arrived within months of each other as well as in the design of a house in Switzerland.

The first office building was for the new headquarters of the Department of Housing and Urban Development (HUD) in Washington, D.C. Karel Yasko was in charge of selecting architects for the huge federal office buildings being built by the government's General Services Administration (GSA). Originally appointed during John F. Kennedy's administration, he kept his position and power under Lyndon Johnson and had a great influence on changes in procedure that allowed commissions to go to prestigious architects rather than to political hacks, as had been the case all too often in years gone by. He himself was an architect, originally from the Midwest where he had been familiar with Breuer's work at Saint John's Abbey. While Breuer no doubt had to present his work in a competitive interview in Washington, we had the impression that the HUD commission was virtually handed to him.

There was a difficult negotiation over fees, since the government was famed for paying bottom dollar. A contract was finally signed based on a percentage fee that was, in Breuer's eyes, very low but that eventually proved to be a bonanza, since it was to be multiplied by a construction budget that was many times larger than anything the firm had handled before. This was converted into a lump-sum fee that fortunately did not decrease when the project later came in significantly under budget. In many ways, the most important feature of the HUD commission was the fact that it came from the United States government. It made Lajkó feel that he was finally an American.

Breuer proposed a variant on the double-Y scheme he used for office buildings, and the design was approved. Its ten stories required a much heavier scale in the size of its tree columns and bearing-wall window frames than had been the case in its predecessor, IBM La Gaude. In comparison to IBM's three stories, HUD looks like a grown-up, heavily muscled older brother. The jambs, or side members of the windows, were sized to carry the accumulated weight of the stories above but also to house the duct risers of the air-conditioning system. Since the air was supplied from both high and low points in the building, the windows have heavier frames at the top and the bottom of the building than they do in the middle. This distinction, while not immediately noticeable, gives the facade a subtle complexity. Jeff Vandeberg worked late on the drawings just before Lajkó's return from Europe and sketched some concrete walls near the main entry that had a curvilinear form not in the usual Breuer vocabulary. Herb was hesitant about Jeff showing the unauthorized sketches to the master, and both heaved a sigh of relief when Lajkó pronounced them "very nice." The rigorous use of concrete, both poured and precast, had the government estimators worried, and they eliminated many of the more "luxurious" materials—such as granite pavers in the forecourt—before they would allow bids on the project. The bids came in four million dollars under budget because of the inherent economy of the repetitive elements, but the GSA wouldn't restore the granite and used the savings to help out other architects' projects that were over budget.

Later in 1964, Breuer was offered the chance to design the tall office building he had been waiting for. Cabot, Cabot, and Forbes (CC&F) asked him to join a developers competition for the New England Merchants' Bank building that was to be built right next to Boston's fine new city hall. CC&F eventually bowed out of the competition without even submitting the design that Herb had presented, but the forty-two-story scheme was a classic embodiment of Lajkó's direct approach to office-building planning.

The Koerfer house in Moscia. Breuer's answer to Falling-water hovers over Lake Maggiore.

Herb also worked on a dramatic concrete house for Jacques Koerfer, the former head of BMW, that was built into a hillside overlooking Lake Maggiore in Moscia, Switzerland. Jeff did much of the drafting for the project and describes a classic Breuer mixture of rough and fine materials at one doorway in which a "barn door" was built up of three layers of fine oak planking mounted on custom-designed bronze pivots above a split-face granite floor and within a bush-hammered concrete frame. (Bush-hammering involves the breaking up of the concrete surface by pounding it with toothed mallets to expose the aggregate within.) The site was very steep, and the house was so carefully integrated into the landscape that it was very difficult to photo-

graph. The principal facade could be seen only from the lake, but I know of no photographs taken from the water. Koerfer had a fabulous art collection that was so valuable that his insurance company insisted its masterpieces travel with him when he moved from homes in Zurich to Moscia to St. Moritz in a flotilla of BMW station wagons. I visited the house in the summer of 1984 when Koerfer was off in Zurich. His housekeeper apologized for several blank spaces on the dining-room wall, but I noted that the paintings that were in place included small Picassos and other works by instantly recognizable artists. The house was almost hidden in a jungle of luxuriant foliage and its concrete showed stains of mold from the humidity, but its interior and view of the lake were breathtaking.

A major commission came in from the University of Massachusetts for a campus center at Amherst. It featured a complex program that included the small and large rooms typical of a hotel along with other student facilities that had to fit into a very small site. Herb's interpretation of the program put many spaces not requiring natural light underground in a great stepped podium. On top of the podium was placed a ten-story building with three differently scaled facade panels that reflected the various occupancies. Jeff Vandeberg, looking for historic precedents, suggested to Breuer that the stepped base for

The University of Massachusetts campus center in Amherst. The stepped base marks the vertical transition between the huge windowless rooms underground and the multipurpose tower.

The all-star Interama design team. Ed Stone, José Luis Sert, Breuer, Lou Kahn, Bob Browne, Edwin Muskat, Harry Weese, and Paul Rudolph all worked on parts of the never-realized trade fair.

the building was really the stylobate of a classic Greek temple. Lajkó rejected the comparison, either because he didn't find it apt or because he didn't like to acknowledge that any of his ideas grew out of the past.

In 1965 Herb also started work on a second house for Rufus Stillman in Litchfield, Connecticut, that was built of white stucco and fieldstone and bore the same relationship to his first house as Lajkó's own two houses in New Canaan had to each other. By this time, Breuer was preoccupied with the larger commissions the office was receiving and essentially left Herb to design, or overdesign according to Ruf, the second Stillman house. That didn't prevent Lajkó from exploding over the height of some shelves destined for herb bottles and asking why Herb hadn't shown him the drawings before they went out.

As the office grew, Lajkó had to spread himself thinner and delegate much of the design work to his partners and staff. The trick was to know when to check ideas with him. By and large, he backed us up before clients, even when something wasn't exactly what he would have done if he had had the time.

Two other projects that occupied Herb's time during these years came to naught. One was a vast permanent trade fair intended for the exhibition of

North and South American industrial products. Located in Miami, Interama was to feature the work of Edward Durell Stone, Harry Weese, José Luis Sert, Paul Rudolph, and Louis Kahn, as well as Breuer. Lajkó's project was highlighted by battered stone walls borrowed from the Aztec and Egyptian traditions. The other project was a small Episcopal church called Saint Luke's for a congregation in Fairport, New York. They weren't able to raise the money for the whole building, but their request to use only plans of the basement was turned down by Lajkó.

In early 1963, just as I was getting ready to leave for Europe, Breuer was selected as the architect for a new Whitney Museum of American Art in New York. It was to be the third home for a collection begun in the 1920s by Grace Vanderbilt Whitney. It was first assembled in a Greenwich Village townhouse and, since 1949, had been shown in an add-on to the Museum of Modern Art on West Fifty-fourth Street, which confused most people, who thought it was a part of its more famous neighbor. There had even been an earlier plan to house the museum in a wing off the Metropolitan Museum of Art.

By the time the Whitney trustees came to Breuer, his assignment was clear: to design something that would work as a museum (as opposed to the Whitney's judgment of the recently completed Guggenheim) and put the Whitney back on the map as an independent entity. The choice of architect had very much been guided by the museum's chairman of the board, and granddaughter of the founder, Flora Miller Irving, and her architect husband, Mike, who wrote the museum's program. Mike received a very enthusiastic endorsement of Breuer from his friend and neighbor Pierre Lutz. Pierre was an accomplished watercolorist who earned some part of his living making architectural renderings. He had worked for Lajkó for years as his illustrator of choice, and the two were great friends.

Once he had his contract, Lajkó retired to the country for a weekend and returned with one 8 ½-by-11-inch sheet of carefully drawn and dimensioned freehand sketches of the plan and elevations that, to those who saw them, completely defined the building that was eventually built. It is, at least for New Yorkers, Breuer's best-known building and one of his most successful.

In the quest for identity, the Whitney was designed to be instantly, almost outrageously, recognizable. Lajkó presented the outer shell to Matt Lévy for structural development, assuming it would be a completely homogeneous concrete structure. Matt pointed out that the audacious cantilevers would be severely compromised by the added dead load of their own weight and convinced Breuer that a steel and concrete composite, however impure, was the way to go. Aside from several adjustments in the coursing of the granite veneer to cover the final structural members, the original sketches were built essentially as drawn.

A design team was assembled under Ham Smith, who served as co-architect and made major contributions to the design. The team included Paul Willen and Crane deKamp, and so great was the drama surrounding the project that the entire office was sworn to secrecy on the subject of the Whitney. The building was conceived to fit tightly within its Manhattan street corner, respecting the street planes of its neighbors on Madison Avenue and Seventy-fifth Street, while being hollowed out to "suck you in" (in Mike Irving's words) along a symbolic bridge across the moat below, intended for the display of outdoor sculpture. Later, when the building was threatened by Michael Graves's proposed addition, the critic and architect Michael Sorkin wrote in his book *Exquisite Corpse* of "the out-stepping of the mass as it rises until its uppermost part presses against the street-wall, like Marcel Marceau limning a window." Lajkó used to say that the great hooded windows were designed to lead the eye diagonally to the spacious street intersection rather than straight across the relatively narrow streets. The canopy, which so dramatically marks the entry bridge, was an after-thought to protect from the rain. And Breuer held out almost to the end for a great sweeping spiral staircase from the lobby to the lower level, but the building code imposed the present switchback.

A number of young draftsmen were involved in the Whitney project, including Dick Meier. Ham took Paul Willen aside one evening during the course of the project, after most of the staff had gone, to show him a drawing on Dick's board: "Now *this* is an amazing drawing. Look at how beautifully it is laid out." It was not only the quality of the draftsmanship but the thought behind its organization that Ham was pointing out—a model to be emulated but also an object of wonder.

Another young draftsman, Don Cromley, had been hired to work on the Whitney on the recommendation of his MIT classmate Stan Abercrombie. He kept being moved to other projects and returned only to design a perforated granite wall on the lower level of the museum. According to Don, the wall doesn't exist anymore, having been replaced by a bronze plaque honoring the person who gave the money to tear it out.

The building was designed, drawn, and built with great economy within an incredibly brief two and a half years. At forty-five dollars per square foot, HRH, the successful bidder, came in 15 percent below its nearest competitor—a price that reflected the company's eagerness to get the job and grow out of its reputation as builders only of housing. There were fears that the contractor's inexperience would hurt the project, but according to Bernie Marson, who acted as clerk o' the works, their principal naïveté was in not paying off the authorities. There was one big incident over the pouring of interior concrete walls that were to be left exposed to view after having been "bush-hammered." A Redi-Mix truck had been held up in Manhattan traffic and arrived with its load of concrete already beginning

The Whitney Museum under construction. Breuer and Jackie Onassis stand in front of admiring steelworkers.

to set up. When it was finally poured, a "cold," or non-adhering, joint appeared between it and the previous pour, to which it was supposed to bond, and it was clear that no amount of bush-hammering would disguise the ragged crack. The builder agreed to remove a part of the concrete surface, and the very thin granite tile that now surrounds the second-floor elevator doors was Lajkó's solution. My favorite little flaw is one small piece of formwork that somehow floated loose and is enshrined by its imprint high on the first-floor wall.

The ground floor and lower level have some of the largest sheets of glass that had ever been installed in New York. They were made in Europe, and several had been cracked when a truck driver misjudged the height of a highway overpass. Bernie was on the phone to Breuer when the replacement shipment arrived at the job site. While they were talking, the handlers dropped another piece.

The subcontractor for woodwork was a meticulous craftsman from central Europe, Naftaly Weiss, who was new to us then but later became our cabinetmaker of choice. He was unable, or unwilling, to produce the shop drawings that would demonstrate exactly how he planned to follow the architects' design. Instead, he offered to make a full-size mock-up of a turning in the main-stair handrail, which is one of the glories of the building interior. It was crafted with such care and innovative contribution to the design that Breuer waived the need for shop drawings.

198

The Whitney Museum of American Art. The museum presents one of Madison Avenue's most startling facades.

*The "Today" show.
Breuer was inter-
viewed when the
Whitney Museum
opened.*

As the Whitney was nearing completion, Rufus Stillman suggested to Lajkó that the museum open with an Alexander Calder retrospective. Breuer liked the idea and asked Ruf to see whether Sandy would be willing. When Breuer made the suggestion to the Whitney, he was turned down; just because he was the architect didn't mean that he could choose the artists.

The Whitney opened in September 1966, and I was back just in time for the grand event. The building had been clear of its scaffold for some time and was the most talked-about structure in Manhattan. I was in a taxi with Lajkó one day as we drove past the nearly completed museum, and he chuckled at the disparaging remarks of the cabbie—Breuer sensed that fame was finally to descend upon him. On the day of the opening, the Whitney staff suddenly realized that many more people had accepted the invitation to the festivities than had been predicted and that, if they all attended, the legal occupancy of the building might well be exceeded. The museum asked the Fire Department what might happen in such a case and was told that the event would be closed down. Hasty conferences with city officials resulted in a call for every available fireman to be posted at the entries and exits. The party crowd seemed to consist of more fire uniforms than black ties.

During 1964, Ham had been briefly diverted to work on the scheme of a house for Johnny van der Wal in Amsterdam. The design, which exists only in a beautiful perspective, was a free composition in poured concrete that had to be abandoned because of a shortage of building materials in Holland—everything available was being used for social housing. Van der Wal, a wealthy and influential captain of industry, could have gotten special permission for his house but decided not to take the heat of what was sure to be the attendant publicity. Lajkó understood but was disappointed, since the special design had been a labor of love for his good friend. Laurie Maurer worked on at least fifteen schemes for its fireplace. Lajkó gave her more than usual freedom to contribute her own ideas. "After he said 'Try this' and then 'Try that,' he added 'Then try anything else you can think of.'" Breuer was rarely that explicit, but it was understood that members of the staff, provided that they had genuinely tried to work out his own suggestion, were free to show him their own ideas. Woe to the draftsman who had no evidence of having tried to do what he was told before coming up with another approach. Gabby Sedlis learned that he could improve the chances of having his own suggestions accepted over those of Lajkó by drawing Breuer's idea on yellow tracing paper and his own on white.

In 1964 New York University asked Breuer for another laboratory adjacent to our previous buildings on the University Heights Campus. The result, Technology II, vividly shows the development in Lajkó's vocabulary over the eight years that separated it from Technology I. The original laboratory had used concrete as trim for the dominant yellow Roman brick of the campus.

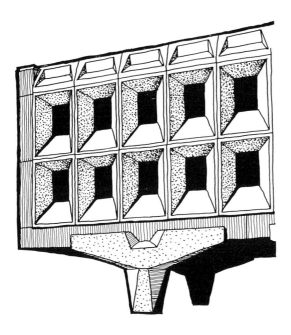

NYU Tech II (after Ben Schnall). The visual vocabulary was much heavier than that employed at Tech I.

201

The library at Saint John's (after Bill Hedrich). Two many-branched tree columns are spectacular structural/ sculptural feats of ingenuity.

The second building was boldly composed of confident tree columns and strongly sculpted window panels including "blind" units that covered the service corridor—an adaptation of our experience at Brookhaven.

During 1964–65, Saint John's University also came back: the school decided to complete the two remaining "walls" of the forecourt of the abbey church with a university library and a science hall. The library, like the science hall that was to follow it, is sheathed in a relatively modest facade of concrete, granite, and sun-shielding terra-cotta flue tiles intended not to compete with the sculptural bell banner that stands opposite. This calm exterior gives no hint of the structural explosion within. Taking his cue from the Hunter College program of limiting the number of columns in order to maximize freedom in the layout of the library floor, Breuer decided to design two tree columns that would end all tree columns. The relatively modest spans of this building could easily have been handled in a light steel structure, perhaps requiring no columns at all, but that was not the point. The building needed drama, and drama it got. From each of two squat trunks, twelve arms branch out that support a coffered, or egg-crate, ceiling whose deep ribs are flush with the outside fascia. The form of the columns is clearly sculptural in intent, although structural in effect. Dan Kistler, who acted as clerk o' the works on the project, used to speak of them as two caged animals. Matt Lévy puzzled over them with Paul Weidlinger while fearing that the limbs of the trees might just fall off under their own weight. Eventually Paul and Matt convinced each other that their angle was just right for the translation of shear forces into pure compression as those forces traveled down the arms of the mighty structures.

Norbert Schikel was living in Ithaca, New York, where he and his brother had a successful business as developers of Federal Housing Authority (FHA) housing, for which the clients were largely faculty and graduate students at Cornell University. The developers wanted to build on a modest-sized site not far from the campus, which they dubbed Fairview Heights, and asked Breuer to be its architect in the early 1960s. Although he had been positively challenged by the rigors of French housing regulations, Lajkó was less than excited by FHA strictures and left the design mostly in the hands of Ham and his job captain, Laurie Maurer. The tight urban composition of one tall block with several town-house groupings completing the surroundings of a square was quite successful. Fairview Heights is considered a desirable place to live, although Cornell architecture students are surprised to hear that they have a Marcel Breuer building in their own backyard. Breuer may not have given the project his full attention, but it is clear that his vocabulary, when spoken by those who knew the language, could produce fine buildings with distinct parentage.

One of Tician Papachristou's first duties after he was hired in early 1965 was to find new office space for Lajkó's expanding practice. The light-filled loft above Schrafft's was simply not big enough. Tician located and negotiated the lease for part of the twelfth floor of 635 Madison Avenue, at the corner of Fifty-ninth Street—a banal, 1950s-style office building with strip windows above metal spandrels and a dreadfully pretentious lobby. The building has since been retrofitted in stylish black granite with an even worse lobby.

The office layout was clear and functional, with Lajkó's office at the end of a long line of secretaries serving him and his partners, who worked in internal cubicles. The cubicles gave onto both the drafting room and the secretarial bullpen and thus acted as inadvertent passageways for those in a hurry. Each partner had a desk, drafting table, cork-covered walls for displaying drawings and photographs, and no doors. Lajkó worked behind a back-to-back pair of teak desks. At the other side of Breuer's private office was a massive gray granite conference table, this time on sturdy granite legs. Lajkó's cork wall held favorite photos and knickknacks, and the office was dominated by a floor-to-ceiling photo-mural made from a black-and-white shot he had taken of the enormous Finger of Constantine in Rome. The drafting room was spread out along windows on Fifty-ninth Street on one side and a light well between us and our neighbor on the other.

Even this space proved to be inadequate, and we eventually took over the entire floor plus a "company cafeteria" on the fifteenth floor. Breuer regretted the good old days when we could all go out to lunch together and consciously sought to regain the former sense of family. He hired a woman to make sandwiches every morning, which were served to all comers at a subsidized fifteen cents each together with coffee, apples, and so on. Breuer had lunch with the group whenever he could, and everyone tried to call him

Lajkó, but the staff grew past thirty and the atmosphere inevitably changed. The partners had lunch in Breuer's office every Monday, more often when the need for further business discussions arose. The noble lunchroom experiment lasted for a year or so but finally disappeared.

Breuer found that there was another Schrafft's on Madison between Fifty-eighth and Fifty-ninth Streets, and as he ate lunch more and more frequently with the partners, it became our routine since the short walk was easy on his aching back. (Mary Farris asked him one day if he had ever tried yoga for his back: "Connie and I eat it all the time but it doesn't do any good.") Lajkó got up early to catch the commuter train from New Canaan to Grand Central, and shortly before noon he was hungry. His memorable habit was to approach each partner in turn with the code words "Are you with us, or against us?" (The luncheon coda was equally predictable: "Well, back to the old drawing board . . .") He liked to carry big bills around with him and apparently often used them to pay his lunch tab. When a couple of the partners happened into Schrafft's some time after his retirement, a waitress asked, "How is that nice old gentleman with the fifty-dollar bills?"

Lajkó asked Joe Neski to come back into the office in 1965 when he heard that Joe's current partnership had folded, and he returned for a year or so, working directly with Breuer in the capacity of a partner but without the title. By the time I returned from Paris, it was clear that Joe's pride precluded his return at a second-rank status, and he left again for good.

Dino Gavina was the manufacturer and distributor of a line of high-style, overstuffed modern Italian furniture that was very much in vogue all over Europe. He approached Breuer in the early 1960s with the idea of reviving many of his old pieces on which the copyrights had expired and which were not generally available except as second-rate knockoffs. In return for calling them the "official" Breuer line, he would give Lajkó a royalty. All the old drawings were resurrected and updated to suit slight changes in the size and weight of average people. There was also to be a new line of desks (which Breuer used in his private office) and other pieces that would be gradually introduced to the market.

Thonet had sold Breuer's furniture by model number, but Gavina demanded names, which was the origin of their present-day identification. The first tubular-steel armchair of leather or canvas slings, the "Wassily," was named after Lajkó's good friend Wassily Kandinsky. The cantilevered chair of chrome, bent wood, and cane became "Cesca" after his mother's nickname. A line of wooden desks took "Canaan" from his adopted hometown of New Canaan. The redimensioning of the low-slung Wassily was not at fault when Breuer, with backache, called to Mary Farris one day: "Get me out of this damned chair!"

Dino was a salesman and charmer, and for a while the arrangement

Dino Gavina and Breuer with an unidentified woman, Bologna.

flourished. We learned from a friend in the business that Dino took on the Breuer line as a "gift to history" rather than with hope of commercial success. When he later found himself overextended and in financial trouble, it was ironic that Knoll bought him out principally in order to absorb the Breuer line into its own catalog. While business was good, he was lavish in his gestures, entertaining Breuer royally on trips to the factory in Milan and giving extravagant presents. He sent Lajkó a painting by Lucio Fontana for Christmas—a green canvas slit three times by razor blade. Today it would be very valuable. Lajkó hung it in "Alice's Restaurant" (as we called the company cafeteria) where it got spattered with Coca-Cola one day; when I last saw it someone had unceremoniously dumped it in the garbage. Mary Farris had difficulty with Dino's English on the telephone and in letters, which arrived in bad grammatical shape. After puzzling over one such letter, Lajkó dictated, "My dear Gavina—please, please, please—write in Italian."

The sisters at the Annunciation Priory in Bismarck, North Dakota, were so happy with their convent that they asked Breuer in 1965 to design Mary College on an adjacent part of their windswept hillside. Ham designed the master plan, and Tician worked on the actual buildings with Lajkó. The two complexes, seen from the air, look like two great rafts adrift on a sea

The Annunciation Priory and Mary College. Inward-looking courtyards were some protection from the raw Dakota landscape.

of grass. The college buildings included many materials and design features from the convent; taken together, these structures represent an extensive and varied statement of Breuer's design philosophy and vocabulary of the 1960s. The first stage of the college was planned as the start of a growing presence for religious education in the area. Since that time, the world-wide decrease in the number of women choosing to become nuns has caused all plans for expansion to come to a halt. Mary College also marked the entry of Tician into our design partnership, which was to be formalized a few years later.

In August 1965 Lajkó had the first of a series of heart "accidents" that were to recur in later years. It had perhaps been provoked by a travel schedule that was quite demanding for a sixty-three-year-old man. No one ever spoke of this as a heart attack, but it was serious enough to put Breuer in New York's Doctors' Hospital for a week and to send shivers of apprehension through the family and staff who had come to think of him as immortal. Marvelous get-well cards were created, and either Herb, Tician, or Paul Moore, who had just joined us from Dublin, introduced Lajkó to the limerick (each claims credit). Every raunchy rhyme they knew was contributed to a ten-page "definitive" document. Herb eventually replaced it with a larger collection that he found in a bookstore and presented to Lajkó, who kept it on the table at his bedside for the rest of his life.

Lillian Leight joined the firm as our controller in 1965 while I was in Paris. She replaced a long line of bookkeepers with a new infusion of experience and energy that made her an indispensable fixture for the next fifteen years.

Lorry Roeder worked in the office from 1963 to 1967 and is best remembered as the organizer of many light-hearted pranks and souvenirs. For one of Breuer's birthdays he went to heroic ends in assembling a Rube Goldberg contraption out of switches, buzzers, lights, a red plastic dome, and black boxes—all purchased on Canal Street. He presented it to Lajkó at a four o'clock office meeting over coffee and cake. It was described as a machine to design buildings, and the switches on the side were all labeled with familiar Breuer trademarks—precast, bush-hammered, board-form, and so on. As Lorry fed blank paper in at one end and turned a crank, out came, in sequence, a five-dollar bill, a fantastic collage of favorite building parts, and a *Playboy* centerfold. Lajkó was enthralled and in later months frequently called Lorry into his office to demonstrate the machine to clients and friends.

Through Mario Jossa's uncle in the Vatican, Cardinal Egidio Vagnozzi, Breuer was commissioned to design the Olgiatta Parish Church for Rome in the mid-1960s. It was abandoned when the Bank Immobiliare collapsed. Don Cromley was working on the design and had been thoroughly briefed by Lajkó as to his intentions before leaving on a trip abroad. The project quickly fell into place, and before he knew it, Don had run out of specific instructions to follow. So, rather than kill time at something else, he decided to carry it a bit further than authorized and, by the time Breuer returned, had a complete set of preliminary plans and elevations ready for his review. Breuer thought about it a bit and then said simply, "Donald, you drew it wrong"; it wasn't what he had in mind. Don has obviously thought about this often and speculates that it was as if he considered Don's hands his hands and that something had gone wrong with the mechanism.

Part of a get-well card for Lajkó. John Manton drew the cartoons of the New York staff.

Marcel Breuer and Associates. Partners Gatje, Papachristou, Beckhard, and Smith flank Breuer at the granite conference table at 635 Madison Avenue.

Madison
Avenue:
1966-1971

The office I found upon my return from Paris was a complete change from the one I had left on Fifty-seventh Street. The staff numbered close to forty and reflected the hierarchy that Breuer had established in order to use his time most effectively in carrying out larger commissions. It was even more of a contrast to the informal outpost I had left behind in Paris. Both Lajkó and I often remarked upon the sense of "home" that we felt on returning to rue Chapon for business trips, something I was to do on a more or less monthly basis until the early 1970s.

Until the twelfth floor of 635 Madison Avenue could be taken over in its entirety and remodeled to fit our needs, I was lodged on its third floor in temporary space I shared with my new secretary, Lynda Green, and a small group of designers who were assigned to work with me on projects. One gesture that helped ease me back into the New York scene was the belated presentation of my very own Marcel Breuer sweatshirt. Lorry Roeder had cut the silk screen based upon a favorite photograph of Lajkó and made up a batch for most of the office in celebration of Breuer's birthday the previous May.

The Armstrong Rubber Company was a small, family-held tire manufacturer whose executive offices and main assembly plant were located in West Haven, Connecticut. The company's symbol, a charging rhinoceros familiarly known as "Tuffy," had been almost forgotten as Armstrong shifted production more and more to the replacement tires it manufactured for Sears and Roebuck under the Allstate label. Over the years the company had become the principal supplier to Sears, and Sears had certainly become the princi-

BREUER

Lorry Roeder's sweat-shirt silk screen.

pal customer of Armstrong. Sears and Roebuck was not happy with this state of affairs, since it found it impossible to bargain hard, as was its style, with any supplier so dependent on its business that it would go bankrupt if ever orders were canceled. As it had done with other principal suppliers in the past, Sears decided to intervene directly in the management of Armstrong in order to build a stronger, independent manufacturer of tires in all sizes that would not be entirely beholden to what was then practically its parent.

Armstrong named Joseph R. Stewart, a retired brigadier general in the Marine Corps, its vice president and second in command to Frank Dwyer, who was scheduled for retirement as president in a few years time. In 1966 Joe Stewart was the first to admit that he knew nothing about architecture. When he approached the mayor of New Haven, Richard Lee, about purchasing a pivotal piece of land in the Long Wharf Redevelopment Area, he was unprepared for the mayor's interest in who the architect might be. Dick Lee explained that the site under consideration would mark the gateway to New Haven for traffic coming off the Connecticut Turnpike and heading into town. He insisted that anything built on the site should have an architectural presence and be designed by a master. Joe asked who he had in mind, and Dick pulled a well-worn list from his top desk drawer. Having previously participated in the selection of Saarinen, Rudolph, Johnson, Bunshaft, Roche, Venturi, Moore, and Kahn by Yale and other New Haven clients, his list was getting shorter and Marcel Breuer was at the top. Joe had not expected this development but promised to discuss it with Armstrong and Sears. A few days later, he was in our office to talk with Lajkó (whom he always addressed as "Mr. Breuer," although he never quite got the pronunciation right, his gentle Southern accent rendering it variously as Brewer or Broy-*air*).

Speaking ten years later at an anniversary celebration, Joe said he had done his homework before that first meeting and was prepared to be "charged an arm and a leg" for the services of such a famous architect. When it came to discuss fees, he was pleasantly surprised to hear that Breuer's proposal was reasonable, and the firm was retained on the spot. Joe continued, "He had just finished the HUD building in Washington on time and 10 percent below budget—that's the sort of thing any potential client likes to hear. Our building came in 2 percent over budget and it was all our fault."

Fresh from Paris with no other assignments, I was the obvious candidate for partner in charge of the job. Since I had never risen above the rank of T/5 during my brief army career, I was somewhat worried about dealing with a former brigadier general. Joe Stewart turned out to be one of the best clients we ever had—strong, fair, and decisive but always deferring to the architect when it came to aesthetics. Susanne Strohbach was the job captain, and we wondered how Joe would react to our choice of a woman for such a responsible position, particularly when it came to site visits and facing up

*An informal confer-
ence between Gatje
and Breuer, 1967.*

to the builders. They hit it off famously—Joe was the consummate gentleman and Susi was tough as nails.

Armstrong had a clear program of requirements. The company needed
two or three floors of administrative office space and assumed it would be
placed at the front of the site where it could easily be seen and admired from
the turnpike. In addition, the research and development laboratories were
to be moved from West Haven as a sort of showcase. A one- and two-story
structure with high ceilings to house it was planned for the back of the site
since tires are tested to destruction, and when an airplane tire blows, it
makes a lot of noise. The problem was that the land that had been reclaimed
from the railhead, at the edge of the old harbor, was about twenty feet below
the roadbed of the turnpike, which effectively dammed it against the sea.
The project as envisioned would have resulted in a view of several acres of
roof from the passing cars above. Happily, we didn't have to wage this
battle; Mayor Lee saw it coming. He decreed that nothing short of a ten-story
tower (he originally had a vision of eighteen) would do justice to the site.
Armstrong was unhappy and couldn't imagine building something it neither
wanted nor needed.

Lajkó listened to all this carefully and had a solution in mind before we
started any drawings. When he presented his thoughts after they had been
drawn up, it was to propose that the office floors be put atop the two-story
research and development wing at grade and then—in order to satisfy Dick
Lee—that they be raised clear of the roof below and "hung from above," leaving a two-story-high slot between the two building masses that could be
filled with expansion space at a later time. Two levels of R&D plus two floors

of air, with five floors of offices and a top level devoted to mechanical equipment between deep trusses, which were going to do the "hanging," equaled ten floors.

Armstrong recognized that it would be paying a premium for these acrobatics and asked Breuer what the additional cost would be. He hazarded a guess of between 5 and 10 percent, and events proved him to be just about right. The company knew that it was buying a symbolic structure that would indeed put Armstrong back into the public eye. Breuer's proposal also improved Armstrong's view of the New Haven harbor and skyline, and the schematic design was approved without further debate. Joe Stewart used to joke afterward, "When people ask me what we're going to do with that hole in the middle of our building, I say, 'That's where we're going to put our vault, if we ever make any money.'"

The entire building, which was a composite of steel structure for the tower and long-span concrete T-beams for the high-bay test area, was sheathed in precast-concrete panels of varying scale and design, depending on the function they enveloped. The precast concrete was made of white cement and a dark aggregate that was exposed by a light sandblasting; it married well to the gray concrete poured over and around the huge aerial trusswork and its supporting stair towers. I was deeply involved in shaping the crystalline forms (Breuer preferred his own term, "crystallic") that expressed the steel trusses within but did not suggest that the concrete was doing the work. The side facade of Armstrong remains one of my favorites. Matt Lévy fought long and hard in favor of a "light" facade for the suspended tower. Breuer agreed with his economic logic but stubbornly insisted on the architectural unity that one material would give to its two disparate parts.

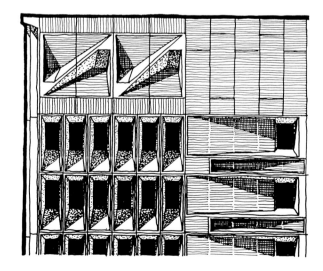

Half of Armstrong's great truss (after Ben Schnall). The faceted concrete sheathing above the windows interprets the steel members within.

Just as we were to start the working drawings, Joe Stewart announced that a program reevaluation had determined that Armstrong really didn't need all the office space it had asked for—in fact, one whole floor could be eliminated. It seemed clear that the impulse behind the reevaluation had been designed to cut costs, but we were never asked to reexamine the concept of the building. We argued in favor of building the extra floor while leaving it unfinished for future expansion, but the company was adamant about saving the entire cost of that floor. Finally, Lajkó relented and the tower grew shorter. It had never been all that tall, and anyone comparing the original rendering with photographs of the final building would have to conclude that it lost a certain grace in its proportions. Unhappiness was evident in the drafting room, and some questioned whether Breuer had really fought hard enough for the integrity of his original design. Other, more "formal" architects might have complained loudly, but that wasn't Lajkó's style. He recognized that Joe had a responsibility to his shareholders and respected the fact that he was trying hard not to derail the entire project. Therefore, giving him a building that was almost as good in appearance was good enough. I seem to remember Lajkó expressing regrets once on his first visit to the job site after the frame was up, but he never showed anything but pride in the result to Armstrong and Mayor Lee.

As the building took shape, it began to provoke much comment in New Haven and at the tollbooths on the Connecticut Turnpike, since it could be seen prominently from both directions. Board members asked Joe what the sign on the roof was going to look like, and he asked us what we had planned. Breuer explained that the building would soon be famous and known to everyone as the Armstrong Building. No sign was required; in fact, any rooftop sign would damage the distinctive silhouette. Armstrong was in a state of disbelief—how could anyone imagine that it would spend all that money for a building without identification? So Breuer suggested a free-standing sign in front, and we sketched a powerful concrete structure almost three stories high, with two broad sides where the Armstrong name and logo could be attached. After receiving the client's approval, we filed the revised drawings with the city of New Haven, only to learn that a signage ordinance restricted the height of signs along the turnpike.

New Haven's planning officer said, "If we let Armstrong put up a tall sign like that, there is nothing to prevent every gas station and trailer park in the vicinity from doing the same." I replied, "But you *would* allow a sign on the roof of the building?" The planning authority responded, "Yes, and we agree that it would be ugly and deface the building."

At this point, someone in the discussion looked at the drawing and observed that the robust sign structure looked big enough to be a building itself. I'd like to claim credit but I suspect it was the planning officer. The question became "What makes a 'building' out of a 'structure'?" "It has to

The Armstrong Rubber Company sign structure. This "building" has had its name changed three times but is still standing in New Haven.

serve some purpose and enclose some space." "What if we put a door in the base and used it to store gardening equipment?" "It becomes a gardener's building, and yes, it could have a sign on its two sides."

By the time the contractor got around to pouring the concrete for the base of the gardener's building, it was late in the day. Susi Strohbach was at a job meeting when the forms were being stripped, and everyone could see very bad "folds" in the pour. The contractor volunteered to patch the surface, but Susi said no, since surface patching in the Northeast rarely lasts through two or three freeze-thaw cycles. There was about a cubic yard and a half of concrete involved, and its removal by jackhammer would cost many thousands of dollars. The contractor assumed he could easily appeal over Susi's head and went straight to Armstrong. Joe asked Breuer if he agreed with Susi, and he backed her up completely. Lajkó once told me privately that he often found his staff more demanding in defending his intentions than he was willing to be. The concrete was removed and poured correctly and still looks fine today.

The building has recently been threatened with demolition since Pirelli, which took over Armstrong, decided to give up its headquarters function. The city has vague plans for a regional shopping center at Long Wharf, which might have spelled its doom. I've been very pleased to participate marginally in the efforts of Dr. Peter Swanson's Alliance for Architecture to recognize its quality. Swanson, a self-described architecture buff, has finally succeeded in getting the building listed in the Connecticut Register of Historic Places.

The Kent School was a very old and proper boys' school in Kent, Connecticut, run by the Episcopal church. It had expanded in the early 1960s, adding 225 girls to its 300 boys and approached Breuer in early December 1966 about designing a chapel for a Girls' School, which was located a few miles away from the Boys' School. We went to visit the beautiful campus, meet the headmaster, and begin our introduction to the arcane art of bell ringing. The chapel was an interesting commission: it was to contain a new organ, space for a large choir, and at times, even the full community as it shifted services from one campus to the other in an orgy of ecumenical correctness. But it was the bell tower that attracted everyone's attention.

The Boys' School chapel contains a significant installation of what I remember as eight great bells made at the Whitechapel Bell Foundry in England. The tradition of ringing "the changes" by hand rope from a platform just below the belfry was deeply embedded in the lore of the school. The boys selected for this honor—and it was reserved for the best in the school—stood in a circle facing one another, each with a bell rope in front of him. The boy in charge gave visual direction to the others. A sharp, powerful tug on the rope was needed semi-seconds before the peal of the bell above was to sound—a difficult job of time-delay management. Not only was it important for the rope to be grasped at just the right moment, it was equally important to let go in time. The bell ringers risked being yanked off their feet by the inertia of a swinging bell weighing several thousand pounds; they could even crack their head on the wood ceiling above, through which the ropes passed to the outside.

Lajkó and I watched transfixed through one session of bell ringing, and I became fascinated and enmeshed in the geometry of hanging six of these monsters in such a way that the ropes coming off their wheels would fall in a circle. Breuer proposed that they be hung high in a freestanding tower that resembled others of his twisted-plane conceptions and was probably a direct spinoff from a clock tower he had recently and unsuccessfully tried to sell to IBM for La Gaude. (Recalling his work on the La Gaude tower, Jeff Vandeberg remembers Lajkó critiquing his sketches with "No, no, it's not clumsy enough!")

The chapel was an ingenious "square within a square" that enabled the normal complement of girls on its flat central floor to be enlarged by adding boys in each of four sloping corners. Stained-glass windows, niches for the organ pipes, and the entries were expressed as hooded shapes pushed out of the battered concrete walls of the chapel itself. It was a neat idea that unfortunately fell prey to the decision by Bishop Paul Moore that the mission of the Episcopal church in the troubled 1960s would be better served by outreach programs than by "bricks and mortar."

In the spring of 1967 we received the first hint of IBM's interest in giving Breuer a second major commission, for Boca Raton, Florida. The La Gaude laboratory had become a favorite of the Watsons, and it took no great selling job on the part of El Noyes to add Breuer to the company's roster of domestic architects, a list that already included El himself, Eero Saarinen, and many well-known commercial firms.

In preparation for running the job, I took a week-long whirlwind tour of comparable IBM assembly plants with Arnie Richter, then a brilliant young project manager with the real-estate and construction division. First I showed him our work at Saint John's, and then we went on to Rochester, Minnesota; Boulder, Colorado; and San Jose, California. The trip cemented a friendly relationship that continues to this day. Arnie had hands-on experience with the building of the Colorado facility, and the chance to tour each of the plants with a local construction representative—to share his gripes about the buildings that had been designed, and see them all in operation—was a valuable introduction to a job that was to occupy me, on and off, for almost twenty years. Each of the plants had addressed the problem of growth and expansion in different ways, and it was a great challenge to design the first parts of an interlocking puzzle the ultimate size and use of which was impossible to predict, given the turbulence of the computer industry.

IBM Boca Raton. The smaller brother of La Gaude grew to over two and a half million square feet.

We started with three components: three-story office buildings that might include laboratories; single-level manufacturing "modules" roughly three hundred feet square; and taller, one-story warehouses. All would be interconnected and served by a central cafeteria. The trick, as Lajkó liked to demonstrate by holding up his hand, was to allow each "finger" to grow along with the entire "hand" without any conflict or interference. An interlocking network of Y shapes quickly developed to serve as office-building components. The buildings were deeper than those at La Gaude since American practice allowed for many more windowless offices; the tree columns were smaller; and the structure of the load-bearing exterior walls became deep fins that projected out as sunshades rather than being folded inward. Otherwise, the two projects bore a strong family resemblance. After trying round manufacturing modules and squares touching corners around triangular courtyards, we settled on a checkerboard of buildings and courtyards. The precasting industry in Florida was very strong—probably the only part of the country where this was true—and we got favorable bids from three manufacturers. Each of them was retained in the interests of speedy, continuous delivery to a project that was "fast-tracked" to control escalating costs in the hot building climate of the 1960s. Each part of the project was big enough to provide economy of scale even though each one had a different height and even a different planning module. The warehouses used increments of five feet to match their steel structure and pallet sizes, while everything else was designed in four-foot increments.

The initial master plan showed how IBM might build up to one million square feet of buildings on the six-hundred-acre site, which was largely a mangrove swamp when I first saw it. Twenty years later we were up to almost four million square feet, including planned buildings, and the number of cars fighting their way onto the site in the morning rush hour approached ten thousand. The company was the single biggest employer in Palm Beach County, and the roads around the site, which were unpaved dead ends in 1967, had grown to six-lane divided highways with overpasses and traffic lights.

Construction started in 1968. In order to build in a swamp, the water level had to be lowered and the buildings raised. This was accomplished by dredging two huge circular lakes—one at the center of the project, surrounded by the branching arms of our Y-shaped office buildings, the other in the middle of the swamp. These lakes became quarries for the sand that was piled up on the sites of future buildings. Ground floors were placed at twelve feet above sea level (there were no basements), and parking lots and pathways at eight feet above sea level, where they might, and did, get covered by occasional floodwaters. I had been working on the drawings for many months before the site preparation began, and I thought I understood what was involved. The next time I visited Boca, however, after the contractors had started moving sand around with great dredges sporting tires that towered above me, I looked out across a 1,200-foot-diameter lake that was only a four-inch circle on my drafting board. I remember a muttered expletive.

In 1967 Breuer received a letter from the head architect of the canton of Lucerne in Switzerland, Beat von Segesser. He wanted to talk about another convent assignment, and he and Lajkó eventually met between planes at the Zurich airport restaurant. Von Segesser had been the professional adviser to a Franciscan order of nuns who ran a girls' school and teachers' training facility on the shores of a small lake, Baldegg, not far from Lucerne. They wanted to construct a central "mother house," or *Mutterhaus*, particularly as a place of refuge for nuns returning from missionary duty across the globe. A competition had been held among the architects of the canton, as was the almost universal custom. When the winner was chosen by the jury, however, the sisters didn't like the proposal and wouldn't commission it. (They had to pay a substantial fee in order to get rid of the winner.) Von Segesser had just been elected to his advisory post, and he suggested that the only thing they could do would be to select a non-Swiss architect with such impeccable credentials that the local architects would not have the courage to object. The sisters asked who that might be, and after doing some research that included Saint John's Abbey and the Convent of the Annunciation, von Segesser suggested Breuer. The sisters wondered if such a famous man would work for them and were overjoyed when von Segesser reported the success of his airport meeting with Lajkó.

I flew into Lucerne late in October 1967 and was put up in a magnificent lakeshore hotel that had been a tuberculosis sanitarium—it still looked the part. My room was all white, and it had a huge, sunny balcony under a broad white awning straight out of Mann's *Magic Mountain.* The whole thing was a bit intimidating, and I asked for a downtown hotel on future trips. Von Segesser introduced me to all the important sisters, including the Mother Superior, and between my high-school German and their variable English, we got along fine. I was given the grand tour of the existing buildings, a strange composite of turn-of-the-century Victorian structures with some recent modern additions. The next morning, I returned to the building site early to walk the hillside that had been proposed for the project. There was still a light mist in the air, and the only sound I heard was a glorious rumble of cow bells, each with its own tone to identify the huge beasts eating their way across the greensward. Upon my return I made a very enthusiastic report to Lajkó, and we began work on the design with Susi Strohbach as job captain (her home was in Stuttgart and her German proved useful). The other member of our team was a young Swiss, **Beat Jordi.** He had just arrived at the New York office in a miracle of good, but unconnected, timing.

The plan for the convent was similar to that of the Annunciation Priory since the programs of each reflected the classic separation between the inner sanctum, or "clausura," where the sisters lived and worked, and the

The Baldegg Convent. One of its four courtyards is formed of Breuer's favorite materials at the time.

areas they shared with the public—school, chapel, and so on. The materials—rubblestone and precast concrete—were also from the same palette. The sites, however, couldn't have been more different—the barren Dakotas were in startling contrast to Baldegg's lush green lakeside with an adjacent apple orchard.

The chapel we designed for Baldegg had a square plan that was roofed by a diagonal grid of deep concrete beams. It had originally been laid out according to the liturgical requirements of 1967, but in the middle of construction many changes had to be made in deference to Vatican II. Beat Jordi was devastated by the prospect of a total shake-up, but Lajkó seemed to welcome the challenge. On one visit to Baldegg he rolled up his sleeves and stretched a roll of tracing paper over the plans. In a single day of work with the bishop, the interior had been transformed with no damage to the exterior concept. Many have noted that Breuer seemed to welcome the "accidents" that might throw a carefully crafted plan off-kilter—the sort of thing that would infuriate Mies or Corb.

The periodic visits by Lajkó, whether to Paris or, later, to Switzerland, were moments of high anticipation and nervousness for our overseas staff. Beat remembers one lunch—the first in his new apartment in Bern—for which his father was a particular adviser, insisting that such an honored guest deserved a great wine. Lajkó watered down the wine, saying that wine made him sleepy after lunch; Beat never had the heart to tell his father.

Like many of us, Beat was frequently more rigorous in defending the architect's original intent than the architect himself. When the sisters of Baldegg objected to split-slate flooring at one point—whether because of cost or ease of cleaning—Breuer immediately suggested a vinyl tile with a stone surface pressed into it. Beat was horrified but kept quiet and only later convinced the sisters that they should have the real thing.

The sisters were actually somewhat intimidated by the fame of their architect and rarely made any objection to what he proposed. Sister Basilda once remarked to Breuer that the windowsill of the full-size mock-up that had been made of the typical residential unit was "perhaps a little high." He replied, "But Sister, you must understand, this is not a room, it is a cell." And they accepted it. The sisters polished the dark wood cabinetry so constantly that Lajkó thought it looked more like a mirror than wood. And they kept doilies on the backs of their easy chairs. (Breuer always carried on a love-hate relationship with the Swiss, who were a little neat and clean for his taste. One day he read with glee in the *New York Times* that Zermatt had been closed to tourists because of overflowing sewers.)

Shortly after the Baldegg Convent was completed in 1969, I received a telephone call from John Morris Dixon, the newly appointed editor of the magazine *Progressive Architecture*. He noted that it had been years since *P/A* had published any of Breuer's work and asked to come to the office to look at what was on the boards. I showed him around, and he was particularly interested in publishing the convent. We made an appointment for him to meet Breuer, which, as it happened, coincided with a morning on which I was delayed in getting back to the office from a job-site meeting at Armstrong. Instead of going on without me, Breuer kept John waiting in the outer office for an hour until I turned up. The interview, understandably, started off on a frosty note that was not helped when Lajkó announced that he had "promised" the convent to Peter Blake at *Architecture Plus*, something of which I was totally unaware when I set up the meeting. Although John promised to consider several other projects he was shown over lunch, our relationship with *P/A* continued in the deep freeze.

Considering the reputation that Lajkó had gained early on for his work on interiors, it is not surprising that he kept a group of interior designers on staff, although he wasn't always successful in getting his institutional clients to hire him for their interiors. His wife, Connie, had been in charge of the department for many years when she decided to retire. She passed the mantle to **Suzanne Sekey** in late 1967.

Sue was intrigued by the fact that all the Breuer chairs in the office were older versions from Thonet via Wohnbedarf, rather than the Knoll/Gavina "official" versions then available. "Yes," Connie explained, "the real ones are so expensive." Some years earlier, when Sue was working for I. M. Pei, she had ordered the "real" ones for Pei's office. They arrived with rosewood arms that had not been specified. When she called Mary Farris, thinking Breuer would be horrified, his response was, "Italians like rosewood," and accepted the departure from the classic quite calmly. (The solid wood also stood up better under scratches and table marks than did the original ebonized light wood.)

Sue worked on the interiors of Mary College at the Annunciation Priory and was taken aback when Lajkó suggested white velvet for the proscenium curtain in the auditorium: "Won't that be hard to keep clean?" Breuer responded, "Oh no, the nuns are very good housekeepers." On the other hand, when Sue suggested a theatrical red carpet for the space, rather than saying he didn't like red carpet, Lajkó objected, "It will be hard to maintain." Later, when she was working on Armstrong, Breuer suggested white wool for the upholstery of sofas in the lobby: "Connie and I have white bedspreads. If it's wool, it's easy to keep up." Sue asked, "But what about the workers in their grimy overalls?" "Let them stand!" was Lajkó's answer.

Breuer liked to speak Hungarian with Sue, who always considered him more Hungarian than German or American. Her friends in the Hungarian expatriate arts community were annoyed with him, since he never showed them any favoritism as political émigrés during the 1956 revolution. Breuer did often repeat two old Hungarian jokes: "If you have a Hungarian friend, you don't need an enemy," and "A Hungarian is someone who can enter a revolving door behind you and come out in front of you." When Sue left after a few years, Jane Yu took over the interiors department.

I was in Paris in late January 1968 for meetings with Eric Boissonnas and the Flaine group. Construction was proceeding apace, and there were many last-minute details to be arranged. We made a three-day trip into the valley walking and skiing across land that I knew better as contoured drawings and climbing around concrete skeletons beginning to rise from foundations that had been asleep for so long. We stayed in the workers barracks, still painted in the bright red, yellow, and blue that Breuer had casually suggested. These were gradually being converted into student housing so that a first group of young skiers would be able to try out the slopes before the official inauguration, which was now set for the holiday season of 1968–69. While the barracks functioned as a student camp, the Boissonnas' daughter Sylvina, who worked as a sometime barmaid, had designed a swinging nightclub at the end of one of the huts called the "Juglotube." It was decorated with highway signs, flashing lights, and emergency sawhorses that had been ordered in Paris. When their delivery was threatened by a highway truckers' strike, her uncle Rémi was drafted into service and drove a truck laden with decor up from the capital at the last minute.

Before I left Paris, Eric asked if I would accompany him on what he thought would be largely a courtesy call to a graphic artist whose work had been recommended to Sylvie by her cousin Madame Couve de Murville, the

Changing the guard at Flaine, 1967. Standing in the valley are Mario Jossa (who was taking over), Fred Berlottier, Rémi Boissonnas, Gatje, and a person unknown.

Cassandre's alphabet. Backlit bronze lettering identifies all the buildings at Flaine.

wife of the foreign minister. The artist had designed a new alphabet that could be used in print as well as in three-dimensional letterform on buildings, and perhaps Flaine would be a good place to try it out. We took a cab to a shabby district in southwest Paris, and as we climbed the rickety stairs to the third floor, Eric mentioned, "By the way, the artist goes by the name of Cassandre." I should have been struck dumb by the knowledge that I was about to meet one of the giants of graphic art—designer of the great *Normandie* posters, the Dubonnet man, and thousands of images of France between the wars. But there was something so casual about the identification that it didn't sink in at that moment, and certainly there was nothing remarkable about the old couple who opened the door and ushered us into their faded apartment.

Around the walls of their living room, as a sort of cornice just below the ceiling, was a series of brown paper sheets about eighteen inches square on which were charcoal cartoons for an entire alphabet that included numerals and ligatures. The paper was thick with impasto since the shapes had been painted out and reconfigured. The old man brightened a bit as he introduced us to each of the letters and described their particular charac-

223

teristics. The alphabet had a timeless cursive quality that had been developed from an old Carolingian tradition. It bore more than a passing resemblance to the intertwined "YSL" that Cassandre had just designed for Yves Saint Laurent. I liked it instantly, and Eric was pleased to have my support. He bought the rights within the week, and the alphabet began to appear in public graphics all around Flaine later in the year. Cassandre's son and biographer, Henri Mouron, acted as his agent and took charge of all the major layouts long after Cassandre's death a few years later.

I wondered at the time how someone so talented and famous could have been reduced to such a sorry state. It was only years later that I read of his personal history of collaboration with the Nazis and the shunning of him by all his old clients after the war. This no doubt influenced the hesitancy with which Eric had approached our interview, but it couldn't detract from the beauty of Cassandre's creation. I wished that we had met the great graphic artist earlier, when Eric commissioned ICPA for the logo in 1965.

Working as I did for the first months of 1966 on the third floor at 635 Madison and spending at least one week of every month in Europe, I was somewhat cut off from the busy times upstairs with Lajkó, Ham, Herb, and Tician. Tician was working on a large public high school for Boston's Roxbury district. It had been the hope of Mayor Kevin White that, by combining the budgets of three different high schools into one mega-school, a special benefit could be created for the disadvantaged neighborhood. Two schemes were developed—low- and high-rise. Tician and Carl Stein tried to dissuade Breuer from using precast window panels, but he was adamant and the low scheme was built, combining the panels with a split-face concrete block that was surprisingly rich in texture.

It's difficult now to know if Tician was right in saying that the public was tired of Breuer's precast vocabulary or whether it was just that the people in the office were tired of doing the same old thing. I suspect that perhaps only history will prove whether Lajkó was correct in persisting in his search for an all-purpose system of exterior enclosure. The high school passed a careful architectural review by a board that had Pietro Belluschi, the dean of architecture at MIT, as its head. Tician had dealt with Belluschi during the architectural selection process that had chosen I. M. Pei for the National Center for Atmospheric Research in Boulder and knew that Breuer had not been chosen by the dean for its short list. There was a testy moment in Boston when Belluschi exclaimed to Breuer, "I know that you don't like me," to which Lajkó, most uncharacteristically, replied, "You're absolutely right."

In 1968 Ham and Lajkó shared a monumental commission for the design of the Grand Coulee Dam's third power plant in Washington State. The dam is on such a remote site on the upper waters of the Columbia River that the

The Grand Coulee Dam. Breuer designed the third power plant with heroic folded plates and an inclined elevator that runs up the face of the dam.

project is virtually unknown to the public, even in its home state, and yet it is one of Breuer's masterpieces. Normally, its design would have been entrusted entirely to engineers, but the Bureau of Reclamation had recognized that its great dam sites were attracting more and more tourists and wanted to pay more attention to welcoming and orienting visitors. This included capitalizing on the exhilarating view of moving water in conjunction with the vast structures themselves. The power plant is 2,000 feet long, 84 feet high, and 125 feet wide, and its construction took many years. Ham would return from his inspection trips filled with a wonder that was hard to express: the great penstocks—forty feet in diameter and sculpted by the dramatic needs of the water that would soon fill them, yet never to be seen again by human eyes; masses of concrete so huge that they had to be honeycombed with cold-water piping to cool them while they were setting; an unusual elevator that climbed the inclined face of the dam itself, carrying tourists to the crest for a panoramic view. But the real drama was the architectural form of the folded concrete plates that supported the roof of the turbine house and a crane that ran along its top that was capable of carrying loads of up to 550,000 pounds. The building is pharaonic in scale, but as Ham had said, "Not even Tutankhamen ever dreamed of folded plates."

Based on the success of his headquarters for the Department of Housing and Urban Development, the U.S. General Services Administration returned to Breuer with a second major commission for the District of Columbia. A design was being prepared for a multilane underground highway that was to pass under some of the best remaining building sites in Washington. It would require several vast ventilation ducts, which, if they weren't designed carefully from the start, risked conflict with future buildings above. The project was to design a hypothetical building, tentatively named the Air-Rights Building, that would house the great vertical tubes and span the underground highway. Herb helped fashion a square building that stretched between the four ducts at its corners and was suspended, like Armstrong, from floor-high trusses above. Once approved, the project was shelved until the need arose, several years later, for a headquarters for the new Department of Health, Education, and Welfare, which adapted itself very well to the plans as drawn. The structure was eventually inaugurated as the Hubert H. Humphrey Building with a stirring dedicatory speech by its namesake just two weeks before his death in 1978.

After Thomas Hoving became parks commissioner under New York's Mayor John Lindsay, in 1967 he developed a plan for the reuse of part of the old New York World's Fair site in Queens as a sports park for the city. According to his deputy, architect **Arthur Rosenblatt,** Hoving was something of a jock who proposed building a series of monumental sports facilities that might serve a future Olympic bid. Together they assembled a design team, with Breuer at its head, that included the well-known Japanese architect Kenzo Tange, who had completed many similar structures for the Tokyo Olympics a few years earlier, and Lawrence Halprin, a prominent landscape architect and planner from San Francisco. Since Herb was *our* resident jock he became nominal partner in charge and traveled with Lajkó and the Parks Department crew to San Francisco to visit Halprin's office and, according to Arthur, a topless shoe-shine parlor, which Breuer found fascinating. I can

The Department of Health, Education, and Welfare. Breuer's second departmental headquarters in Washington, D.C., started out as an air-rights exercise to see how best to build over a large underground highway. Its exhaust towers are part of the building's fabric.

personally attest at least to the fact that Lajkó loved having his shoes shined and wondered at how good a polished pair of shoes made him feel. They went on to Tokyo, where Breuer kept pretty much to his room, having just recovered from another heart scare at Doctors' Hospital in New York. Unfortunately on the one day he did venture out to walk the streets of Tokyo he fell backward into an excavation pit while composing a photograph and injured the back that had already long been tormenting him.

The project that developed was dramatic and ambitious. According to Arthur, "Breuer and Tange divvied up the buildings and Halprin filled in what was left." David Vachon, a new designer on staff, was working on the structure of the great arenas that had been assigned to him when Lajkó stopped by his desk. Breuer took soft black pencil in hand, hovered over the drawing for a short minute or so, and then, while using one of his favorite phrases, "It should go zis vay . . . ," slowly defined a great concrete "bent" almost six hundred feet long. Everyone watching caught their breath at the audacity of the gesture, but as Dave puts it, "He was, of course, exactly right." Tange was always accompanied on his trips to New York by a young associate who had studied architecture at Harvard and spoke excellent English. The associate, who was quite tall for a Japanese, welcomed the trips to New York, where he could find suits and shoes that fit him. His name was Yoshio Taniguchi, and in 1998 he received the prestigious commission to enlarge the Museum of Modern Art in New York.

The work was quite far along and preliminary sketches had been praised in the press by critics such as Ada Louise Huxtable of the *New York Times* when Breuer noticed that no one was paying our bills. The agreement with Hoving had been on the basis of a handshake, and working on the contract was giving Tician a monumental headache. Meanwhile, Abe Beame, the city's comptroller and later mayor, was not about to pay anyone until a final contract was signed. It never was. Beame discovered that Tange and Halprin were unlicensed to practice in the state of New York, and even though the initial contract was for planning only, that put an end to the project. Halprin eventually sued the city, and Breuer joined the suit—for which I think we recovered ten cents on the dollar. I have always faulted Hoving for irresponsible naïveté, since he promised something without checking to see that he could deliver it, while Breuer looked him in the eye and trusted him.

In the early 1960s Washington, D.C., was still without an FDR Memorial when an international competition was launched by a committee of friends, relatives, and politicians for an appropriate design at a site on the Tidal Basin. The winning scheme was designed by a group of young New York architects who received fame and a certain notoriety for a project that was widely criticized in the press and unfairly nicknamed "Instant Stonehenge." After several years of controversy, including the eventual opposition of the Roosevelt fam-

The FDR Memorial. Lajkó's emotion-laden turbine wheel of granite blades failed to impress the Fine Arts Commission of Washington, D.C.

ily, the project was canceled, the winners were paid off, and the committee once again had to face a selection process. Another competition was out of the question—the committee wanted consensus. Such was Breuer's fame and universal admiration at the time that, after a low-key selection process, he was chosen for the job and unhesitatingly accepted by the critics.

During 1966 he worked hard on its design, taking the creation of a monument to one of his personal heroes as a labor of love. The scheme that resulted featured a huge cube of polished black granite, thirty-two feet on a side, at the center of a series of wedge-shaped rough gray granite walls that radiated out in a pinwheel plan. Breuer compared them to the blades of a turbine; the dynamic force represented that of Franklin D. Roosevelt. Herb worked closely with Lajkó on the project; and it was well along when I happened to share a trip to Paris with Breuer.

We were both invited to dinner with the Boissonnas family, who had as a special guest Ralph Kirkpatrick, a world-renowned harpsichordist and professor at Yale. Breuer brought the talk around to the subject of the FDR Memorial—what he had decided and what was still unresolved. He was determined to avoid the traditional statue, which was prescient, considering the controversy that much later raged in Washington as to whether Roosevelt should be depicted standing or sitting and, if sitting, in what. Lajkó was guided by his own memories of FDR, which were dominated by his voice on the radio and newspaper photographs. Acousticians were already working on Breuer's proposal to project selected sections of the great radio speeches by means of special speakers that would address the visitors to the memorial in the low tones of a personal radio.

The incorporation of newspaper photographs had him stumped, and we tossed many ideas around over coffee and brandy. I suggested that, since newspaper images were made up of dots in the form of a half-tone screen, these could be enlarged perhaps a hundredfold to the point where each dot would be about an inch across. The pattern could then be sandblasted into the side of the polished black granite of the central cube. The dot would be shiny black while the background would be the soft gray of rough stone. Close up, the pattern would become a geometric abstraction; seen from some distance, the full photographic image would emerge. Everyone liked the idea, and Lajkó even went so far as to choose that evening one of the photographs he would propose: the famous shot of FDR at the rail of a naval ship, holding a gray fedora, his black cape blown back over his shoulder by the wind.

Once we were back in the office, we ran some tests of the technique, and a very convincing one-foot square of black granite, which had been sandblasted through a rubber template, became a part of Breuer's tri-

Breuer chose this famous photograph of the president as one of the images to be sandblasted into the black granite cube at the heart of the memorial.

The nose and eye-glasses of FDR. The half-tone dots that make up a newspaper photo would have been transformed into squares of polished black granite against a light gray sandblasted background surface.

umphant presentation to the all-star commission that marched into our office one day. It included members of the Roosevelt family, Anna Rosenberg, Senators Eugene McCarthy and Jacob Javits, and Congressman Eugene Keogh, who was the chairman. With their approval it looked like clear sailing, although there remained the matter of the Fine Arts Commission in Washington, which had to give its blessing to any important building or monument in the nation's capital. It was assumed that this would be no more than a pro forma stamp of approval, and Breuer and Herb confidently made a Friday afternoon presentation. We learned only years later that the architects on the commission, led by Gordon Bunshaft of Skidmore, Owings & Merrill and including Kevin Roche, had already decided to reject the scheme based on the drawings sent ahead, and that Bunshaft was furious when some members wavered after hearing the eloquent presentation made by Breuer. He is reported to have said something like "Oh, come on! You're not going to approve this scheme just because you like the guy, are you?" Lajkó and Herb first got word of the rejection on the front page of the Sunday *New York Times*. It was a crushing blow. Half-hearted attempts to revive the scheme were made after new members joined the Fine Arts Commission in later years, but all came to naught.

Morris Saady was a wealthy English developer who in 1967 was negotiating with the Penn Central Railroad to buy the air rights above Grand Central Terminal in midtown Manhattan. The railroad owned the land and, provided that the recently landmarked building itself was not touched, could presumably use the air above the structure for any purpose it chose. By careful interpretation of the zoning laws then in force, it was determined that a fifty-three-story office building could be built "as of right." Still, perhaps aware of the possible controversy that such a massive structure in the heart of one of the most densely trafficked spots in the world might provoke, Saady was advised to select a distinguished architect to give the project added credibility. He chose Breuer.

There is reason to believe that Lajkó hesitated before accepting the commission, since he well remembered the criticism that had damaged Walter Gropius's reputation after the construction of his Pan Am Building right next door. In overcoming his qualms, he may have reasoned, and certainly later asserted, that the damage was done—the Park Avenue vista was forever blocked by Pan Am. As for Grand Central, no one had ever claimed that this hack, eclectic bit of political chicanery was good architecture. The designers, Warren and Wetmore, had elbowed the competition winner aside in the early 1900s on the strength of being related to Commodore Vanderbilt, and even that partnership's scheme showed an office tower over their station. The Grand Central area was without doubt a traffic nightmare, with taxis and pedestrians at grade and trains, a shuttle, and the subway below. It presented at the same time an enormous challenge: to try to rationalize all the conflicts that had arisen during years of inattention. If Breuer asked anyone's advice before accepting the commission I never heard of it, although many people say today that they would have said "no" if asked. I wonder.

The chance to build his first skyscraper in New York must have been irresistible, and Breuer began work on it with Herb in late 1967. In order to analyze the incredibly complex three-dimensional jigsaw puzzle presented by Grand Central, Breuer pulled Don Cromley off the Cleveland Museum job, saying, according to Don, "I don't want anyone but Donald."

The first scheme placed the tower over the waiting room, which would have to be transformed to receive the columns and elevators from above. The great concourse, however, was to remain untouched, and the lower levels of station and subway were to be rearranged to relieve many bottlenecks. The process could have resulted in a major contribution to city life in the area. The project was totally defensible, if one were inclined to defend it. Within the office, there was some opposition, even by members of the staff who were working on the project. Don Cromley considered resigning from the office. Ham was heard more than once advising Lajkó against the idea. I was peripheral to the project but supported it at cocktail parties whenever the subject came up, as it began to with increasing frequency and urgency.

What completely escaped us at the time was the subtle redefinition of "landmark" that had taken place since the destruction of Pennsylvania Station only a few years earlier. We still felt that a landmark was a building of high architectural quality, and we missed the role that sentiment and memory were now to play. People admired Grand Central not so much for its looks but for their associations with it. I learned later to make this same distinction by using the lions in front of the New York Public Library as examples. No one would claim them as great sculpture, but no one, including me, would vote for their removal.

By this time Breuer knew that he was in for a fight, and when it came time to prepare for hearings before the Landmarks Preservation Commission and other public bodies having jurisdiction, he lined up an impressive list of friends and experts who would testify on behalf of his proposals. But he was chagrined to learn how many of his friends and admirers declined. Some said they would simply remain uncommitted; some joined the increasingly vocal opposition organized by Philip Johnson and Jackie Kennedy. Lajkó was essentially blindsided. He was surrounded by a client and consultants who all shared in enthusiastic pride of authorship, and the roar of protest outside was yet to be heard from. (Not that Saady had been an easy client. According to Murray Drabkin, Saady's lawyer, Breuer defended architectural integrity on more than one occasion with a soft-spoken "Yes, you could do that. But in that case I think you would have to find yourself another architect.")

After the parade of distinguished critics who testified against the project before the commission, it came as no surprise when it was turned down. The project, an enormous tower hovering over the south facade with its clock and heroic sculpture, was not convincing. James Marston Fitch, who found that many architects supported the project, chose not to take sides. He did suggest to Herb that the building would have looked much less threatening if the perspective had shown it from below, at street level, rather than with the bird's-eye view that was used in the presentation.

Many suggested that it would be better to tear down the southern facade rather than have it visually "crushed" by the tower above, so Breuer went back to the drawing boards to work on a second scheme. He told Rufus Stillman at the time that "saving the old stuff is irrelevant, considering the indecent shops down below."

This time he was nervous and went so far as to give his old friend I. M. Pei a private and confidential viewing of the final product. Pei later said that although he thought the second scheme was better than the first, he still told Breuer that he would not support it. (The two frequently vacationed together with their families but rarely spoke of architecture. Pei later told me that Breuer had never complimented him on his work, except as a student, but had been grateful for I.M.'s praise for the Doldertal when he had seen it in Zurich.) Pei's criticism hurt his old friend deeply. Breuer went on to present the second scheme to the Landmarks Preservation Commission and to see it too turned down.

Murray Drabkin then arranged to have Saady's suit appealed to the Supreme Court, and when it was defeated there in 1978, all the world knew that however great or admired the architect, in the future no one could tamper with properly dedicated landmarks. Many people have said that Breuer paid a terrible price in friendships and critical standing because of this project, but no one ever heard him utter a second thought. He was still convinced that the important thing was to improve the life of the pedestrian in and around Grand Central Terminal, through which he walked almost every day, and that what went on above the concourse was secondary.

In late June 1968 we all flew out to the one-hundredth convention of the American Institute of Architects in Portland, Oregon, where Lajkó was to receive the AIA Gold Medal—the institute's highest honor. In a cruel irony of timing, the press coverage of what should have been the crowning moment of his professional life was tarnished by simultaneous mention of the Grand Central controversy and the criticism he had received as a result of it.

Later in 1968, the University of Virginia awarded Breuer its first

The second Grand Central scheme. Sculpture and clock were no longer threatened—they were removed.

A Breuer self-portrait. This affectionate sketch is from the personal files of his secretary Mary Farris Drabkin.

Jefferson Foundation Medal and said, "The jury [has] chosen him among all the living architects of the world as excelling all others in the quality of his work."

One of the goals of Nelson Rockefeller's governorship of New York State was the creation of a great state university system, SUNY, rivaling that of California. It was to have, and today does have, branches scattered all over the state. Many of them were based on existing college campuses but others were to be built from scratch. To guide this enormous undertaking—programming, development, and construction—Rockefeller established the State University Construction Fund (SUCF) under the dedicated leadership of Tony Adinolfi, one of his most loyal and effective administrators. What was then called the University of Buffalo had been absorbed into the system and was run by the state on a crowded site in the middle of the city that had no possibility for expansion. The strength of the university was its medical school, which was to become its specialty within the state system. The construction fund proposed building a new campus on open farmland in Amherst, a few miles from downtown Buffalo. It was to be the largest college campus in the world—and it was to be built in ten years.

Breuer was asked in 1966 to join forces with nine other architects in developing the master plan for the State University of New York at Buffalo/Amherst and then, specifically, to design the faculty of Engineering and Applied Science. This mouthful was eventually boiled down to the acronyms SUNYAB and E&AS. It quickly became apparent that this project was going to be plagued by problems, starting with the ecology of Amherst and ending with the collapse of the state's economy. Breuer was engaged in the early discussions of the master plan, which involved principles of city planning on a large scale: pedestrian versus automobile traffic and parking, mass transit (there was to be a monorail connection to the downtown campus), the use of industrialized building techniques that would gain time and save money, uniformity versus variety in building materials and shapes. All were debated in the context of the activist 1960s, and the discussions were lively, verging on the raucous. Hideo Sasaki, through his planning/landscape firm in Watertown, Massachusetts, was the chairman of the group, which included Breuer, Harry Weese, Ben Thompson, Armand Bartos, Davis Brody, Hellmuth/Obata/Kassabaum, Bob Coles, and others. A consensus finally developed in favor of a large central open space defined by densely planned "faculties" that were to be interconnected by ring roads at different distances from the center and the eventual monorail. The entire complex was then surrounded by acres of parking.

At New York State's direction, Sasaki imposed campuswide measures, such as the interconnection of buildings by bridges at the second level (it snows a lot in Buffalo), earth-colored brick and concrete (preferably precast) as principal materials, and rational patterns of service by vehicles—none of which gave us any problems. As money grew tight and tempers wore thin, the initial spirit of cooperation within the design group dissolved and was replaced by a series of competing fiefdoms that barely communicated with one another. When Breuer heard that the great central open space for which he had fought so hard was to be filled with a multipurpose megastructure designed by the Sasaki firm, he essentially washed his hands of the project and left me to manage it as well as largely to design the four buildings (out of the sixteen originally planned) that were finally built.

Breuer said that he liked the project, which he saw only in photographs, but he never included it in any publication. Long before we finished with the last building, in 1978, Tony Adinolfi had died, Rockefeller had left the governorship, and the bureaucracy that remained was run by petty individuals who gave their architects a hard time in terms of fees and contracts. I spent a lot of time explaining to my partners why this job just couldn't make money and yet there were times in the lean 1970s when we were glad to have it around just to have something to work on. The buildings that did get built were assembled from by then predictable, but strong, precast concrete window units and dark brown brick; the interiors were dominated by polished gray concrete block walls and black millwork punctuated by more red exit signs than I had ever seen any code impose. Office interiors had one wall in a bright color, selected from within a restricted palette that we proposed, and the Civil Engineering Building had a photogenic row of metal bins containing sand, gravel, and cement painted in seven rainbow colors.

The Civil Engineering Building also contains the principal earthquake simulator in the eastern United States, a pet project of Bob Ketter, who was

The faculty of Engineering and Applied Science, State University of New York at Buffalo/ Amherst. Our design responded to a program that asked for all-weather connections in one of the state's snowiest corners.

the university president during part of the time we were working on the project and, subsequently, a professor of civil engineering. Just as we were finishing the drawings for the building, a similar earthquake installation went into operation in Mexico City that, when it was first turned on, tore the building housing it to shreds. Our engineers did some fast recalculations and beefed up our structure in response.

A project of this magnitude was certainly not without some joys and satisfaction. Among the high points were a nationwide tour of state-of-the-art laboratories, which gave me my first look at Lou Kahn's great Salk Institute in La Jolla; our first friendly master-planning sessions in Watertown at which Ben Thompson filled our lunch breaks with his personal collection of slides of signs and shops from all over the world, which would become the basis of so much of his later work for Rouse at the marketplaces of Boston, South Street Seaport in New York, and the Baltimore Harbor; receptions in the two great Frank Lloyd Wright houses in Buffalo, then used by the university to house its president and provost; the shock of having our first building for Environmental Engineering and Library Sciences come in two million dollars under budget as the Buffalo building market collapsed in the early 1970s; and finally seeing built for Chemical Engineering the idealized office/lab/service-corridor scheme that we had first developed for Dick Dodson so many years before at Brookhaven.

The Chemical Engineering Building at SUNY Buffalo/ Amherst. More patterns of precast grew out of the state's demand for fast-track construction methods.

Flaine opened officially to the public at Christmas 1968. The month before-hand had been one of chaotic last-minute preparations. Sylvie Boissonnas personally swept the floor of the main lift station, hung curtains, and even scrubbed toilets as the opening day approached. When the newly ordered Aalto chairs arrived for the hotel lounge, she was aghast to learn that they had been shipped "knocked down" without adequate instructions. Breuer, who was nearby, got down on the floor to examine the "kit," discovered that an essential part was missing, and was able to improvise a fix.

Lajkó and I participated in some pre-opening festivities for the design team. Talking to Yves Tayssier of COTEBA over cocktails in the lounge of Hôtel B—now christened "Le Flaine"—he reminded me that the floor we were standing on was actually cantilevered out over a cliff that fell several hundred feet to the valley floor below. He suggested that we should paint a prominent dashed white line across the midpoint of the lounge, where it became airborne, with a cautionary label such as "Warning! From here on you are in the hands of the architects."

Flaine was far from presentable its first year. Only two hotels and one apartment house were up, and the rest of the resort was just a building site with excavations and foundation work visible everywhere, although largely camouflaged by the snow. Still, it was very exciting to see the resort finally in operation when I returned a month later with a group of thirty skier friends from the United States and Europe. It certainly helped to be known to the owners and the pioneering staff, and we were completely spoiled as one of the first paying ski groups to arrive.

Le Flaine was at that time owned and managed by the Provenaz family, which also owned a four-star resort hotel in Aix-les-Bains. Monsieur Provenaz was a very stiff, traditional *hôtelier* who wore a suit every evening and seemed to expect that we should have come in evening clothes rather than parkas, sweaters, and slacks. Eric Boissonnas assured us that the presence of Provenaz gave Flaine credibility in the financial and social world of France and we forgave him his eccentricity, particularly since the food and service were excellent. The next year he had unbent a bit—he wore a turtleneck under his suit jacket. There was a proper concierge in the entry lobby—a man weighing close to three hundred pounds but with a splendid uniform and a jolly disposition.

Lajkó visited Flaine shortly after the opening and had lunch with the Boissonnas family on the dining terrace outside Le Flaine. During the elegant meal, complete with fine linen napkins, silver service, and a smiling maître d'hôtel pouring wine for Breuer, Sylvie erupted, "Lajkó, isn't it remarkable? Just a few years ago this spot was a wild and inaccessible desert and now look at it. Why, it's just as if someone had waved a magic wand!"

In addition to the new buildings, there were several old shepherds' barns remaining in various spots in the valley, and each was eventually

Hôtel Le Flaine. Its audacious cantilever as seen from below became something of a trademark for the resort.

Lajkó, Connie, and Sylvie at Flaine for the inauguration of the new ice sculpture, 1971.

turned into a rustic restaurant-bar that made a good foil for our modern architecture. One of the more enterprising developers in this line was a smiling German who ran the Hôtel Gradins Gris (Gray Steps)—"Daddy Joe" Wilkehr—who became a great favorite of our groups over the years and arranged late-night fondue parties up on the slopes with most people afterward sliding down the mountain on trays while yodeling in the moonlight.

An architect is lucky to receive some compliments at the opening of a building and perhaps even favorable reviews in the press. Never, however, has any project given back to its architects as much pleasure and satisfaction over many years as Flaine has to me and, I hope, to Lajkó. He usually visited once a year and was certainly honored by the Boissonnas family and their important guests, but he was no longer the skier of his Obergurgl days and walked with difficulty around town. In my case, I had the thrill of using a piece of architecture I had helped design. Weeklong visits with admiring friends and family meant seeing the town not just with an eye to publishable photographs but in the evening as the lights came on, or in the early morning before the ground fog had lifted, or from high above at the start of a descent on skis. We visited our "competition," Avoriaz, one day, and I admired the fantastic wood structures that its Belgian architects had sculpted out of cedar shakes. They also had confronted the automobile problem, and their solution—reindeer-drawn sleds—was very picturesque. Eric Boissonnas had been disappointed to see this upstart open a year before we did, due to his political problems, and worried about our ability to catch up. On the contrary, in a few years, the press called Flaine a couture "Balenciaga," comparing it to Avoriaz as a trendy, ready-to-wear "Dorothy Bis." I never returned to Avoriaz, but I heard later that its wooden shingles had weathered badly in the alpine winters and that the last of the reindeer was to be seen running wild in the woods.

In the middle of summer 1969 Eric Boissonnas organized a one-week "retreat" for the design team and principal staff of Flaine in order to assess the first year of operations and to learn from one another's experiences. We met at the Grand Hôtel d'Albion in Aix-les-Bains, under the still watchful eye of Monsieur Provenaz, its owner. At the farewell banquet, which was held at a beautiful restaurant in the middle of a lake, everyone was so relaxed, or drunk, that the staid assembly descended into a sort of food fight with bread balls being lofted at the instigation of Denis Creissels, our lift designer. Earlier, during the course of the meeting, Emile Allais had asked that the minutes record an obligation that the architects be "required" to visit Flaine once each year during the operating season to see their work in actual use, as opposed to our inspection trips during the construction in summer. He felt this would enable us to better appreciate the day-to-day problems that might arise with real people on real skis. No one took exception to this brilliant idea, and I visited Flaine to ski every season for the next ten years.

Rumors of a possible expansion of IBM La Gaude had begun even while I was still living in Paris, but for one reason or another, despite occasional meetings, new buildings were delayed. In the meantime, a village of "temporary" trailers had sprung up at the bottom of the site, and internal communication within the lab was severely compromised by people having to shuttle back and forth from one site to another. It finally took an architect, El Noyes, to blow the whistle, especially on a site that had just been given official landmark status by the French government.

Expanding the facility in 1968, which had been designed in 1960 at a stand-alone maximum size by dictate of the company, was not going to be easy. The northern wings of the double Y, which faced downhill toward the open part of the site, already stood on columns twenty-five feet high, and the hillside just kept falling away, making any horizontal extension impossible. Since the new program stipulated deep laboratories without windows, we proposed and it was decided that it could be built partially underground at the foot of the last column, with a roof of grass, connected to the existing building via an elevator tower that leaned against its downhill end. Great walls of rubblestone defined huge "scoops" out of the hillside, and two major expansions, each as big as the original building, were constructed in this fashion during the subsequent years. The design work was done in New York; working drawings were made under Mario Jossa's control in the Paris office. Mario developed close relationships with the Paris office of IBM France that were eventually to feed a jealousy that grew between Paris/La Gaude and New York/Armonk, drowning future expansions in interoffice politics. It got so tense at one later point that Breuer threatened to resign the commission over President Baron de Waldner's insistence on working only with our Paris office, which was convenient for him and the staff of IBM France. Jacques Maisonrouge, the head of IBM World Trade, intervened to save the day. In 1968 all this was ahead for us, and initially everything went smoothly; we were happy to see such dramatic growth at the site.

Computers in the late 1960s were still unknown in the practice of architecture, and Lajkó was fascinated on one of his trips to La Gaude to be shown on screen a perspective drawing of one of his tree columns that was made to appear to tumble in space. The company suggested that if he was interested he should visit a shipyard in Marseilles, where one of its computers was not only designing the complex shape of ship hulls but also laying out templates for each of the steel plates in such a way that they would "nest" economically before being computer-cut from sheets of rolled steel. Breuer was very interested but didn't want to make the trip, so I stopped by on my next visit to La Gaude. It was impressive, particularly since the entire cost of the computer installation and program had been financed by the savings in formerly wasted steel.

Although Breuer was not a graduate of Harvard, his many years of teaching there had left him extremely loyal, and the university was soon to return the favor with an honorary doctorate in 1970. In the autumn of 1968 Harvard offered Lajkó a commission for a new building to house the biology and chemistry departments, which was to be shoe-horned into the center of the campus. The building committee was chaired by Ronald Vanelli and included two Nobel Prize winners (there were four in the departments). I was partner in charge and enjoyed many stimulating meetings with the distinguished committee. Ron ran a tight ship, and the committee was supportive of the scheme that developed, a variant on the service-corridor plan that had originated at Brookhaven. (In fact, some of our old scientist friends there had recommended us for the Harvard job.) It had been approved when two bombs fell. James Watson, of double-helix fame, was on the faculty but had not served on the committee. When he was shown the drawings, he realized that one result of the very efficient service corridor was that he would have a window only in his office, not in his laboratory. He hit the roof and set about sabotaging the project. We briefly considered buying him off with a corner laboratory where a window would be possible, but Ron was against such favoritism and the project was put on hold while the faculty tried to calm things down. Shortly afterward, then President Richard Nixon announced major budget cuts in National Science

Foundation funding, which Harvard had been counting on for support, and the project came to a halt.

In late 1969 Breuer began work on a book to update the record of his work. He chose as its original editor Steve Kliment, a well-known architectural writer, but soon switched to Tician. Perhaps it was a matter of editorial control, which Lajkó wanted and Steve was unwilling to give. At any rate, Tician thoroughly enjoyed the daily sessions with Breuer, and their detailed discussions provided Tician with a unique opportunity to catch up with the rest of the partners in terms of an understanding of Lajkó's intent. The choice and composition of the photographs were entirely in Breuer's hands, and the text resulted from easy-going conversations characterized by a subtle sense of humor, pride, and self-confidence without a trace of the prima donna. The book was published with Tician's byline in 1970 in at least three different-language editions. The only controversy that Tician remembers was Breuer's displeasure at the color of the linen binding, chosen by the publisher, Gerd Hatje, which he called "shit brown."

The Baldegg Convent was nearly complete when the sisters asked Beat Jordi whether he thought it was time for them to have their habits redesigned, since everything else around them was being updated. Beat volunteered to approach some of the great designers of the day—Saint Laurent, Cardin, and

Courrèges' original sketch for the nuns'"city" habit at Baldegg.

243

Courrèges. The only positive response came from Courrèges, who was an architect by training. Beat's wife, Elsbeth, accompanied a committee of two nuns (both professors of art history) on their interview trip to Paris. After lunch at a tea room opposite the Madeleine, they proceeded to the designer's studio, which was a spare, modest attic space painted all in white. Ushered into his office, the sisters found it furnished with four stools and a drafting table. Courrèges himself entered dressed in pink nylon jacket and knickers and wearing large white-framed glasses. He was both friendly and businesslike as the nuns discussed their needs for Sunday, holiday, and work habits—they blanched a bit at having to describe their undergarments. He made some quick and elegant sketches of his first ideas, which included robes divided into a four-part checkerboard of black and white over white ribbed turtlenecks.

After the interview, the sisters stopped by several of the designer showrooms in the neighborhood, and Elsbeth reported that the two digni-fied nuns created quite a sensation. When they finally sat down for tea, Elsbeth asked, with some trepidation, how they had liked Courrèges. "Oh, he was fine! Just our man," they replied. Elsbeth was surprised: "Didn't you find his outfit a bit outrageous?" "Oh no, it was just what we expected," they said. Courrèges visited the convent a few months later to present his final designs—navy blue for everyday, white for Sunday, and black for holidays— and brought along a tall, beautiful model to show them off. The sisters were very pleased, but worried, "because we don't really look like her." The designs were finally adapted by "sister tailors" and have been in use ever since. Courrèges never charged them a fee.

Shortly after the convent opened, Beat was able to arrange a public-relations coup for the sisters. Shelby Collum Davis was the United States ambassador to Switzerland and the father of an old friend of mine who had often joined us at Flaine. Both Beat and I had met the ambassador at an ele-gant black-tie dinner he gave after one of our yearly ski trips. Beat cultivated the acquaintance of the ambassador and arranged for him to visit the con-vent during Breuer's next visit. The sisters were beside themselves with pride—their famous architect and the American ambassador on the same day! Davis was a prominent figure on Wall Street and a heavy contributor to Richard Nixon's war chest. He had served longer than any other ambassador to Bern and was generally rated a very successful diplomat. He also always wore a red carnation in his buttonhole. I regret that I didn't prep Breuer for their meeting. All he could say when he got back was, "Who was that glad-handing American I met? He was right out of an operetta!"

Sister Basilda Umbricht had worked closely with Breuer during the entire design process. She later recalled, "Mr. Breuer radiated calm and con-fidence. We all felt very much at ease in his presence. He treated us as equals and never tried to show off as a know-it-all. His warm-hearted humanity inspired confidence. All the sisters instinctively trusted him, recognizing his great abilities as an architect—from both his artistic and practical spirit."

Breuer was invited to receive an honorary doctorate from the University of Budapest in 1970. His mother and sister had been visiting Vienna when the Russian tanks rolled into Budapest in October 1956, and they had never returned home. Lajkó himself was reluctant to revisit Hungary while the Communists remained in power, but he relented for this occasion. He took the opportunity to show Connie all the scenes of his youth, including Pécs and Lake Balaton. Attending a high-school reunion held in Pécs in his honor, he was astonished to find most of his classmates still there, practicing, for the most part, their fathers' professions. He let one of the sisters at Baldegg, who came from Hungary, read his acceptance speech. She was surprised at his use of the language, which was full of terms more suited to a peasant than to a world-famous, sophisticated architect.

In 1969 the first stage of our project for IBM in Boca Raton was racing toward completion, and it looked as if we would have other buildings to design as soon as the first group of six had been finished. At twelve people, the team in the drafting room was one of the largest we had ever assembled, and it worked efficiently under tremendous time pressure and the whip of Bodo Schneider, our Swiss job captain. Bodo was a growling, foul-mouthed taskmaster who had recently joined the firm with high recommendations. Unlike almost everyone else in the firm, he had no aspirations to be thought of as a designer—he was just a very hard-working "production man."

As opening day grew near, the frantic pace picked up, and I seemed to be in Florida every other week. Breuer had chosen six or seven works of art for the main lobby at Boca from among the major art collection that IBM kept ready for just such occasions. Arnie Richter was amused by a kinetic sculptural piece that "very slowly" changed its colors through polarized light. "Very slowly" became a running gag for years to come in response to all sorts of questions. Arnie had a last-minute crisis on his hands having to do with the dedication plaque, which was to include both Breuer and myself as credited architects. Lajkó had suggested sandblasting the letters into the concrete of one of the tree columns by the side of the entry. When the rubber stencil was stripped off, the letters were found to have crumbled to illegibility. Literally overnight, Arnie had to find a piece of granite, engrave the names, carve out a depression in the column, and have it in place for the unveiling.

When IBM realized that employees in the laboratories on the east side of the central lake would have to walk around it to get to the cafeteria, the company asked Breuer to design a bridge across the lake. Lajkó came up with the idea of building a square island near the center of the lake that would be connected to either shore by short bridges. He proposed building a version of his beloved project for the Cambridge War Memorial on the island (although it wasn't identified as such). The "lake island" appeared in the final renderings and was much admired. For economic reasons, it was put on hold for the moment, which extended into years. Yet it was mentioned by Thomas Watson Jr. in a much later lecture at Harvard as a promise he felt he had made to Breuer that would some day be fulfilled. I kept reminding succeeding generations of CEOs of that promise but was finally told by the Real Estate Division to "shut up already."

The opening day for IBM Boca Raton arrived March 31, 1970. Eastern Airlines, the only carrier serving the area at that time, was on strike. I called IBM to tell the company that some architects were likely to be missing unless one more corporate jet could be made available, as had been provided for its board members. The jet was arranged, and Barbara and I joined Connie and Lajkó at Westchester Airport at noon on March 30. Our flight was presided over by Arthur Watson, the World Trade head whom we had last seen in connection with La Gaude—in fact, the pilot was one who remembered Breuer from a flight in France. Connie did not like to fly, especially in small planes, and when Watson asked her if he could get her something to drink, she enthusiastically agreed. The choice was Coca-Cola, ginger ale, or Seven-Up, evidence of the puritanism of his father, which still reigned supreme in the company. Connie was disappointed.

The next day the sun was out—in fact, we were roasting in the first row of seats, and Connie tried with her program to shield Lajkó from the hot Florida sun. Anita Bryant, the Florida orange-juice queen, sang the national anthem, and Thomas Watson Jr. gave an appreciative speech that made it all seem worthwhile.

I organized an office party in Bedford in January 1971, on what turned out to be a beautiful, sunny, snowy Sunday. In the few years since the last such party my family home had grown, but not nearly as fast as the office. More than one hundred people, including families, attended. There was mulled wine down by the lake, where we'd cleared enough of the ice to provide good skating. Parties of five or six were shuttled over to "Suicide Hill" at the Golf and Tennis Club for tobogganing on excellent fresh snow. The hill, alternatively known as "Cardiac Hill," was not actually all that steep, but it was quite long and no one I knew had ever ridden it all the way to the stream at the bottom. My secretary at the time, Sue Bassett, decided to pile as many of the office heavyweights as she could fit onto one of our toboggans, which took off like a shot. They got to the bottom, to the ice that covered the stream, and crashed through it with great hilarity and drenched clothing. It recalled Susi Strohbach's misadventure on our own

The Atlanta Central Public Library. If the Whitney had any descendants it was this. The walls are of striated concrete.

lake six or seven years earlier. Home movies show Lajkó helping her remove her foot from a hole in the ice after which Murray Emslie emptied her boot of frigid water.

I interrupted my ski trip to Flaine in February 1971 to fly up to Rotterdam for a meeting to discuss a parking garage to be built next to the De Bijenkorf Department Store. It was not a particularly challenging project, but Lajkó was pleased to see a client so loyal fifteen years after the construction of the original building. In fact, a great deal of our work in this period, which was otherwise slowing down as the building industry ground to one of its periodic halts, involved repeat commissions for old clients. Flaine, Bayonne, SUNYAB, and IBM Boca Raton kept expanding, and the Sacklers asked us back to add on to Laboratoires Sarget in Bordeaux.

After the enormous Grand Coulee Dam, Ham had the chance to work on two small, elegant projects, one for the Southern New England Telephone Company (SNET), which wanted to build on property next to the headquarters of Torin (Rufus Stillman made SNET hire Breuer before he would sell it the land); and the other for the Bryn Mawr School for Girls in

Pennsylvania. He also began work on a large public library for Atlanta, the dream of its head librarian, Carleton Rochelle. The design was a development of shapes that Breuer had used at the Whitney Museum, although the exterior material chosen, striated concrete, was dictated by a budget more modest than the one that had allowed for the Whitney's granite. The project was put on hold for about year while the economy recovered, but we had a persistent client and the building was finally and successfully built. The huge expanses of concrete have weathered extremely well over the years, especially since the pattern of grooves, or striations, in the concrete forces the rain to follow predictable paths; thus, whatever staining has resulted serves to reinforce the composition of opposing diagonals that were part of the original intent.

Tician and Carl Stein worked closely with Lajkó in 1969 on a large school for the mentally retarded in Nassau County for the New York State Health and Rehabilitation Agency. It was a large and complicated program that seemed logically to fit within a one-story scheme. When Carl questioned Tician as to why they were studying only a two-story version, his answer was, "Because Lajkó wants it." The Nassau school was one of many victims of the economic collapse of Governor Nelson Rockefeller's grand dreams for his state.

Lajkó returned in October from a European trip that had taken him to Flaine and Bayonne; Eric Cercler had been his guide and translator. On his first day back in New York, Breuer asked me into his office and announced that Cercler would have to be fired. He had been embarrassed by some of Eric's physical mannerisms during the trip, such as a tendency toward nervous giggling, which was certainly exacerbated by being at Breuer's side. There was no way to dissuade him with reminders of almost ten years of loyal service. He was adamant: "I can't afford to be represented by a jerk." We were to let Cercler go as soon as possible. Despite my mixed feelings, I had to agree with Breuer, and with Mario well installed, we had a perfect, experienced replacement in hand as head of the Paris office. Still, I had hired Eric as one of our first employees in 1964, he was a great friend of my good friends, the Chevaliers, and he had essentially cut his ties with his French career in order to serve us.

Boarding the plane at Kennedy Airport for a sudden trip that I could not explain in advance was a very sad occasion, and I elected to meet Eric at my hotel in the afternoon of my arrival. He certainly knew that something was awry, but there was no way for him to have been prepared for the shattering news I broke as gently as I could. I used all the rationales that Breuer had given me—an incompatibility of personalities, a desire to be represented by Mario. None of it was very convincing, and Eric just stared at me while I talked and then thanked me for my personal courtesy in delivering the message. We briefly discussed the generous severance terms that Lajkó had authorized and said good-bye. I have never seen him again.

I didn't stay in Paris too long—it was rainy and cold—and after checking in with Mario the next day to work out the details of his takeover, I got back on the plane for home. Jean-Pierre Chevalier told me a year later that Eric had had a complete nervous breakdown within days of my departure and, after a period of institutionalization, had found a job in the construction department of one of the great banks where, so far as I know, he may still work.

Public relations and advertising for Flaine had been handled for several years by Hugette Imber-Vier and her Parisian firm, ICPA. I had tangled with her on several occasions—proposing an alternate logo for the double skis with which she spelled Flaine, openly disdaining the colors she chose as trademarks. In fact, her proposals have worn well, and we later patched up our differences. In the fall of 1971 she brought us an important commission for beachfront development on the Côte d'Aquitaine, part of the French coastline north of Biarritz along the Bay of Biscay just before it turns west to join Spain. The Côte d'Aquitaine is largely unpopulated. The seas are rough, and the fragile dunes have been overprotected since Napoleon had his engineers plant huge pine forests to catch and drop the wind-driven sand. When Jacques Chelban-Delmas became prime minister after years as the mayor of Bordeaux, he created an interministerial commission to see whether the logjam between warring ministries couldn't be broken and permit the careful development of the coastline for tourism to take some of the pressure off the overcrowded Côte d'Azur. The commission divided several hundreds of miles of beachfront into ten parcels, with natural buffers in between, and assigned each to a different group of planners. Somehow, Hugette wangled parcel number 6 for a team headed by Breuer with Max Stern and the BERU along with ICPA. We were the only non-French architects, and it proved to be a fascinating planning project.

The area contained nothing but two tired old beach resorts and a paper mill that spewed noxious gases over the area when the wind blew from the wrong direction. I visited the site the following spring after my family's annual Flaine trip and found the towns of Mimizan and Mimizan-plage to be quite charming. Our scheme involved a new network of protected bays and was drawn up about a year later; it garnered favorable attention in Paris. Unfortunately, shortly thereafter, the French satiric newspaper *Le Canard Enchainée* made some scandalous revelations about the prime minister, and his favorite project was shelved forever.

*Breuer at Kabul air-
port. He is met by offi-
cials of the ATO with
Nick Ludington on
the left.*

Kabul:
1971–1973

An old friend, Nick Ludington, was working for an American advertising agency in London during my years at the Paris office and gradually assembling a set of public-relations clients on his own. Some years before in the United States, he had met Zalmay Mahmood Ghazi, then attached to the Afghan Embassy in Washington and by 1966 the Afghan ambassador to France. Nick had suggested that I meet Zalmay, with whom we had an elegant dinner.

During a trip Breuer and I took to Paris in 1968, Nick arranged another meeting with his friend Zalmay. We met at the Afghan Embassy on avenue Raphael, an ornate nineteenth-century townhouse. On the coffee table in the reception room was a book of Breuer's work, which I had sent a year or so before. We discussed the possibility of designing the Afghan exhibit at an upcoming trade fair in Paris, and Lajkó sketched a ziggurat on a cocktail napkin while we were at a restaurant. Nothing came of the assignment, perhaps because of lack of funding, but all of Nick's careful coaching was certainly making the Afghans aware of Marcel Breuer.

Sometime during late 1971 I got a postcard from an old classmate, Greg Votaw, postmarked Afghanistan. He worked as a manager at the World Bank and was in Afghanistan after a visit to India with the bank's president, Robert McNamara. The bank had recently decided to encourage tourist development in countries where such activities offered an opportunity to earn significant amounts of hard currency. The card said simply, "I think we have something for your firm. I'll call when we are back."

Greg called later to say that the bank had decided that Afghanistan had a number of potential sites for good-quality hotels and was looking for an architect of standing who could survey the field and make some recommendations. A trip to the country would be required. If Breuer was willing to travel, they would nominate him as architect to the Afghan Tourist Organization (ATO), which would be paying for the first master plan with financing from the bank. Lajkó was not particularly enthralled by the prospect of such a long journey, but he agreed to go to Kabul in the summer of 1972 at the tail end of a European trip he had planned that was to include Flaine.

Breuer turned seventy in May, and his friends arranged for a gala birthday party at Estia, an old Greek restaurant on Eighty-sixth Street, which was taken over in its entirety for the evening. The party included a belly dancer at whose appearance Breuer took obvious pleasure and a cake that the cartoonist Saul Steinberg decorated with a pastry bag. The party featured lots of food and drink, and no one remembers what the cake finally looked like. Since everyone else speaks vividly of this party I have long wondered why I wasn't there. It was only when Mary Farris pinned it down to Monday, May 22, 1972, and I consulted my agenda, that I realized that I was at that moment flat on my back with hepatitis. At any rate, I did recover sufficiently to be able to travel to Afghanistan in early July when Nick Ludington and I were invited by the World Bank to join Lajkó for a preliminary survey of the tourist potential of the country. On the day of my departure, I had to dash up to an adoption agency with which Barbara and I had been negotiating. I reviewed a Korean orphan's file that had been received just that morning. Margot, our third daughter, arrived just before Christmas.

I flew ahead of time to Paris for meetings with Mort Sackler and his lawyer about a new job for Purdue Frederick in Germany, and Nick arrived a few days later. Lajkó had come down from Flaine a bit sooner than expected, feeling uncomfortable at the high altitude. We discussed again whether he really had to fly to Afghanistan, but after listing the number of people who would feel let down if he were to be a no-show, we agreed to meet at Orly Airport on Wednesday, July 12, for an Ariana Afghan Airways flight to Kabul. Breuer had asked for permission to fly first class due to his age, but Ariana didn't have first class. Then again, Ariana didn't have many passengers, either, and we had been assured that we would have plenty of space to stretch out.

The flight was scheduled to last for almost twenty-four hours with stops in Frankfurt, Istanbul, Beirut, and Teheran before landing in Kabul the next morning at six o'clock. (The time difference was four hours.) The timing was important because the summer sun in Kabul Valley causes the heated air to rise during most of the day, and cold winds that rush down from the Hindu Kush (the Afghan name for their branch of the Himalayas) create bad cross-winds on the only landing strip in Kabul. The moment of atmospheric equilibrium was at that early hour, and most planes (of which there were not many) were scheduled to land and take off about then. The runway was not long enough for jumbo jets, so Ariana owned only a modest fleet of 727s (which needed all the refueling stops). When we checked in at the ticket counter at Orly, we were told that the aircraft coming from Kabul was running four hours late, and we were invited to amuse ourselves until an expected departure for Frankfurt at about two that afternoon. We were also advised to take three seats together: "It's going to be a full flight."

With hindsight, if ever there were warning signals suggesting that we should abort a trip, they were flapping in our faces that day. I think the only thing that kept Breuer going was that he had noticed that Orly had a movie theater playing *Divorce, Italian Style,* a film about which he had heard good reports, and the illicit chance to take in a movie in the middle of a working day proved irresistible to the old fan.

I was pleased to note as the door to the plane closed that we were only five people on the flight. Convinced that I had simply misunderstood the information about all seats being booked, we spread ourselves all over the cabin and Lajkó went promptly to sleep. The first stop was Frankfurt, where who should join us but the entire annual incoming contingent of Peace Corps volunteers—a once-a-year phenomenon that resulted in Ariana's only full flight. The volunteers had flown all night to Amsterdam, made the connection to Frankfurt, and were by now in a high state of excitement about the start of their two years in Afghanistan. It did not look like a sleepy group. On top of it all, Nick and I had been separated from Lajkó when we chose our seats and never did get back to his side. None of us got much sleep, and Breuer ended up sharing his row with a couple of ebullient twenty-somethings who didn't stop talking all night.

We deplaned at about ten o'clock the next morning onto an actual red carpet and were greeted by a delegation of senior officials from the ATO. They recognized our need for sleep and whisked us off to the luxurious Kabul Intercontinental Hotel after canceling a welcome luncheon. As we were handed our keys, Lajkó suggested we call each other later in the afternoon.

Not an hour later, I was awakened by a phone call from Breuer. His voice was very strained: "Bob, come quickly—I'm very sick." I found him a dismal gray, obviously in great pain, and fearful that the problem was his heart. I got on the phone to the front desk and found that the hotel doctor had just left for lunch and the staff didn't know where he had gone.

My next call was to the ever-resourceful Nick, who immediately suggested we call the American embassy. Fortunately, Nick had thought to notify the embassy several weeks before of the arrival of a noted American architect. An embassy ambulance with a nurse and a Care-Medico doctor pulled up in front of the hotel about fifteen minutes later. Lajkó had been very quiet and composed during all this frantic commotion, which is more than I can say for myself. Our relief as the no-nonsense Dr. Moede strode into the room was

253

explosive, and his preliminary exam resulted in good news and bad news. The bad news was that Breuer had apparently suffered a heart attack. The good news was that the doctor thought the crisis was past and that tests at the American embassy dispensary would probably confirm that. Lajkó was taken away on a stretcher, and we were told to call in a few hours for an update.

When Nick and I got to the dispensary later that afternoon, Breuer was resting comfortably, although he was somewhat groggy from sedation. He had, however, begun to think things through, and he gave me two assignments. I was to notify Connie, but since she was also in delicate health at that moment, I was to do so in such a reassuring way that she would not fly out to be with him. I was also to pack up only a few of his essential belongings, including a favorite gold toothpick, which I would find in the right-hand change pocket of the suit hanging in his hotel closet.

Years later, Lajkó told me that he was sure he was going to die and, having studied the last words of famous men, had given the matter some thought. His plan was to utter "Let's go." But he said that when he saw the look of abject terror on my face as I came into his room, he realized that he "couldn't do that to Bob—all the bother of shipping a body back to the States—and would have to live."

The hotel told Nick and me that all telephone calls into and out of the country traveled by radio and had to be booked several days in advance (we later learned that the World Bank could have put us through immediately). I doubted my ability to be convincingly "reassuring" in a telegram but didn't feel I could delay in sending some kind of message to Connie. We composed the best one we could think of and sent it off.

In response to my telegram, and before my phone call could be booked, Connie got through to me thanks to Chris Herter Jr., an old friend of the Breuers in the U.S. State Department. She had, of course, made a reservation to fly to Kabul the next day, and my only real contribution to this sorry state of affairs was to impart to her the sense of confidence and calm that we genuinely felt in the presence of Dr. Moede and the dispensary staff. She agreed to wait for a few days, and as all the reassuring tests came in, she finally found the strength to obey Lajkó's wishes and await his return, which would only be three weeks later. That was, and still is so far as I know, the standard recuperation period, and Dr. Moede was a very experienced internist from Baltimore who knew the rules.

After notifying our client of the situation the next day, we visited the dispensary and found Lajkó propped up in bed, looking positively chipper. His color had returned, and he was being spoiled silly by a round-the-clock team of nurses who normally had nothing to do between embassy pregnancies. He always said that it was the best hospital experience he had ever had, and we were certainly relieved as we started to plan what we might do during a survey trip that had suddenly tripled in length.

The World Bank's resident representative was a Burmese named Kyaw Myint who was a close friend of Greg Votaw's. He arranged for our first visit to his good friend the head of the ATO—and the brother of our Paris friend Zalmay—Sultan Mahmood Ghazi, who was also the minister of tourism and president of Ariana Afghan Airways.

The meeting was understandably somewhat strained. Ghazi graciously inquired after Breuer's health and assured us that we were the guests of the Afghan government during the three weeks we would have to stay in the country. Cars, drivers, airline tickets, and hotel rooms were all at our disposal both for completing our survey of the tourist potential of Afghanistan and for making our time there as pleasant as possible under the circumstances. He was as good as his word, and the weeks that followed were an eerie composite of fear and worry about Lajkó and awe and interest in the country we were to discover.

Although Ghazi was perfectly fluent in the bank's official English, he seemed more comfortable in his university French and was pleased that we could conduct our meetings in that language. We agreed that a survey of available hotel sites in Kabul would be first on our agenda, and then, if we felt comfortable leaving Lajkó for a few days at a time, we could visit the other potential sites at Mazār-e Sharīf, Bāmiān, and Herāt.

The vice president of the ATO, Mr. Sultani, acted as our guide in his native city of Kabul. Although he was very proud of the recent "modern" buildings that lined the main street downtown, there was no mistaking the nostalgia with which he would walk us through the old alleyways of the original Kabul, framed in two- and three-story mud-brick structures. He showed us six or seven sites that might be considered for a new hotel, most of them already occupied by older ones that could easily be replaced.

Our assignment was to site and design a hotel that, in contrast to the luxurious Intercontinental, was more appropriate to the Western tourist on a modest budget who was beginning to find Kabul an exotic stopover after India and Nepal. Of the sites we were shown, our favorite was a broad, tree-shaded square in the middle of downtown that was then occupied by the Ministry of Tribal Affairs. (The Intercontinental was a long taxi ride out of town.)

We were in Kabul in one of those rare bubbles of time when two westerners could wander the city day or night and receive welcoming smiles at every turn. The "Great Game," which the British and Russians had fought for centuries, was currently being played by the Americans and Soviets, but there was no apparent tension in Kabul. Americans were to be seen everywhere, while Russians stayed behind the walls of their compound on the outskirts of town, as did an equally large contingent of Communist Chinese.

After being driven around for a few days, we got the lay of the land and were able to navigate on foot, exploring the old bazaar streets. Breuer was

Gatje at Bāmiān airport.

fascinated by the stories and trinkets we brought by each evening, and one day we finally felt ready to take off on our first side trip—a two-day jaunt to Mazār-e Sharīf, which was near the northern border with the Soviet Union.

We crossed, or rather wound our way through, the passes of the Hindu Kush in one of the Fokker Twin Otter turbo-props of Bakhtar, the internal Afghan airway. After landing, we were shown a fine hotel site near the old shrine to Ali, where relics of Mohammed's son-in-law were supposed to be lodged. We stayed overnight in a "new" hotel built by the Soviets that was dreariness personified.

The next day we picked up a young photographer from *National Geographic* who had just crossed the border from Samarkand. Together we visited the spectacular old markets of Balkh and Khulm and walked around the circular mound of sand that marked the easternmost advance of Alexander's army.

After reporting dutifully on our impressions to Sultan Ghazi and Breuer, we flew to the great valley of Bāmiān, the most famous tourist attraction in the country. It is bounded on one side by the Hindu Kush and on the other by a sheer sandstone cliff out of which were carved, in the third and fifth centuries, the two tallest freestanding statues in the world (180 and 125 feet tall), both representing Buddha. The valley floor resembled a great carpet—rows of potato greens defined by the serpentine pattern of irrigation ditches. The village itself was a mud-brick market town, and we stayed in a hotel made up of yurts left over from the filming of *Caravans* a few years earlier. The yurts were traditional nomadic tent structures of saplings

The yurt village of Bāmiān as seen from the head of the Great Buddha.

Nick Ludington in front of his yurt with the Great Buddha in the background.

and goatskins huddled together on a cliff opposite the wall of Buddhas and were to be incorporated into whatever new hotel we could dream up.

We drove back to Kabul from Bāmiān in six very dusty hours so that we could see the Salang Pass and some of its native villages. On leaving Bāmiān Valley we passed by the ruins of Shahr-e-Gholghola, the "City of Shrieks" or "Palace of the Daughter," after a famous Afghan legend involving treachery and slaughter.

A trip was arranged to inspect the new airport at Qandahār, which had been designed by an American firm, Hellmuth/Obata/Kassabaum (HOK), and built with USAID funds only a few years before. I think the idea of the inspection was to judge whether it could serve as a model for the new airport that the World Bank hoped to finance outside Kabul. The airport itself was a complete shock. It was a scaled-down version of a parabolic-shell structure that HOK had built somewhere in the American Midwest and was completely out of scale with the modest countryside. The further surprise, however, was that it was completely deserted. Ticket counters and baggage carousels stood silent accumulating layers of dust and sand. It looked like a movie set after the film was finished. We learned later that its sole purpose was to act as a visual excuse for an airstrip that was planned to help future CIA operations.

Our last side trip was to Herāt, far to the west, a city that is more Persian than Afghan. At the time, it featured some sixteen minarets and the ruins of beautiful blue-tiled domes. It was very hot in the middle of the summer, and Mayor Rafik, a friend of Greg's, had had the foresight years before to line most of the principal streets with fast-growing pine trees. They gave welcome shade and whistled in the constant winds, creating an impression of cool comfort. The steady wind from the north was also captured, architecturally, by mud-brick and plaster "wind scoops" that topped every farmer's shallow dome and directed moving air to an underfloor network of channels that served to make the dark interiors quite livable year-round.

A few years earlier, a legendary Peace Corps architect, Bob Hull, had designed and built a local office for the ATO in Herāt. He used traditional methods of brick construction including centerless vaults and domes in a style reminiscent of Lou Kahn. It was that beautiful small building that led to my meeting Bob a few years later and hiring him to work on our project.

Everyone recommended a visit to see the firing of the "noon gun," and we took a taxi to the base of a sandy hill that looked out over the entire town. At the top we found a bronze cannon and a turbaned timekeeper who had just loaded his piece and had begun to consult the myriad wristwatches that covered each of his arms, as well as a couple of pocket watches. Once he had a consensus, he touched taper to fuse and a large boom rumbled out over the valley below as people looked up from their labors and noted noon. Before bidding him goodbye I checked the muzzle of the venerable cannon and was surprised to read by its cast inscription that it had been the

FRIENDS,

COUNTRYMEN,

MASTERS!

I CAME TO BURRY LAJKO BUT I HAVE TO PRAISE HIS FIBERS. HE WILL BE WITH YOU SOON, ON THE FIELD OF BATTLE. GREETINGS AND MANY THANKS FOR YOUR THOUGHTS, FOR YOUR FLOWERS AND OBJECTS.

YOURS LAJKO'

Breuer's thank-you note. He mailed it from the embassy dispensary in Kabul to Mary Farris for typing.

property of King George III, undoubtedly left behind after one of several vain attempts made by the British to subdue the Afghan tribesmen.

We finally received word from Dr. Moede that Lajkó had made such splendid progress that he could be released a few days early on the condition that he make a stopover at the American Hospital in Paris. He could then proceed to meet Connie in Boston where she would drive him up to what Lajkó always affectionately called "the Cape Cod." We made a hurried last-minute trip to the markets. On the night before our departure, Nick and I laid out on Lajkó's bed a splendid assortment of jewelry, blouses, sheepskins, and woodwork and invited him to make his choice for personal presents. With his unerring eye he chose a single rustic earring for Connie that was indeed the finest thing we had found.

On our way to the airport on August 1, we drove Breuer around to see the city and confirm our choice for the Kabul hotel site. He was in high spirits—whether it was because of the chance to share the wonders of which we had been telling him, or the knowledge that he was about to leave the country, we couldn't tell. Happily, we didn't have to follow the slow route of Ariana on our return. We were dropped off at Teheran where we continued on to Paris in the wide-bodied splendor of TWA. Dr. Lancry, my old

259

doctor at the American Hospital, gave Breuer the green light to return home, and we saw Lajkó off to Boston the next day.

Once back in New York we sent our report to the World Bank and the ATO and then waited for over a year before the project moved forward. Although Greg and Sultan Ghazi were prepared to continue with us, the Tourism Department of the bank was staffed by Germans who had apparently promised the Afghan project to an architect from Düsseldorf, Walter Brüne. It became a political battle of wills between Greg's department, which was responsible for the area that included Afghanistan, and the Tourism Department staff. Neither was willing to budge. Finally Greg asked me whether a joint venture might be a way out of the impasse, and a meeting was arranged in the neutral territory of the Ritz-Carlton in Boston on July 16, 1973. Breuer and I flew up to Logan Airport with all sorts of reservations but the meeting was a total success. We were impressed by the Germans' credentials and charmed by their two principals—Brüne and his head designer, Milko Arseniev, from Romania. They immediately deferred to Lajkó's senior standing and agreed that we would produce the design while they would be responsible for the working drawings and supervision of construction.

There remained only the details of a contract and fee to be negotiated, and I was appointed to represent the joint venture in what proved to be the worst negotiation nightmare of my professional life. I made three or four visits of several days each to Washington, D.C., to negotiate with a very tough contract officer at the bank who was taking his orders from a new vice president in charge, someone far less committed to the development of tourism in Afghanistan than Greg's previous boss. I stayed with Greg each time and we would commiserate over dinner. Breuer had set some pretty stiff conditions, considering the difficulties of working together at such a distance, and the bank was more used to dealing with complacent second-raters. On more than one occasion Lajkó ordered me by phone to break off the talks and come home, but finally we reached a deal via some last-minute concession involving acceptance of German marks as the currency of the contract. We were set for our next trip to Kabul.

The hotel at Mazār had been dropped from the program, but in compensation there was the possibility of being involved in the new airport. I had called Bob Hull in Washington State, and he had agreed to come to New York to work on the project. We were later joined by Rafi Samizay, who had been chairman of the Department of Architecture at Kabul University. Frank Richlan, who was by that time one of our most trusted senior associates, was put in overall charge of the job.

I met our newfound friends in Germany later in 1973 after having heard by radio on the morning of my departure that the king of Afghanistan had been overthrown by his cousin, Prime Minister Daoud. Our sources at the bank assured us that all could proceed as planned since it was already in contact with the new government.

The weather was cooler on arrival in Kabul and delightful in Bāmiān with some early snow on the foothills. The only evidence of the new, opportunistic government was their confiscation of a copy of *Playboy* upon our arrival at the airport and its return, considerably dog-eared, upon our departure. During this trip, I met our hotel consultant, a Bavarian named Arne Krüger, who was a well-known German television personality, the author of many cookbooks, and the owner of a string of *Weinstübe* where the project was roundly toasted. We revisited most of the sites, and I was beginning to feel like an old hand.

We didn't have much time for shopping during a hectic five days, but Walter picked up two "antique" rifles in Istalif, which had probably been made the week before. Our ATO guide offered to ease our jewelry shopping by bringing selected pieces to our rooms that evening. One pin was described as having been found in the ruins of Shahr-e-Gholghola, which, if true, would have placed it somewhere in the twelfth century. I chose, and choose, to believe the man.

We went back to New York to begin work on the design, and Milko came over to work by our side during the process. A modest three-story modern hotel was developed for Kabul and a romantic informal assemblage of rubblestone prisms designed for the clifftop in Bāmiān. We prepared presentation of the Bāmiān project in photomontage by superimposing it on a slide I had taken from the head of the Great Buddha. We were able to demonstrate convincingly that the new hotel would be virtually invisible from the opposite cliff.

After making a successful presentation to the bank, a third trip to Kabul was scheduled. Our presentation to the ATO went well, and we had compliments from Sultan Ghazi who, by now, could hardly wait for construction to start.

Preparation of the working drawings was well underway when the first oil crisis occurred and the price of an Ariana Airways ticket doubled overnight. Ghazi and the bank assumed that that was the end of tourism in Afghanistan and pulled the plug on our project. All our protests went unheeded. They were right, of course, although for the wrong reasons. The Russians moved in five years later.

Marcel Breuer, 1979.

New York:
1971–1976

After leaving the New York City Parks Department, Thomas Hoving became the head of the Metropolitan Museum of Art, bringing Arthur Rosenblatt with him as vice president for planning and buildings. Sometime during late 1971 or early 1972 Arthur was approached by an ad hoc committee consisting of Tician, Rufus Stillman, and **Lily Auchincloss** to discuss the possibility of an exhibition of Breuer's work at the Met.

Arthur took on the responsibility of convincing Tom Hoving that a one-man show of a living American architect, although never before undertaken at the Met, would be a good idea and one that would upstage the Whitney and the Museum of Modern Art. Breuer was arguably the best-known and most respected architect in America at that time, "and besides, Tom, after that fiasco at the Sports Park, we owe him one."

Rufus and Lily went about raising the funds to support the exhibition and found willing donors, including almost every one of Breuer's appreciative clients—an eloquent tribute to the satisfaction they felt with the projects he had designed for them. Breuer laid out the exhibit personally, and Ivan Chermayeff designed a handsome catalog for which, according to Arthur, he insisted on "perfect binding," which promptly fell apart. New models of all the major projects were built of wood and cork, including many in sumptuous teak. The tours-de-force were three-quarter-size white mockups of the La Gaude tree column and the great many-limbed column from the Saint John's University library. One-quarter of that column sat in a corner of the gallery, and wall-mounted mirrors rendered it in the round.

Naftaly Weiss built the display cabinets, and by the time the exhibition opened in late November 1972, we all felt as if we had participated in a remarkable theater piece. The show received rave reviews, and large chunks of it traveled to the Musée des Arts Décoratifs in Paris and eventually to the Bauhaus-Archiv in Berlin, where many of the models are today.

Everyone thought that the exhibition would be a tremendous boost to business. As the years went on and the office—along with most of the rest of the profession in the mid-1970s—slowed considerably, we realized that things weren't working out that way. We hired a succession of public-relations consultants, with Breuer's grudging consent, but nothing seemed to work. We realized later that the exhibition had been counter-productive in terms of business-producing potential. Some people simply assumed that any architect who had done so many things over such a long period of time must be dead. Of the potential new clients, there were those who apparently thought Lajkó was out of their league. And in truth, everything looked so splendid that it was impossible to imagine the hard work it had taken on Breuer's part to make something memorable out of what were often unpre-possessing projects with very tight budgets.

Based on their success with Sarget in Bordeaux, the Sacklers had launched a new German affiliate to be called Mundipharma. As a site for its head-quarters, they chose Limburg, a charming medieval town on the Lahn River not far from Frankfurt. When Mort approached us about designing the new building, he already had some specific thoughts in mind. He had fallen in love with the Saint John's Abbey church at the Metropolitan Museum show and wondered whether his new headquarters might somehow resemble it. He wanted to get away from the appearance of a two-story building while still maintaining its usefulness for his manufacturing methods. I had to agree that we had often found one and three stories easier to design, but the idea of starting with Saint John's was so far-fetched that Lajkó told me, in effect, to take over the job and do the best I could.

The layout of the plant was very similar to that of Sarget. We found that if we mounded the earth in a berm below high strip windows around most of the ground floor, the rest of the building, including the floor and roof thicknesses, could be wrapped in tall precast panels defining a box that seemed to float above the strip windows at grade. I worked on the building and its subsequent extensions during a ten-year period and can't tell whether Mort's idea was inherently a good one or whether I just got used to it. At any rate, I like it better than Sarget, and the heroic facade panels do bear some relationship to the folded plates of Saint John's and UNESCO.

We were having a hard time finding engineers and local architects in Frankfurt who were willing to work with us on a consulting basis (as opposed to trying to take over the job) when Breuer had the idea of hiring

*Mundipharma,
Limburg. This was
our second corporate
headquarters for
Mort Sackler.*

the engineering consultants on the staff of Philipp Holzmann, the great builder of his two Harnischmacher houses. No one, myself included, could quite imagine how our interests could be served by professionals who would be captive to the contractor rather than professionally independent. What Lajkó knew, and what we began to trust, was that it would all work out if the contractor was rigorously honest and responsible.

Since the client didn't quite believe in negotiating directly and only with Holzmann, we worked out bidding terms whereby the firm's professional fees to that date would be absorbed in the cost of construction if Holzmann turned out to be the low bidder; otherwise the firm would take on an independent consulting role. We never had to face that eventuality, since Holzmann did deliver a very attractive low bid.

I had a disagreement with Mort over his insistence on a rooftop sign that would dominate the building when seen from the autobahn. At the beginning of construction, the site was semi-rural and I tried to convince him that freestanding letters hovering over a nearby line of evergreens would do the trick. This time we lost the rooftop-sign battle, but a few years later the site was surrounded by industrial buildings of every sort and any niceties of building graphics would have been overwhelmed. The company name can still be seen from the autobahn in spite of the new buildings built in the foreground, and our later addition to the warehouse has bold new graphics.

After his August 1972 recuperation on Cape Cod, Lajkó told his partners that on the advice of his doctors he was going to start slowing down a bit and proposed that he come into the office only for half days. Since his back pains woke him early, he tended to be in during the morning and return to New Canaan after lunch. Eventually, the daily commute got to be too much for him, and he and Connie moved back to the city. They sold their beloved stone house to Gerry Bratti, a masonry contractor who hired the firm to renovate and enlarge the house some years later. Herb did such a great job with it that Lajkó told him it was a better piece of architecture than when he had lived in it. (Of course, it helped that Gerry had more money to spend on it than Breuer had when he originally built it.)

Despite occasional health setbacks, Breuer began to feel stronger, and particularly after the move to the apartment on Sixty-third Street, he was spending more and more time in the office. His bad back made it difficult to walk any distance and also made for restless nights. He had strong sleeping pills, which he tended to avoid taking until absolutely necessary. Since that was often at four or five in the morning, he sometimes turned up very groggy at the office. He was stoic about the pain and would more often speak about it in the abstract than let on that he was hurting at the moment.

During the run of the Metropolitan Museum exhibition, we indulged in a flurry of business entertaining, and it did seem, for a while, that some new contacts were developing. We had a very interesting approach from Stratton Mountain in Vermont about doing some planning for a destination ski resort à la Flaine, and IBM Boca Raton seemed to be stirring as well. In addition to commissioning another assembly plant for Torin, this time in Australia, Rufus asked for yet another house. Breuer combined elements from the stick structure of his Wellfleet cottage with rubblestone painted white that warmed Tician's Greek heart as he worked on it. After happily living in it for several years, Rufus eventually moved back to his first house and asked Lajkó which, of the three, was his favorite, guessing that it would be the first. Breuer responded, "No, Rufus, it's the third. You got your nose too much into the first one . . ." Rufus was floored. He thought he had been an ideal client.

Sidney (Bill) Morrell had been brought to our attention as a public-relations consultant for Flaine in the United States in the 1960s, and we turned to this charming Australian for new-business advice. We were aware of a vague diplomatic life in his background, which turned out to be a spectacular career in the Office of Strategic Services, and a number of the staff that he put to work on our account seemed to have come from the same world.

By 1973 Flaine was in full operation, and the original group of buildings that surrounded the former small shelter was complete. More than five thousand skiers visited on an average winter weekend. Life in the main town square, called the Forum, was alive with cafés, ski shops, and ski schools

Emile Allais surrounded by skiers at Flaine, 1972. Most of those posing in this publicity photo were members of the original pioneering staff of instructors and shopkeepers including the Gatjes' au pair Marie-Jeanne Pouchelon.

*Flaine, 1972. At the
time of this photo-
graph the ski resort
was almost complete.*

Design discussion in Breuer's office. Lajkó, Claes Erickson, and Gatje review the model of the Hôtel Résidence.

sporting bright banners, umbrellas, and signposts. Sylvie Boissonnas was a bit nervous about the visual clutter and asked Lajkó if he thought all this was going overboard. "Not at all," said Lajkó. "It's just what I wanted and expected."

I was walking with Sylvie along the path at the edge of the lower slopes on a particularly brilliant Sunday, surrounded by happy visitors and their children. Although she herself was not a skier, she was well known to the community and, in her long fur coat, recognizable from a distance. I made a reference to all the years of troubles, now safely behind us, and suggested the joy it must give to her, knowing that she had, in effect, made Flaine possible. She responded, "Oh yes, it's marvelous seeing all these people enjoy themselves, but what is even better is seeing all of you men— Eric, Lajkó, Max, and yourself—finally vindicated in what you worked so hard to accomplish."

In 1982 Sylvie was interviewing me for a book to be written about Flaine, and we fell to reminiscing about the final size and shape of the resort as it was being completed. She said the best proof of its independence and stature was that when she moved about town she could now overhear the comments of tourists and shopkeepers with no fear of being recognized. She added, "Why, when I order something I even have to spell my name!"

The next step in the development of the valley was to build at the crest of the cliff that looked out over the Forum. The narrow plateau, known as Flaine Supérieur or Flaine Forêt, was only wide enough for a double line of

The Hôtel Résidence. This apartment hotel on the bluff at Flaine Forêt overlooks the center of town.

buildings on either side of the access road. In order to reduce the over-powering visual impact of a line of buildings along the top of the hill, tall hotels and apartment buildings, averaging eight or ten stories, were kept to the north or uphill side, while three- and four-story apartments climbed down the hill opposite on stilts; bridges connected their upper levels to the sidewalk. We developed the master plan in New York under Breuer's watchful but increasingly less-involved eye.

The first and largest hotel at the eastern end, the Hôtel Résidence, was softly Z-shaped in plan and organized as an apartment-hotel under the recently liberalized rules of the French Ministry of Tourism. Eric asked that we use more wood on the facade, partly because he wanted a different look above the town center. The main reason for the wood, however, was that the precasting plant was becoming increasingly expensive to operate with the fall-off in production as the annual building program slowed, and wood covered the rough character of poured-in-place concrete structures. The new hotel was developed within our architectural guidelines but without Lajkó's

The ecumenical chapel. Breuer broke all of his own rules at Flaine in this marvelous building.

direct input, and I was heartened to hear him say after it was built that he thought it was the best-looking building at Flaine. I was further pleased to hear that the Boissonnas family had sold their apartment in the town center in order to live in the penthouse of the Hôtel Résidence.

One of the last and best of Breuer's personal contributions to the town was the ecumenical chapel, which Eric finally found financing to support. It was built in the midst of a tall stand of dark pine trees that had been reserved for it from the inception of Flaine. When I heard that we had received the go-ahead, I immediately began gathering program data and assembling a design team. With some hesitation, but firm resolve, Breuer said simply, "No Bob, I want to do this one by myself." I immediately backed off, and he chose a draftsman from the crew. The jewel that they created was the exception to every architectural rule that we had established at Flaine. The structure was of wood, sheathed in an almost iridescent skin of black slate tiles. The walls inclined inward as they rose, and the forms that resulted intersected one another at surprising angles. Built in 1974, it could have belonged to the

1990s deconstructivist movement in architecture. I had never seen Lajkó sketch or talk about anything quite like it, and it was a source of great pride for him when the chapel was recognized as proof of his continuing inventiveness and vitality.

I'm not certain that Breuer ever got back to Flaine to see it finished. According to Sylvie, at one point during the last trip that he did make, they stopped to survey the whole valley from the approach road above. Lajkó said, "One can't see anything; that's good." Daniel Chiquet, who was on that same trip, as a courtesy took Lajkó around on a general tour of what had been built in the past year, knowing of his gradual retirement from direct involvement in the project. He was completely astonished at Breuer's familiarity with every detail of what he was being shown.

In order to minimize the need for vehicular connections between the upper and middle plateaus, we designed an inclined elevator—a sort of modern funicular—that continuously travels up and down between the two stations without an attendant. The red-orange cab has become something of a symbol of the resort. The design of its two stations was assigned to a new draftsman in the office, Claes Erickson, one of the brightest recent additions to our staff. We were shocked when his wife called one day to say that he was in Bellevue Hospital; he had been stabbed in the eye the night before at an East Side restaurant in a fight with a man who had been bothering her. It was clear that Claes would lose the sight in that eye, but we were heartened when, after a week or two, he was able to return to work on a part-time basis. Breuer was personally solicitous of his care and comfort. Two weeks later, however, an embolism, resulting from the trauma, suddenly took Claes's life. We were shattered. No urban violence had ever before intruded into the small family of our office.

In 1972 the European Investment Bank had commissioned a new headquarters in Luxembourg and was required by charter to hire an architect from the Common Market. The choice was Denys Lasdun, an English architect based in London. Breuer was selected as architectural adviser to the bank. Lajkó may have been given some off-the-record hint by the bank that it would have preferred him as its architect, but in any case, he entered the relationship with the impression that it was to be a collaboration and he prepared a scheme. According to Tician, the meetings went from bad to worse until a moment came when Breuer ordered Lasdun out of the office at the top of his voice. A scheme was finally completed and built by Lasdun, but Lajkó would have nothing more to do with the project.

In December 1974 Bill Morrell and Tician took an exploratory trip through the Middle East to scout new business possibilities through some of Bill's wartime contacts. Many other American architects were doing the same thing,

The Paris office, 1974. The staff is posed at the windows of 48 rue Chapon.

since business was very slow in the United States while the Arab economies were booming. The trip was quite successful, and after Tician made his report to the partners, it was decided to invest in sending him and Judy to live in Teheran for what turned out to be a year. Breuer was uneasy about the venture, but most of his architect friends were doing the same thing and he reasoned that they couldn't all be wrong. Tician left in March 1975.

Mario Jossa was running the Paris office very well, and the affection that Lajkó had felt for him on their first meeting developed into a professional relationship that only deepened with time. Breuer always considered his business trips to Europe as half holidays (as, frankly, did I), and he felt very much at home on the rue Chapon. His first order to Mario on arrival was invariably, "Let's organize a lunch for the office." This might mean taking everyone, including the secretaries, out to a restaurant commandeered for the occasion, or the spreading of a vast array of hors d'oeuvres over several drafting tables.

Breuer was often accompanied by Connie, especially while their daughter, Cesca, was at school in Switzerland. Mario acted as their chauffeur on trips to Holland and Switzerland to see old friends and clients. (Connie did not trust Lajkó's driving any more than the rest of us did.) Everywhere,

273

Lunch in the Paris office. Lajkó joins Harry Seidler (in the bow tie) and most of the staff in 1974.

Breuer was received as a visiting dignitary. But it was in Italy, where he was greeted as "maestro," that Mario felt most proud of the fuss that was made over Lajkó's arrival. A dinner with Mario's cardinal uncle caused some family flutter because Cesca had nothing but miniskirts with her, but the cardinal didn't seem to mind. A later dinner with Pier Luigi Nervi was threatened by a strike of waiters and busboys in Rome, but so great was the management's respect for the famous engineer that it opened his favorite restaurant to his honored guests for just one night.

On an earlier drive to Italy with Mario, Lajkó had insisted on taking the wheel and suggested the pass rather than the tunnel for crossing the Alps: "I know this pass like the back of my hand." Having apparently missed an early warning sign, they drove on through one hairpin turn after another—the snow by the side of the road getting deeper and deeper—until finally they were met with a barrier that told them, belatedly but definitively, that the pass was closed. Mario regained the driver's seat.

On these trips together, Mario felt that he got to know Breuer very well and had long discussions with him about history, cinema, and travel, but never about architecture or other architects, except as they might crop up in stories. Talking about the Bauhaus with Lajkó was always in terms of the parties or his bike trips with Herbert Bayer, never its influence on him or modernism. Mario felt, finally, that Lajkó considered the Bauhaus to be a "design" school and that he wanted to be thought of not as a designer but as an architect.

There came a time in the early 1970s when business in the Paris office was very slow, and Mario felt a twinge of conscience about drawing a handsome salary with little to show for it. It was also a point in his professional life when he was wondering whether he should be heading out on his own, possibly in association with some of his European friends. He discussed the matter with Breuer, who counseled against it. Lajkó wisely observed, "Mario, you don't know what a good thing you have going for you. We supply the capital and new business support. All you have to do is design. I never had that opportunity myself, and I would have welcomed it had it been offered." On reflection, Mario agreed and stayed in the position.

Harry Seidler had prospered in Australia and, as one of that country's leading architects, was a logical choice to design the new Australian embassy in Paris in 1973. The embassy staff had tentatively selected Bernard Zehrfuss, Breuer's old UNESCO partner, as his associate architect, but Harry rejected him after their first interview in Paris. He went to the rue Chapon to discuss the matter with Lajkó, who was fortuitously in town, and in a few hours the two of them hammered out the terms of a contract that was to lead to fruitful collaboration. The Australian government then had to be convinced that a partnership of "equals" who spoke the same architectural language would work. Harry's practice had been so strongly influenced by his studies alongside Breuer and his years in the office that the handsome building eventually built on the quai Branly resulted from a very happy and truly joint effort.

One of Harry's principal associates, Graham MacDonald, moved to Paris from Sydney and worked with Mario during the development of the design. It began with Harry's site plan of two opposed semicircles and incorporated some very Breueresque window patterns together with marvelously warped columns and canopies descended from the hand of the late Pier Luigi Nervi via his sons. (Harry had met Nervi many years before and had employed him as his structural engineer for several huge projects in Australia. They both spoke German but had to use an interpreter since Nervi, after the Nazis blew up his great airplane hanger in Rome, swore never again to speak German.) Over all the years that I have known Harry, I have never seen him angry or heard him raise his voice. But according to Mario, Harry's mercurial temper punctuated the calm of rue Chapon on many occasions during the process of working out the design, whenever neither Breuer nor his partners were present.

I happened to be in Paris at the time of the springtime grand opening of the embassy and had been warned by Mario to bring black tie for the festivities, which were to include the French minister of culture, André Malraux. Graham MacDonald picked me up in a taxi at my hotel, and I was amused to see that he was wearing a bright red sweater under his dinner jacket. The practical Aussie had noticed that the evening was getting cold, and most of the ceremonies were to be out of doors.

The wife of the ambassador to France who was chosen to live in the elegant new chancery loved the French antiques of her old residence on the rue Las-Cases and hated all the new Knoll furniture that Harry had selected for their top-floor residence overlooking the Seine. It was actually a magnificent apartment with huge rooms, splendid fireplaces, glorious views, and paintings by Australia's most prominent young artists. But she would have none of it. There were several sheltered courtyards in the midst of the enormous apartment that were open to the Paris skies, and before long a couple of important pieces of modern furniture had been left out in a courtyard to be ruined by rain. When word of this got back to Harry in Sydney, he was enraged and, with the help of his political friends, had parliament pass a law making it a federal offense to harm government property, including most especially the furnishings of overseas embassies. The ambassador and his wife were shortly thereafter transferred to a more traditional post.

While Tician was in Iran, and I continued shuttling back and forth to Europe, Ham was working with Breuer on a visitors' center for the Grand Coulee Dam. The original scheme was a magnificent muscular monster raised up on huge legs to improve the view. It was immortalized in one of the most beautiful teak models displayed in the Metropolitan Museum exhibition. Unfortunately, it exceeded the budget set by the Bureau of Reclamation, and a more modest structure had to be substituted. Ham also co-authored a couple of smaller projects for the American Press Institute in Reston, Virginia (1971), and the Clarksburg Library in West Virginia (1973), his wife's hometown.

During 1974 Herb was busy finishing several projects. These included the headquarters for the Department of Health, Education and Welfare (HEW) in Washington; a residential hideaway for one of our old clients at the Esalin Institute in Big Sur, California; and the design, largely on his own, of the Strom Thurmond Federal Office Building and U.S. Courthouse in Columbia, South Carolina, a commission he had won with the vigorous help of friends made at the GSA after all his good work on HUD and HEW.

Breuer had always encouraged my participation in the American Institute of Architects although he was not interested in any of its committee work. He recognized the value it had for the profession and particularly praised its standard forms of contract and the annual awards program, in which he figured often and prominently. In the autumn of 1967 I was elected to the executive committee of the New York Chapter and served on it for several years before eventually being named the chapter's president in 1975.

I was in Atlanta in May 1974 for the national AIA convention, just about to start my year as president of the New York Chapter. I was also being inducted as a fellow of the institute. One of Breuer's old friends in the AIA had nominated all of Lajkó's partners as fellows, and we were all eventually so honored for the design work that we had done at Lajkó's side.

One of the more colorful characters Judy and Tician met in Teheran was a Redi-Mix concrete contractor named Bahman Batmangalidg. His father was Turkish but had moved to Iran to make his fortune in building, and "Batman," as we called him, was determined to multiply the money he had inherited by entering the development business. He had already built himself a flashy mansion on the northern, fashionable edge of town complete with a glass-walled swimming pool that could be seen from his bar and was embarked on a joint venture with General Aghaghian to develop a ski resort on Mount Tochal, which loomed over Teheran in the Elburz mountain range. General Aghaghian, the minister of tourism, derived his considerable political clout from having taken a bullet intended for Shah Reza Pahlavi and was the only Christian in the cabinet. I found his steely blue eyes totally intimidating and often said he was great to have as a friend and ally but I never would have wanted to have him as an enemy. Although Tician had no drafting force in Teheran, we accepted the commission to design a luxury hotel. We had always planned to send any work that he landed back to New York for design, and I was assigned to work on the project.

Batman drove me to see the site he had chosen for the first of his ski hotels on a plateau high above the city that was perhaps one-third the way up Mount Tochal. The sun was going down, and he was playing a cassette of *La Bohème* at full blast in his top-down convertible Mercedes as we wound up the hairpin turns of the dirt construction road. The view was breathtaking when we wheeled onto the rough-graded site. The project called for a long, low resort hotel with a swimming pool and tennis courts that would

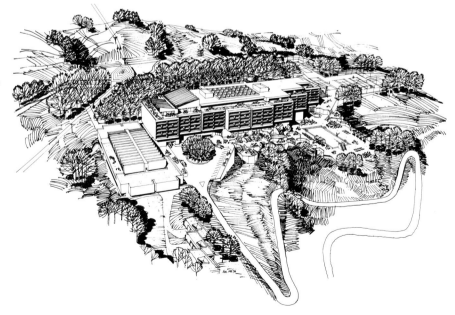

The hotel for Mount Tochal, Teheran. Larry Perron drew Batman's dream.

277

largely be hidden by the brow of the plateau when viewed from the city below. Access was to be via a *téléphérique* that would start at a parking field at the base of the mountain and, after one stop at the hotel, take visitors up to a panoramic ski pavilion at the top of the mountain.

Construction on the pavilion, which was not part of our job, eventually got underway, and I heard General Aghaghian describe the delivery of the trapezoidal panels of double-glazing at the summit by military helicopter. One of the panels was cracked, and I shuddered to think of the fate of the guilty party at the hands of the general.

Another Middle Eastern assignment that Tician and I shared long distance in the late 1970s was the assembly of a team of consultants to go after a large USAID-financed planning job for the government of Egypt. The project involved the creation of an entirely new satellite city along the Nile delta just outside Cairo—Sadat City. Tician had heard about the job on his tour with Bill Morrell, and with Baltimore-based Wallace McHarg & Roberts as our principal planning consultant, we became one of the finalists. We landed the assignment to design Sadat City and were in the process of drawing up contracts when we were suddenly confronted with the "Arab Boycott" clause, which simply stated that we had never worked for the state of Israel (which was true) but obviously implied much more. We reluctantly signed, but Wallace McHarg balked and dropped out at the last possible moment. The only other American planning firm that I had any personal knowledge of was headed by my old friend Dave Crane, who had been unceremoniously fired from our firm years before by Breuer. I had heard from Wallace McHarg on a Friday afternoon and called Breuer at home to see if he had any problem with taking the Crane firm on board. He had completely forgotten Dave Crane and raised no objection. That Saturday morning I was on the telephone to Houston where I finally found Dave in his office at Rice University and proposed our deal. By Monday his partners had agreed to take on the job, and our team was once again complete. It would be months before all the specialized personnel required were assembled and ready to start work.

I left New York in February 1976 for Flaine, a new-business interview with the U.S. Army Corps of Engineers in Livorno, Italy, and eventually Teheran. The drawings and model of our schematic design for the Mount Tochal project had been shipped ahead, and we had only to hope that General Aghaghian would be able to clear them quickly through customs. Rumors from other professional friends practicing in Iran spoke of months of delay in clearances for those without pull. When my plane taxied to the Teheran airport in an unusually heavy downpour, I saw acres of packing crates sitting unprotected on the tarmac and shuddered.

Just in case the model was damaged in transit, I had in my suitcase three small bottles of lacquer in the colors we had used for the site, roads, and facade. While sitting in Batman's office waiting for the arrival of the model (the general's henchmen had been alerted and were furiously scurrying around trying to find the crate), I told Batman that, despite the careful taping of the bottle tops, one of my T-shirts, which had been meant to shelter them, was stained in tan, gray, and ivory. Batman assured me that I could bill him for the T-shirt and told the following story while we waited: "When I was learning the ropes in my dad's firm, a crusty old Dane supervised the batching plant and always wore a gray fedora while working. One day, it slipped from his head and into the swirling mass of concrete below. Next month, his expense account ended with 'one hat' charged at a nominal value. I was working as comptroller and struck the hat from the total before reimbursement. Next month it was back on the list and I struck it again. The third month it wasn't on the list of expenses, but my Danish foreman had written at the bottom: 'The hat's in there, but you'll never find it.'"

The model finally turned up in good shape, and the project received enthusiastic approval from our client. Preparation of the working drawings was held up by administrative and financial problems. After the 1979 revolution that deposed the shah, Batman would flee to Los Angeles with little more than his life. Of course, we knew nothing of that then, and the rest of my time in Teheran was booked with parties and dinners given by the enormous expatriate American architectural community, of which Judy and Tician were honored members.

One night after a dinner party, we all went to the home of Nazreen Frampton—the head of city planning for Teheran and the former wife of the architectural historian Ken Frampton, whom I did not know at the time. We talked through the night about the magical transformation that was soon to ensure that women in Moslem Iran would be catapulted to a position of equality never seen even in the West.

After that late night, Judy, Tician, and I were lingering over breakfast when the telephone rang. It was Lajkó calling from New York to announce his decision to retire from the firm, effective at the end of February. A recent visit to his cardiologists had convinced him that he had to choose between an absolute end to the tensions of professional life and an increase in heart problems that would end his life. It was a defining moment, but at the time we were all reasonably relaxed about it. Breuer had been withdrawing gradually but steadily from the day-to-day operations of the firm, and we were confident of our ability to keep it going. It was certainly preferable to have our old friend and mentor extend his life in ease and honor rather than slump over the drafting table one day sooner than necessary.

Our lawyers and accountants drew up the appropriate papers shortly after my return to New York a week later, and Judy and Tician came home in April 1976. We had a farewell luncheon for Lajkó, and from then on he would drop by the office as a visitor or we would go to see him at his apartment, frequently bringing along some project or other to receive his ready blessing.

279

The partnership shortly after Breuer's retirement. Standing around Lajkó are Ham, Mario, Herb, Tician, and Bob.

MBA Without Breuer: 1976–1981

The character of the office without Breuer did not change immediately. We had become gradually used to the fact that he was not always there, not always available for counsel or decisions, and we had learned in that case to simply make the choices on our own and check back with him when we could. The possibility of his death or retirement, which had loomed over our heads as a dread event many years before—one that we had discussed with him in terms of insurance and the partnership agreement—had, by the time he was seventy-four, become an event for which we were all largely prepared.

Most of the office staff had never known the easy, personal contact with Lajkó that had been characteristic of the earlier, smaller offices. They were part of a team, and their loyalties were to a tradition of high-quality design and the partners with whom they worked.

When potential clients asked about any continued personal involvement on Breuer's part, we spoke of twenty years of work together (which was true and relevant) and his occasional visits to the office (which was misleading and largely irrelevant). Within the first year, we were to have evidence of the wisdom of Lajkó's doctors' advice.

Harry Parker was an old friend of mine from Bedford who had moved from his post at the Metropolitan Museum of Art to become the director of the Dallas Museum of Art. Before moving away, he had told me of his hopes of building a new museum with Breuer as his architect. By the time Harry was settled and had his fund-raising in place, Breuer was retired and I had to tell Harry that, although we could not promise Breuer's personal involvement, the office would be happy to take on the assignment. Harry explained that, however much he might trust the abilities of our firm, he had to deal with a headstrong group of trustees who would demand the personal services of a "name" architect. The story did not end there. In 1978 Harry hired the architect, critic, and writer Peter Blake as his professional adviser. Peter was one of Connie and Lajkó's oldest friends and was the author of two books about his work. He conjured up the possibility that Breuer might be hired to work on the design of the museum by himself, with only such drafting help as he might need, and then turn the job over to us for the execution of working drawings on a no-questions-asked basis. This would, it was hoped, relieve Lajkó of the stress of arguing over or even discussing the process of design with his partners—rather like the way he had produced the chapel at Flaine, although this would, of course, be a much bigger and more complex program. Lajkó called us for a lunch appointment after discussing all this with Peter and outlined the proposal to his sympathetic, though slightly skeptical, former partners. We knew that we could try to make the process as smooth as possible, but we also knew of the inevitable tensions that accompany any vital act of creation. We had just barely begun to discuss the matter after he had left when we received a call from Lajkó at home. He announced that it couldn't possibly work, that just the effort of explaining things to us had been so great a strain on him that he had returned home with strong pains of angina. So Peter and Harry turned to Ed Barnes, who would design a fine building for them.

Partners' lunches had always been presided over by Breuer, and design work was assigned to a single partner who would work with him. All that had to change. We created a rotating post of managing partner, and each of us accepted specialized administrative responsibilities: Ham Smith was in charge of finances; I dealt with our lawyers and public-relations counsel and led our graphics efforts; Herb Beckhard managed personnel hiring and firing; and Tician Papachristou took care of new business and contracts. More important were the personality strains that gradually became apparent in the years that followed. It was as if we had all been brothers—sons to one strong father who kept us together despite underlying sibling rivalries. Now suddenly we were free to design the way each of us might want to, to run the office in what we might consider the most efficient fashion. Decisions often were delayed by tie votes, although there were at first no predictable alliances. New projects were assigned to the partner who had the most available time, with a second partner available, when asked, as a critic. The crit was rarely requested. Some projects came into the office through the personal activities and acquaintances of one of the partners, and that partner, of course, got first crack at the design. Herb was probably the most active and successful of us in this regard. Tician and I often found ourselves the arbiters in the personal disputes that grew more and more evident between Ham and Herb. Still, to outward appearances, we remained a closely knit team with several years of successful practice ahead of us.

Mario had been running the Paris office since Eric's departure, although I was the titular head after Breuer's retirement, having achieved membership in the Ordre des Architectes Français long before Mario was able to unscramble his Italian, American, and French credentials. At our invitation, he joined the partnership in 1977; in 1980 he bought the Paris practice from us after we decided to abandon that distant outpost.

The space we occupied on the twelfth floor of 635 Madison Avenue had gradually shrunk in response to the falloff in business, but in 1979, after Breuer's retirement, Herb landed the commission for a two-million-square-foot manufacturing plant for Philip Morris in Concord, North Carolina (our competition included the likes of SOM and HOK), and we had to rent new space on another floor. Staff size gradually grew to over fifty, and before our lease ran out in 1980—and a huge rent increase was announced—we started to look elsewhere. Our Madison Avenue landlord claimed that the informally dressed architects were making his elevators look déclassé, even though he had thrived for years on the presence in the building of the staffers who ran the *National Lampoon*.

We found raw loft space on Twenty-sixth Street at the top of Madison Square Park and moved into our grand new quarters in June 1980. We had designed several new, massive granite tables for the space; the granite bases were based on an egg-crate interlock that Lajkó had used for a low coffee table at Madison Avenue. The Cold Springs Granite Company in Saint Cloud, Minnesota, made them for us at cost, remembering our work on Saint John's Abbey. International Contract Furnishings (ICF) marketed the tables for several years, and we earned some royalties from sales to others who also admired heavy granite. The day we had to move in the two halves of the conference-room tabletop was memorable for the three or four heart-stopping inches that the freight elevator dropped when each half was rolled into the cab. We had calculated the dead load of the table and determined that the floor was adequate to support it, but no one had asked about the elevator, which was surely overstressed.

The office stretched from Twenty-sixth to Twenty-seventh Street, and there was so much distance between offices, which overlooked the park and the Flatiron Building, and the back of the drafting room that we seriously considered an overhead public-address system so that our secretaries could find us. We decided that this would give too institutional an image and settled on beepers instead.

In giving written credit for the design of buildings, Lajkó had always insisted upon the names of the two partners involved—Marcel Breuer and Hamilton Smith, for example (even though the press always wrote of "Breuer's Whitney")—and he restricted the use of the firm name to stationery, contracts, and so forth. He had agreed long before that we could continue to use his name after he had left the firm, but we did make a subtle shift from "Marcel Breuer and Associates" to "Marcel Breuer Associates" soon after he retired. Paris had always been "Marcel Breuer Architecte." When we moved to our new office, we decided to invest in new publicity brochures and asked our old friend Ivan Chermayeff for a graphic overhaul. He came up with a stencil-inspired "MBA" logo and designed a delightful announcement. The letters were cut out of the card, and the pieces fell into the lap of the person who opened the envelope. For our opening party invitation Ivan conceived a variant from which confetti fell. Breuer was too sick to make the trip downtown for the party and never did see the space that we had described to him so proudly.

Our new logo. Ivan Chermayeff designed the stenciled letters for the new firm that would carry on without Lajkó for five more years.

In order to show off our new office and maintain professional relations with some of our fellow architects, the partners invited one or two colleagues for lunch in our impressive conference room on a biweekly basis. Among the first were Philip Johnson and John Burgee, in March 1981. As usual, Philip led an engaging and outrageous discussion of what was going on in the profession. At one point he turned to Ham and mentioned the ongoing search for an architect to extend the Whitney Museum of American Art: "Of course, they should give *you* the commission—you're the logical choice." Coming at a time when we knew from other sources that he was one of the strongest lobbyists for Michael Graves, we were shocked, but not surprised, by his duplicity.

Although Ham was not chosen for the Whitney, he did work on important new commissions for the Richard B. Russell Dam on the Savannah River and for NYU while finishing the Atlanta library. Tician moved to Paris and Cairo for a while during the design of Sadat City and a big hotel in Bahrain. Herb had his hands full with Philip Morris and a new headquarters building for Merk Sharpe & Dohme.

I had returned to Boca Raton in 1978, and we designed an additional one and a half million square feet of building before IBM's needs leveled off. There were also assorted adventures in Sinai as we drew up a master plan for its tourism development. Flaine continued to add to its stock of hotels and apartments, and I saw Mario regularly in Paris.

I used to visit Lajkó and Connie on Sixty-third Street once a month or so. Sometimes they would have a small party of old friends; more often it was just a casual drink. On occasion I would bring along some photos or draw-

The new office of MBA. Our reception area looked out on Twenty-sixth Street.

MBA's drafting room. The old loft building on Twenty-sixth Street easily lent itself to the creation of a large, informal workplace.

ings so that he could see progress on projects that he had started; in some cases they were buildings that he never knew. Conversation was easy, with none of the pressures of our former professional relationship. I felt that I was finally able to show, by tone of voice or perhaps a touch on his shoulder, the very real affection that I felt for this marvelous man. I think he had always considered me a bit uptight for his taste and once inscribed a book he was presenting for Christmas "to Generalissimo Bob Gatje"—I took it as a compliment at the time, considering it praise for the valor with which I defended his ideas. But now that we could relax a bit and discuss real life—like the women I was dating (Barbara and I were separated and divorced in 1981)—we were free to open up to one another, much as a father and son toward the end of a competitive life together. I don't remember any breathtaking insights, just a warmth that had been inappropriate in the office setting.

Breuer's office maintained its vibrant activity after his retirement in part because he had assembled a good team to which many important clients remained loyal. While we enjoyed the practice, its founder was increasingly troubled by heart and circulatory problems.

Rufus Stillman attended his old friend during Breuer's final illness, which became severe after 1980. The two often played chess. Ruf noted, "He always won. He wasn't competitive and was always pleasant to play with. Not a great chess player, but . . ." The two drove to the River Café in Brooklyn "for a scotch," and Breuer, looking at the World Trade Center towers, reminisced about the Nazis and Russians competing with the height of their towers at the Paris Exposition just before World War II. According to Ruf, "It was a bad time at the end."

I paid my last visit to Lajkó one evening in late spring. He was confined to bed and barely able to lift a seemingly transparent hand in greeting. Even though I had been forewarned by Connie and Lajkó's doctors, I was shaken when I saw him. Breuer died on July 1, 1981. His photograph was on the front page of the *New York Times* the next morning; his family asked for privacy in the days that followed.

Christopher Wilk had been preparing an exhibition of Breuer's furnishings and interiors for the Museum of Modern Art with Lajkó's reluctant participation. The last thing Breuer wanted toward the close of his life was a major show of a part of his career that he had thought was behind him. The exhibition opened in July, just after his death. It was a distinguished show, and Wilk's accompanying catalog is a major contribution to the scholarly record of Breuer's career. Philip Johnson made some belittling comments about Lajkó's stature as an architect at the opening banquet that deeply offended his partners but especially Connie and made her wish she had followed her original inclination to decline the invitation when she heard that he was to be the principal speaker.

A memorial was held at the Whitney Museum on September 21, and Ham, who had been chosen by the partners to speak for us, delivered a fine professional eulogy. Rufus, speaking from his heart on his long-time friendship with Lajkó, offered most beautiful words. Stan Abercrombie and I were invited to speak at the Smithsonian's tribute to Breuer in Washington, D.C., on October 14. My remarks included the following:

"Stan and I thought we should divide our subject between 'Breuer: His Work' and 'Breuer: The Man.' Only when I sat down to organize my thoughts did it dawn on me how difficult it would be to separate the man from his work. It couldn't be done while he was alive, and it can't be done after his death.

"He was, of course, a most complex man—how could it have been otherwise? He did, however, have a remarkable facility for coming on simple. He was soft-spoken and genuinely kind, with a low threshold of tolerance for the pompous. He spoke English and French with a heavy Hungarian/German accent but he wrote the English language with the care and clarity he used in putting building materials together . . . He was a great movie fan and teller of tales sprinkled with old-world proverbs and a good sense of history. All of my friends who met him casually found him modest, unassuming, and very approachable . . . The monks who chose him as their architect . . . admitted . . . that it was because they found him so humble and straightforward.

"If all of the above is true—and it is—it's only part of the story. Well camouflaged, and controlled by a will of iron, was a very considerable ego. He did not suffer criticism gladly and, in fairness, rarely criticized the work of others. He exacted the highest professional standards from those who worked with him. He was firm with his draftsmen, often stern toward his partners, tough only on himself . . .

"Tom Wolfe takes the Bauhaus leaders to task for their rigorous Puritanism, and in a way, he has a point. Breuer had a good sense of humor, but he never joked about architecture. It was something akin to a sacred calling, and he felt a terrible sense of responsibility to his clients and his place in history. His shapes are always strong—he even called some of them grotesque—and all grew out of the inner logic of the architectural program as Breuer perceived it—not always correctly and not always consistently, but assuredly true to his professional bargain. He looked for inspiration in the details of program or site—and then let forms grow under one of the greatest critical eyes and imaginations we will ever know. If the forms were without precedent, all the better, and the materials, in sumptuous juxtaposition, are either from his very varied experience or an extension of the surrounding urban environment . . . The creative process would start with his intuitive suggestion and usually end with its logical derivative.

"He was not a particularly good draftsman himself, but he admired good drawing and was pleased that he had attracted a group of talented designers who could produce a set of drawings of which he could be proud. I remember once going over some old archives with him. We came upon an original drawing of one of his famous houses with the initials 'MB' on the title block. He looked at it wistfully, criticized the draftsmanship, and remarked, 'I could never have gotten a job in this office . . .'

"He was obviously a man of many contrasts who lived a long and productive life during which his work passed through many phases, always inventive, always inquiring. The early experiments in light, taut furniture and his travels by freighter along the North African coast led to an infatuation with ship's rigging, skeletal construction, and asymmetric superstructure that found its natural expression in the balloon framing that he discovered in America. A whole generation of famous, spare wood houses was the result, and they revolutionized contemporary domestic architecture. This was followed by a series of glass curtain walls in which he experimented with solar shading devices . . . But there was something unsatisfactory to his sculptural soul in these light, ephemeral facades, and it was in concrete that he seemed most at home. This facility with concrete dates from what he called the most successful collaboration of his life—his work with Pier Luigi Nervi on UNESCO. The folded concrete plate was to be a recurring theme.

"Breuer didn't invent precast concrete but he became one of its most sophisticated users. It let him buy shape and shadow within most clients' budget . . . Although precast concrete remained an important part of his palette to the end, no one can doubt that he found his greatest joy and some of his greatest success in the use of stone—from the native rubble fieldstone of New England to the shaped granite skins of Saint John's and the Whitney and the slate shingling of his gemlike chapel at Flaine."

I have little to add to my summary thoughts of that evening almost twenty years ago. Their sad tone has been deepened over time by the changing fashions of architectural criticism and the shortness of memory. I cannot accept that the name of Marcel Breuer and his works, which resonate so vividly in my mind, should have faded so markedly from the public scene. Friends say that we have only to wait for the time of reevaluation. Perhaps the time is now.

Marcel Breuer, 1979.

Epilogue

Marcel Breuer and Associates became Marcel Breuer Associates after Lajkó's retirement, and although he had specifically given us permission to use his name in perpetuity, we respected Connie's report that he had regretted that promise during his illness; the firm thereafter became MBA. The practice held up for a while as commissions came in from old friends at the DeMatteis Organization, Millipore Corporation, Purdue Frederick Company, and IBM, as well as from new contacts at General Electric, Xerox, and the U.S. State Department. But gradually the level of activity declined to the point where we had to give up our handsome new office. Chermayeff and Geismar took it over and still use it.

Herb Beckhard had left the partnership in November 1982, and in 1983 we became Gatje Papachristou Smith in shared office space on lower Fifth Avenue. The early 1980s were not particularly prosperous for the profession, and we hung together much longer than we should have in the hopes that one project or another was just about to go ahead. Most reluctantly, the partnership dissolved in 1986, and we each went our separate ways.

With little in the way of work in the mid-1980s, many architects who were eager to overthrow the modern movement rather than correct its excesses wrote and spoke with the same polemical purpose as the modernists before them who had sought to demolish the tired tradition of the Beaux-Arts. This frequently included unnecessarily personal attacks on the giants of modernism, including Breuer.

Of all the affronts to Lajkó's professional reputation and achievement that followed after his death during the benighted heyday of postmodernism, nothing rankled his friends and admirers as much as the intention of the Whitney Museum in 1985 to expand its building under the architectural direction of Michael Graves—an avowed anti-modernist who was to be shown to be unsympathetic to the qualities of the building he set out to destroy aesthetically.

The former Breuer partners were no doubt especially disappointed to see Ham Smith, co-architect of the original building, passed over in the awarding of the commission to expand it, but there was no self-interest in the howl of protest that arose from many quarters following the springtime publication of the first of Graves's several proposals. This was a gaudy collage of historicist allusions that spanned the entire block along Madison Avenue from Seventy-third to Seventy-fourth Street and enveloped the original building in a hostile embrace.

Aside from uncoordinated telephone calls and commiseration among alumni of the office, I was aware of no organized opposition to the project until I received a phone call from Arthur Rosenblatt inviting us all to a meeting at Carl Stein's Greenwich Village apartment in mid-May 1985. Arthur had a good instinct for publicity and civic action, and he was also the president of the New York Chapter of the AIA.

Abraham W. Geller, then one of the grand old men of our profession, was to receive the Gold Medal of the AIA's New York Chapter at its annual meeting a few days later, and he was an enthusiastic contributor to the discussion that night as we began to compare notes and consider alternate strategies. We were far from convinced that there was any way to block a private owner from ruining its own building no matter how strongly we all felt about it. It was still too "young" to be landmarked.

It was at about that point that Arthur announced that Abe Geller, a shy, soft-spoken gentleman, had an announcement to make. Abe explained that he felt so strongly about the injustice that was about to be visited upon Lajkó's masterpiece that he had decided to denounce the action as the main topic in his acceptance speech at the chapter meeting. We were stunned and thrilled to think that this fine architect would chose to deflect attention away from himself at a crowning moment in his professional life in order to speak for Lajkó in defense of the Whitney.

George Lewis had been Lajkó's student at Harvard and had worked in his office in Cambridge for a time. He was the executive director of the New York Chapter of the AIA for many years, and we had strengthened our friendship during my term as the chapter's president in 1975. While not in attendance at the inaugural meeting of what was later to become known as the Ad Hoc Committee to Save the Whitney, George got wind of the activity and specifically of Abe's intention to speak out at the chapter meeting. Although he may have agreed with our credo, George, by reason of his necessarily apolitical role in the chapter, would never have taken public sides in the debate over Graves's project, which was soon to become very heated. He did feel strongly, however, that Abe's plan was ill-advised and inappropriate to its setting in the midst of an annual meeting usually marked by nonjudgmental camaraderie. He also felt that Abe would be doing himself a disservice at a moment of personal honor, and in the course of a long and persuasive telephone call the next night, he convinced Abe to abandon his plan. Abe called Arthur to tell him of his change of heart and began rewriting his speech.

Arthur called me and we both agreed that George was wrong in his timid counsel to Abe. Arthur took on the responsibility of convincing Abe to pursue his valiant gesture. I tried to make sure that Abe's statement would not be wasted. By ten o'clock the next morning, I heard that Abe would proceed, and within the next few hours I had photocopied a few hundred stickers that read "SAVE THE WHITNEY." I also notified a friend at the *New York Times* that, unlike the usual AIA annual meetings, there might be a newsworthy event under the vaulted arches of the Fifty-ninth Street bridge abutment, the meeting's location in 1985.

George Lewis died in 1993, and I never did have the heart to tell him where all the sticky lapel labels had come from at the last minute. When Abe stood up before his audience, he not only saw friendly, admiring faces but also knew from their stickers that they were in agreement with him. Nor did George understand why a *New York Times* reporter had been assigned to cover what was usually such a humdrum affair.

What followed were many public meetings, harsh debates, and articles and critiques of the project, which was revised and resubmitted twice. I. M. Pei told me later of many strategy sessions in Connie Breuer's apartment where Lajkó's old friends decided how best to band together and give public voice to their outrage. Somewhere along the line, the trustees of the Whitney gave up, perhaps at the realization that raising construction funds would be difficult in such a contentious atmosphere. The museum's director lost his job, probably for other reasons, but some trustees were known to have blamed him for getting them into the whole mess.

The Whitney Museum of American Art today stands proudly on Madison Avenue exactly as Lajkó envisioned it, and the lovely old brownstones, so dear to Helena Rosenthal's heart, stand next to it just the way the Friends of the Upper East Side want them to. Recent renovations to one of the brownstones owned by the Whitney, as well as the conversion of the Whitney's top floor to galleries, seem to suggest that space needs can be solved and that the threat to the building is past. A festive thirtieth-birthday party at the Whitney recently reunited many of the original participants—Connie Breuer, Mike Irving and his former wife, Flora, and Lajkó's four partners, Ham, Herb, Tician, and Bob.

Dramatis Personae

Stanley Abercrombie Stan had architecture degrees from the Georgia Institute of Technology and MIT before coming to work for the Breuer firm. He received a masters degree in city planning from Columbia University after leaving the office and worked for some time for John Carl Warnecke. Then he was offered an editorial post at the new *Architecture Plus*, founded by Breuer's friend and biographer Peter Blake. The longtime editor of *Interior Design*, Stan is one of America's most respected architectural journalists. *Interviewed July 8, 1996, in Sonoma, California*

Emile Allais Born in Val d'Isère the son of a local cheese merchant, Emile was a self-taught skier. He became a French national champion and Olympic star, transforming the sport of skiing with his revolutionary technique of shoulder rotation. He became one of the leading consultants in the layout of trails and lift equipment and is credited with the overall design of the ski areas at Squaw Valley, Courchevel, and Telluride among many others. Television viewers of the winter Olympics at Grenoble in 1968 will remember references to the dreaded "Allais bumps."

Lily van Ameringen Auchincloss Lily first met Lajkó and Connie at Cambridge through Philip Johnson while she was a student at Radcliffe College and remained a very close friend—"almost a member of the family," according to Connie. Shortly before her death, she spoke fondly of her long friendship with the Breuers and remembered baby-sitting Tamas, especially Ise Gropius's suggestion that she put his head in the oven if he cried too much. She often went to the movies with the Breuers; although Lajkó was an avowed fan, he was known to snore in the theater. When she first joined the office in the late 1950s, she was introduced as someone to handle public relations. Lily dismissed her prowess as a contact person and didn't stay long in the job. She commented later, "I asked for a job and Lajkó felt sorry for me." *Interviewed July 24, 1995, in New York*

Jean Barets His engineering group—what the French call a *bureau d'études techniques* (BET)—was named after him and abbreviated by everyone as COFEBA. Breuer welcomed the chance to work with the Barets system of prefabricated concrete, in part because it permitted the creation of facade panels that were thick rather than thin and that could be sculpted in depth to provide the deep shadows that Lajkó preferred. Barets would occasionally appear at design team meetings—he was a dour, nervous figure—but more often than not, he would send his lieutenants, of whom the one I got to know best was Pierre Lamy. He drove a tiny Citroën deux-chevaux with absolute abandon and was usually the one assigned to pick me up at Orly Airport on arrival from New York. We would drive at breakneck speed through the early-morning rush hour to a meeting at the SEPAD office on the rue de Villersexel.

Belva Jane Barnes For all the flamboyant impact that B.J. had upon my introduction to the Breuer office and the fact that we worked together for three years, she has turned out to be one of the most elusive characters to pin down in a thumbnail biography. She grew up in Ann Arbor, Michigan, and her mother was the inventor of the Daisy air rifle. It would seem logical that she would have attended architecture school at the University of Michigan, and most of her old friends so assert, but the university has no record of her in their alumnae rolls. She had worked for many of the best architectural firms in New York City before joining Breuer and had been the only woman among the "back-room boys" who labored all night for Wallace Harrison and George Dudley between the design sessions for the United Nations Headquarters Building. After leaving our office, she returned to work for Harrison on the Metropolitan Opera House and married Arvin Shaw, a well-known architect, who took her on a round-the-world cruise. She died of cancer shortly afterward.

Edward Larrabee Barnes Ed was a great friend of Breuer's from the time they met when Ed was teaching at the Milton Academy in Massachusetts. His long and distinguished career shows much of what he learned afterward at Harvard under Breuer. *Quotations from a letter of August 25, 1995, and an interview in the fall 1995 GSD News*

Herbert Beckhard Herb volunteered in 1951 to work in the office without salary: "Hell, I would have had to *pay* to go to Harvard . . ." Herb was working on the Levy house when I arrived, and as he has written, he worked on many of Breuer's residences. Trained in architecture at Pennsylvania State University, he was a ranking tournament tennis player long before it became fashionable in the architectural profession to be a "jock." *Interviewed December 1, 1995, in New York*

Christine Benglia Born in Paris after her actor-father had emigrated from Algeria, Christine was schooled at the Ecole des Beaux-Arts in Paris and at the Illinois Institute of Technology in Chicago. She was introduced to Lajkó by the Parisian architect Edouard Albert, who had designed an elegant modern steel facade on the rue Jouffroy in the seventeenth arrondissement. Breuer had noticed it when passing in a taxi and had tracked Albert down just to tell him how much he admired the building. Christine started work for Lajkó in 1960 and spent two periods with us separated by six months at Ed Barnes's office. She left in 1966 after her request to be assigned to Paris was turned down, moved to Vollmer Associates while preparing for her licensing exam, and married Alistair Bevington, an English associate of Ed Barnes's. She was very close to all the Breuers—Lajkó, Connie, Tom, Cesca, and Cairo the poodle—and spent a great deal of time at their homes in New Canaan and Wellfleet. She says that Lajkó didn't take himself too seriously; she considered him warm, friendly, and unassuming. She also considered Connie to be the perfect, refined complement and commented on the gentle, fluid jazz she played on the piano. When the Breuers moved to New York from New Canaan, they presented Christine and Alistair with a huge avocado tree that had been in their home for years. It was placed in the Bevingtons' high-ceilinged loft at Broadway and Thirteenth Street. When Connie and Lajkó came to dinner shortly thereafter, their hosts tied a couple of avocados to the barren tree—an effective and surprising joke. *Interviewed October 7, 1995, in New York*

Frédéric Berlottier Trained as a civil engineer, Fred had worked for the French government for nine years on reconstruction work after World War II and then in the private sector, which brought him back to his native mountains. In 1959 he had just moved his family to Grenoble when Pierre Carpentier, a government figure, helped bring the Boissonnas family to Flaine. Carpentier told Fred of an opportunity that "would fit you like a glove." Eric Boissonnas made Berlottier the technical director of the semi-public company he established in order to gain control of the land in the valley of Flaine. The grandest ski trail of all, leading down off the Grandes Platières, was named "la Fred" after his retirement. *Interviewed January 26, 1996, in Paris*

Eric and Sylvie Boissonnas The two were French but had lived in New Canaan, Connecticut, for twelve years where Lajkó and Connie were neighbors. Eric, a geophysicist by training and an organist by avocation, was an executive in the Schlumberger oil-exploration firm, which had been founded by Sylvie's father, Conrad, and her uncle, Marcel. Sylvie and Eric had initially lived in Houston for two years, after which it was decided that Schlumberger would build a research laboratory in Ridgefield, Connecticut, with Eric at its head. The building was designed by Philip Johnson, as was the residence the young couple commissioned in New Canaan. This famous house was notable in part for the installation of Eric's pipe organ, which was built into the living-room floor. It was not far from Johnson's own glass house and that of the Breuers. In 1959 Eric left Schlumberger and returned to France. A detailed account of the history of his ski town can be found in his book *Flaine, la création,* published in 1994. In order to organize the Boissonnas family's finances, Flaine was sold in 1989 and is now operated by a subsidiary of Crédit Lyonnais. Sylvie died on October 26, 1999, following an accident. Her obituary in *Le Monde* revealed the modest lady to have been a chevalier of the Légion d'Honneur. *Interviewed January 27, 1996, in Paris*

Rémi Boissonnas Eric's older brother was a banker for many years, principally at the Banque de l'Union Parisienne (BUP). Rémi, a bit of an old-fashioned gentleman, in the early planning days always wore three-piece suits, tab-collared shirts, and a gray fedora, although when he was dealing with the local country folk near Flaine he sometimes sported a beret. At my request he recently wrote of the retirement days of the two Boissonnas families, who live on different floors of the same house in the middle of Paris: "They are surrounded by neighboring gardens and listen to the cooing of pigeons and the hooting of an owl whose ancestors go back to Chateaubriand. They thrill their great-grandchildren by popping champagne corks over the wall and into the prime minister's garden next door." *Interviewed January 28, 1996, in Paris*

Guillermo Carreras Born in Havana, Cuba, where his father was the second in command of the local Chase Manhattan Bank, Guillermo began his architectural studies at the University of Havana in 1951. After the Batista coup in 1952 shootings around the university prompted him to go to Cornell—his father's choice. After graduation, he returned to Havana. Although jobs were scarce, he found employment with a Batista-connected developer who left for vacation in Spain and, after Castro took over in January 1959, never returned. Work with José Luis Sert and Mario Romanach followed. But there came a time in August 1960 when Guillermo had a business meeting with an old classmate, Osmani Cienfuegos, who is today the minister of tourism. He asked, "Carreras, what are you doing here? You're not a revolutionary!" To which Guillermo had to reply, "You're right!" He realized that he had no professional future in Cuba, and his family left within the week. *Interviewed July 8, 1996, in New York*

Eduardo Catalano   After studying with Breuer at Harvard Eduardo returned to his native Buenos Aires. He was very active in the late 1940s trying to get work in South America for his favorite professor. At Eduardo's instigation, Breuer developed a plan for a new college of architecture for Buenos Aires but refused to head it up. A splendid show of Lajkó's work was mounted in his honor, and thereafter he was very well-known in South America. Eduardo and Lajkó together designed the beachside Ariston Restaurant in Mar del Plata, just outside Buenos Aires, and it was surely not their fault that this gemlike floating four-leaf clover, lifted whole from Breuer's Civic Center of the Future model, fell on hard times in later years. My Argentinean roommate of 1954 did not accept my description of it as a restaurant: "It's nothing but a low dive." Breuer designed the basic project and Eduardo completed the working drawings. When Eduardo asked Breuer to bill for his services, Lajkó said, "Please do not spoil our beautiful friendship." *Quotations from a letter of January 22, 1996*

Eric Cercler   A brilliant graduate of the Ecole des Beaux-Arts, Eric spoke passable English and was an experienced administrative architect, though not a strong designer. He could always be counted upon to take either side of any political or philosophical argument, and I never did learn whether he voted for or against de Gaulle in the presidential elections despite our frequent debates.

Ivan Chermayeff   The son of Lajkó's old friend Serge, Ivan is a graphic designer of great distinction. His firm, Chermayeff and Geismar, often worked as graphics consultant to Breuer. *Interviewed August 2, 1995, in New York*

Daniel Chiquet   One of the first, and last, members of the staff of MBA in Paris, Daniel is a man of modest dignity, quite in contrast to the rest of us prima donnas. He worked quietly, intensely, and efficiently while soaking up the culture of the office. He rarely expressed his own opinion until asked and then demonstrated a total comprehension of the problem posed. He became the center for technical information about Flaine and earned the respect and admiration of our clients, the Boissonnas family. *Interviewed January 30, 1996, in Paris*

Donald Cromley   Don studied architecture at MIT and received a graduate degree from the University of Pennsylvania after enrollment in the studio of

Louis I. Kahn. He also worked for a year in Alvar Aalto's office in Finland. Don was in our office from 1963 to 1971. His mother was Japanese, and Breuer frequently introduced him to visitors from Japan as if it would make them feel at home, although he spoke not a word of Japanese. Don eventually became the head of the undergraduate program in architecture at Pratt Institute. *Interviewed June 26, 1995, in New York*

Allen Cunningham Born just outside London, Allen was evacuated to the West Country during World War II. His father, director general of munitions production for Britain, was directly answerable to Churchill—an embarrassment for his pacifist son. Following his first three-month summer with us, Allen returned to England to get his degree (and win the Sikorsky Prize) from Liverpool University, married Sandra Bainbridge of Brooklyn, New York (a happy result of his New York summer), and worked with Sir Leslie Martin in Cambridge, England, for two years before rejoining the office in New York in 1960. For many years he was the head of architecture at London's University of Westminster. *Interviewed October 15, 1995, in London*

Abbot Baldwin Dworschak As the leader of Saint John's Abbey and University during the entire period of its rebuilding, Abbot Baldwin was a strong and supportive client. I saw him for the last time, after his retirement and shortly before his death, on a Sunday during one of the coldest Minnesota winters ever. *Interviewed February 4, 1996, in Collegeville, Minnesota*

Murray Emslie A long-time New Yorker who, like his architect wife, Olive, had gone to my alma mater, Cornell, Murray was about ten years older than Ham, Herb, and myself and vastly experienced in the ways of the architectural world. He had a technical know-how that made him a marvelous teacher and a gentle, wry sense of humor that helped him manage all the high-strung personalities that passed through the office. He was a great friend to all of us, and I owe most of what I know about professional practice, fees and contracts, and technical drawing and detailing to him. When he wasn't smoking, he was chewing gum. I never heard him express a single opinion about design in all the years I knew him.

Mary Farris Mary replaced Connie Moensch as Breuer's private secretary in 1963, after he had rejected twenty other candidates. She recently reported, "He was married to a Connie, the bookkeeper's name was Connie, my predecessor was another Connie, and he kept calling me Connie." Mary grew up in Portland, Oregon, but somewhere developed a charming Southern accent. She commented, "Mr. Breuer needed someone to render his English idiomatic—what he called 'Anglicizing'—although he had a very strong sense of the structure of the language. If I sometimes had trouble understanding what he was saying, the reverse was occasionally true. I once interrupted a meeting and his train of thought to announce a phone call from his son. 'Mr. Breuer, Tom is on the phone.' 'Who?' 'Thomas.' 'Who?' 'Tamas!' *'Who?' 'Your son!'* . . .'Oh.' Later, with some chagrin, he told me the story of almost losing Tom in Paris, as if that explained some consistency." Mary eventually left to marry Murray Drabkin, our lawyer at the time. Breuer always had trouble with people leaving the office, whatever the reason, taking it as some sort of personal affront. (When Stan Abercrombie left to follow his career in journalism, Lajkó said, "You are leaving! I won't forgive you. God will forgive you, but that is his métier.") When Mary finally told him of her departure, after seven years of service, he responded, "Mary, we cannot have all this coming and going!" *Interviewed January 23, 1996, in Washington, D.C.*

Jack Freidin Trained in architecture at Pratt Institute, Jack had worked for two of New York's best designers—George Nemeny and Charlie Warner—before arriving at the Breuer office just before Ham Smith and I did. He remembers being a bit jealous as the office started to expand in the mid-1950s and he had to "share Breuer with more people. We felt that we were working in a studio . . . not employees, but apprentices to the master, and there was a certain bond in this anachronistic specialness." *Interviewed April 10, 1996, in New York*

Isabelle Pack Hyman When Margaret Firmage retired and moved to Florida in 1958, Isabelle became Breuer's personal secretary. She stayed for two and a half years and then left to get her doctorate in art history from New York University's Institute of Fine Arts. She is soon to publish her scholarly biography of Breuer; in fact, she inspired me to write this book as a complement to her academic approach.

John Johansen Jo was one of Lajkó's most devoted students at Harvard and remains a close friend of Breuer's family. He is married to Gropius's daughter Ati. Always a rigorous modernist, he designed a number of houses and theaters that are high modern icons. *Interviewed July 24, 1995, in New York*

Beat Jordi Beat came from Bern, where his father had been on the city council. (His father was also an architect who studied in Vienna and worked for the great Peter Behrens.) Upon Beat's graduation from the ETH in Zurich in 1967, it was suggested that foreign experience would be good for him and Breuer's old Doldertal partner, Alfred Roth, wrote to Lajkó on his behalf. Beat explained to Lajkó shortly after his arrival that he was trying hard to get rid of his Swiss accent. Breuer said, "No, no, you should keep it. It's much more interesting." Beat worked in New York on the Baldegg schematic design and followed the project to the Paris office where its working drawings were prepared. When construction started, he became our site representative working from his own new office in Bern. *Interviewed September 8, 1995, in New York*

Mario Jossa Born in Rome to a family well-connected to the Roman Catholic church, Mario was sent to America to study architecture at Catholic University in Washington, D.C., and later moved to suburban New York. He joined the Breuer office in 1963 as a result of his friendship with Guillermo Carreras. He still doesn't know what led Breuer to choose him for an assignment to Paris, which was first proposed after a long drunken Christmas party in 1965. It was likely one more example of Lajkó's intuitive selection of young people for extraordinary responsibility. Mario was thirty-two at the time and says, "Breuer liked anything that was Italian." *Interviewed June 8, 1997, in Paris*

Frank Kacmarcik As a faculty member and independent art consultant to Saint John's, the Annunciation Priory, and other religious institutions, Frank was an influential supporter of Breuer, as well as a house client. In later years, he retired to the monastic life as a brother at Saint John's Abbey. *Interviewed February 4, 1996, in Collegeville, Minnesota*

Paul Koralek Born in Vienna, Paul escaped with his family to London in 1939 where he studied architecture at the Architectural Association School of Architecture (AA) in the early 1950s. After practice in Paris and Canada, he worked on Flaine for a year; at the same time he prepared his own entry to an international competition for the Trinity College Library in Dublin. He left the office after winning the competition and formed a partnership— Ahrends, Burton and Koralek (ABK)—with two old AA friends in London. Breuer later put them on the short list for the European Investment Bank in Luxembourg, which he served as professional adviser. Despite Lajkó's help they "blew the interview," and Breuer learned a lesson, from the other side of the table, about more than one person talking at the same time. ABK tangled with Prince Charles over their winning scheme for the addition to the National Gallery on Trafalgar Square in 1985; the partners became world-famous heroes of modern architecture even though they lost the commission. *Interviewed September 18, 1995, in London*

William Landsberg Bill, a graduate of what is now Carnegie Mellon University, studied under and worked for Breuer in Cambridge, Massachusetts. He then worked for Skidmore, Owings & Merrill (SOM) in New York for a time before returning to Lajkó's New York office. Gordon Bunshaft, his boss at SOM, told him, "Well, if it was anyone else you were leaving to work for, I'd try to convince you to stay." Although Bill worked, often as the only draftsman in the office, on such projects as the Museum of Modern Art's House in the Garden, the Grosse Pointe Library, and the Neuman house, he is very modest in speaking of his own design contribution: "Lajkó would walk in with a very well-worked-out sketch and it was up to me to draw it up." When I joined the firm, it was Bill's experience in professional practice and the details of construction upon which we totally depended. *Interviewed November 20, 1995, in Port Washington, New York*

André Laurenti A graduate of the Ecole des Beaux-Arts, André worked with Lajkó on the UNESCO team. When Breuer saw the project at Flaine developing into more than just a master plan he felt the need for an experienced French architect with whom he could talk frankly about professional matters, and he enlisted André as a consultant to the design team. André became my indispensable guide in setting up the Paris office a few years later.

Lillian Leight Breuer posted an opening for controller at the New York State Unemployment Office in 1965 and Lillian applied for the job. Lajkó came out of his office to greet her when she arrived for her interview and impressed her as an Old World gentleman. Before long she convinced Breuer that many of his suppliers were stealing him blind, and she was left to negotiate most of the day-to-day purchasing from then on. Her access to personnel files meant that there were no secrets from Lillian, but she was a benevolent and helpful mother-confessor to us all. Breuer's office was quite close to hers, and she remembers being struck by the fact that within ten minutes of the arrival of any new client, roars of laughter were sure to be heard from their meeting. She worried about Lajkó's health and kept track of all the pastrami sandwiches ordered in from the Carnegie Deli. Lillian is convinced that she was the "shadkhn" who matched Mary Farris and Murray Drabkin, however much they deny it, and remembers the day that Breuer named her an associate in the firm as the proudest moment of her life. *Interviewed August 24, 1995, in New York*

Matthys Lévy Born in Basel, Switzerland, Matt was living in Paris when he was marooned in New York during a family vacation in 1939 by World War II. He was educated at New York's City College and Columbia University. Recruited by a consultant to the new Weidlinger firm, Mario Salvadori, who had been his professor at Columbia, Matt eventually became a partner in the firm, and Breuer frequently worked with him. Matt's mother was an artist who had lived in Paris during the 1920s. She later remembered meeting Breuer, whom she considered very much of a bon-vivant and boulevardier. When Matt brought it up, Lajkó claimed he had no memory of their meeting and contested the description. *Interviewed September 19, 1996, in New York*

Bernard Marson Bernie was clerk o' the works at New York University (NYU), as well as at the Whitney a few years later. He had an engineering degree from NYU and studied architecture at Cooper Union. After completing the Whitney he served as Moshe Safdie's partner in Jerusalem for several years in the early 1970s and then continued to practice architecture in New York, aided by occasional referrals from Breuer. *Interviewed August 1, 1995, in New York*

Laurie Maurer Brought up in Brooklyn, Laurie received her architectural degree from Pratt Institute. She is married to Stanley Maurer, a former associate of Ed Barnes, and she worked in our office for five years before returning to Pratt as a teacher. When she gave her notice to Breuer, he tried to dissuade her ("Imagine, one of the great teachers of architecture, trying to talk me out of teaching!") and then asked if she would be interested in freelance work. She maintained that association with the office for several years, working on construction drawings for several of Breuer's houses. *Interviewed August 17, 1995, in New York*

Richard Meier Born in Newark, New Jersey, Richard graduated from Cornell University a few years after I did and came to work with Breuer in the early 1960s. He was a brilliant and hard-working draftsman who hid his very considerable design talent under the proverbial basket while in the office. We worked together on IBM La Gaude and Flaine and I considered him a good friend. When I moved to my newly completed home in Bedford from a rent-controlled apartment at Ninety-first Street and Park Avenue, I turned the lease over to Dick (as he was known then) and received a very nice collage in return. He lived there for several years and might have been killed when some bookshelves that I had installed in the bedroom pulled loose from their anchors. They bowed precariously over his bed with barely enough time for his vast library to be unloaded. After leaving the Breuer office in 1963, Dick tried his hand as a painter in a loft space that he shared with Frank Stella and eventually opened his own office. He was joined by Murray Emslie after Murray left Breuer. Speaking to Stan Abercrombie recently, Richard said, "I learned a lot from Breuer . . . the simultaneous design of inside and outside . . . attention to detail and a wholeness of vision." I joined Richard's firm in 1987 and was his partner until I retired in 1995.

Valerius Michelson Val was working in Percy Goodman's office when I started there in 1952. He was born in Estonia, trained in Saint Petersburg, drafted into the Russian army, and captured by the Germans. Val spent World War II in the midst of Eastern Europe living by his wits while surrounded by indescribable horror. He eventually made his way to the United States where he received his architectural degree from Columbia University and was hired by its dean. *Interviewed February 4, 1996, in Minneapolis, Minnesota*

Julian and Barbara Neski   Bobbie and Joe came to the office while they were engaged. Bobbie had been a brilliant student at the Harvard GSD after attending Bennington College; during that time she visited Breuer's nearby Robinson house and became convinced that she should study architecture. She arrived at the office with a totally undeserved Harvard nickname: "the Dragon Lady." Joe had had an equally successful period of training at Rensselaer Polytechnic Institute and quickly established himself in the office as a brilliant draftsman/designer and genuinely funny man. His nimble wit was used to mimic the accents he heard around him in the office, including Breuer's, and his ability to draw rubblestone just the way Lajkó liked it earned him the title "Count Rubblestonsky." Bobbie left in 1957 to have the first of their two sons, and Joe later drifted into several partnerships; the final, and most productive, was the one he established with his wife. *Interviewed May 27, 1995, in New York*

Tician Papachristou   Born in Athens the only son of a German mother and a Greek father, Tician was named after his father's favorite painter, Titian. But when Tician got his first passport the spelling was scrambled as it passed from Italian to Greek to English. After the harrowing war years in Greece, Tician was sent to study architecture at Princeton and essentially never returned. After his graduation, he moved to Boulder, Colorado, where he developed a thriving residential practice. When Walt Roberts, the director of the National Center for Atmospheric Research, was looking for an architect to design his new headquarters, he asked Tician to join him as architectural adviser, which led him to Breuer. *Interviewed May 19 and July 29, 1995, and February 18, 1996, in Hydra, Greece, and New York*

Jay Ritchie   Jay, who received his architectural degree from Princeton, worked in the firm for two and a half years. He then returned home to Salt Lake City to an architectural practice that has since ranged all over the Midwest. *Interviewed December 11, 1995, in New York*

Yolande Roche   Madame Roche comes from a very old Scottish family, related to the Stuarts, who have resided in France since Charles VIII (1490); they served the kings of France as Scottish Guards and settled in Normandy. Her father was the Comte d'Oilliamson. During World War II she fell in love with a handsome American "GI" (as her disapproving family always characterized him). Tom Roche was a much decorated captain in the Texas Rangers and a graduate of Princeton (and eventually a very distinguished Wall Street lawyer). After the war the young couple moved to New York where they started married life in a small apartment in Stuyvesant Town. After they divorced, she returned with her children to France. Max Stern knew her family well, suspected that she could use a job, and made the introduction. With her idiomatic American English, she became my elegant French voice and I was the envy of every expatriate businessman I knew. *Interviewed July 7, 1998, in Paris*

Lawrence Roeder After studies at the University of Minnesota, the Graduate School of Architecture and Planning at Columbia University, and the Ecole des Beaux-Arts at Fontainebleau, Lorry came to the office in 1963 and amused us for four years. *Quotations from many undated letters of 1997 and later*

Arthur Rosenblatt Born in the Bronx, New York, Arthur studied architecture at the Cooper Union and Carnegie Mellon University. He has practiced in both the public and private sectors and is the coauthor of *The Movie Song Catalogue. Interviewed June 23, 1995, in New York*

Alfred Roth The grand old man of the ETH in Zurich, Roth first met Breuer at the Weissenhofsiedlung in 1927 and worked for many years with Le Corbusier in Paris. Sigfried Giedion suggested that Lajkó join Roth's project at the Doldertal "because Breuer was a friend of Giedion's girlfriend," and Roth, who lived there in retirement, still remembered Lajkó as a very good skier. He died in 1997. *Interviewed by Patrick Jordi in November 1995 in Zurich*

Dr. Mortimer Sackler Mort was one of three brothers in a family of Austro-Hungarian and Polish immigrants. They grew up in an apartment above the family store in Brooklyn. The hard-working and ambitious family sent each of the three through college, medical school, and a psychiatric internship, although none of them practiced medicine for long. The oldest brother, Arthur, founded the ad-rich giveaway *Medical Tribune* and amassed a fortune and art collection that was partly distributed to museums and galleries that bear his name at Harvard, the Smithsonian, and the Metropolitan Museum. The youngest brother, Raymond, and Mort run the United States operations of Purdue Frederick with Ray's son Richard and other family members. They have all been major donors to the Metropolitan Museum and to other museums and universities. When I eventually met "Dr. Mortimer" (as his associates referred to him), he was the fifty-year-old divorced father of two grown children who was circulating through Europe, managing both the overseas operations of the family-held company and his personal life in flamboyant style. Lajkó never quite understood how to deal with Mort and eventually left most of the day-to-day relations to us two Brooklyn boys. I do, however, remember that Breuer was very interested in Mort's sales pitch for Sargenor, the product that lay behind the French acquisition. It was promised to perk anyone up, especially those of a certain age, and Lajkó would try anything for his aching back.

Peter Samton With his brother and parents, Peter fled Germany in 1939, studied under Pietro Belluschi at MIT, and worked for the Architects Collaborative and Hugh Stubbins in Boston. In 1960, while at MBA, Peter, with his brother Claude and Abe Geller, another Breuer alumnus, was one of six finalists in the FDR Memorial competition in Washington. During this time, Peter's wife, Emily, a dancer and physical therapist, had Lajkó on the floor at a party in their apartment doing the well-known Hans Kraus exercises for what was even then a bad back. Peter followed me as a president of the New York Chapter of the AIA and served that organization with distinction. He is a partner in Gruzen Samton Architects of New York. *Interviewed August 6, 1995, in New York*

Gabriel Sedlis Gabby was born in the part of northern Poland that became Lithuania. He spoke Russian, Polish, and Lithuanian, among other languages, and today, after forty-nine years in the United States—most of his life—is chagrined to note that English is the only language he still speaks with an accent. In 1941, when the Germans invaded Lithuania, he entered the ghetto, became a resistance fighter, and fought with the Red Army in the Polish forests. In 1945 he studied in Rome and Turin before coming to the Harvard GSD. On the advice of Joe and Bobbie Neski, he left Skidmore, Owings & Merrill in 1956 to learn architectural detailing with our firm, even though it meant a pay cut. He stayed until 1959 when he was caught in one of Breuer's periodic "bloodbaths" designed to downsize the firm in response to some now forgotten reversal. *Interviewed February 8, 1996, in New York*

Harry Seidler Born in Vienna, Harry was sent to school in England. When the war broke out he was interned as an "enemy alien" and eventually deported to Canada, where he studied architecture at the University of Manitoba. He headed to Harvard on a scholarship as soon as he could to study under Gropius in its master class; while there he met Breuer. After Harvard, on Gropius's advice, Harry studied for a summer at Black Mountain College with Josef Albers who "taught me to see." His parents passed through the United States en route to Australia but he declined to join them, at least at that time. Eventually, after two years with Breuer, he did go to Australia to design a house for his parents, and he stayed there, becoming one of the country's most distinguished architects. *Interviewed April 21, 1996, in New York*

Suzanne Sekey Sue was born in Hungary and studied interior design at the Design Laboratory in New York. She was working for Breuer's old friend Herbert Bayer in 1941 when Breuer and his new bride, Connie, came to visit. Sue had been with many other fine firms in and around New York before coming to us. Reintroduced to Lajkó at lunch by her half-brother, Tamas, who had known Breuer at the Wohnbedarf in Switzerland, she remembers being impressed by the clothes he wore (Lajkó always had his suits made to order once he could afford them) and the way he wore his hair (a wavy fringe combed forward over a high forehead). *Interviewed September 7, 1995, in New York*

Hamilton Smith Ham had attended Princeton and Yale and had worked for several years in Bloomfield Hills, Michigan, for Eero Saarinen before he decided to move back east to his native Garden City, Long Island, to be closer to his family. Ham had, and has, about him a patrician air that suited his position of authority even at the relatively young age of twenty-eight, when we first met. Most of the time it serves to mask a shy, sensitive personality and a bawdy sense of humor. *Interviewed June 3, 1995, in East Hampton and February 21, 1996, in New York*

Carl Stein The only son of one of Lajkó's oldest friends—a student and early employee, Dick Stein—Carl came to us with high recommendations and worked in the office from 1968 to 1971. He was always afraid of overplaying his hand in the office because of an acquaintanceship that went back to the time when, at the age of ten, he had visited Connie and Lajkó with his parents, Ethel and Dick, and had seen his first modern house. Later, when he was sixteen years old and possessed of a learner's driving permit, he remembers Tamas, who was a year younger, badgering him to take his father's Jaguar out for a spin. Tamas was in the middle of a rigorous drivers education course given by his father, and it was a source of some tension between them. Carl worked for us during what is remembered as a hippie period when everyone, including him, sported a beard. Someone told Breuer that it set the wrong tone for the office, but Lajkó's response was to wear a false beard the next day. Carl had a marvelously woolly sheepdog at the time and kept a photograph of it pinned above his drafting board. Breuer studied the picture carefully one day and finally said, "Yes, I can see the family resemblance." Carl recalls a relaxed luncheon with Breuer: "I asked him why he had given up teaching, and he replied, 'And what, exactly, do you think we are doing here?'" When it came time for Carl's going-away party—he left to join his father in partnership—Breuer said, "I understand; too bad we didn't have more time to talk." *Interviewed July 18, 1995, in New York*

Max Stern Born in Paris in 1920 and raised in a not particularly religious Jewish home, Max converted to Catholicism when he was in his late teens. After World War II broke out he went to officer training school, and at the time of the capitulation, he was at the head of a unit whose soldiers guarded word of his Jewish birth from the Nazis. He finished his university training in literature in occupied Lyon. After graduation he joined the resistance, was flown to London, and later parachuted back to the mountains of southeastern France, where he participated in the liberation of Annecy and its surrounding towns. By the time he returned to Paris, he had received the rosette of the Legion of Honor, the Croix de Guerre, and the Bronze Star. In 1956, with a group of professional friends including an ex-priest and several noblemen, he founded the Bureau d'Etudes et de Réalisations Urbaines (BERU), the commercial planners who had been hired to test the market and write the program for a new ski resort. The BERU was a cooperative— an association of radical planners interested in social housing in France and abroad. He remained its elected head until 1968 when he left to become chief aide to Albin Chalandon, the minister of housing and planning in the de Gaulle government. Max knew a lot about politics, particularly French politics, and he became my mentor in many respects—including good food and wine. Max died in January 1996 just after I had flown to Paris for an interview that he was too sick to give. *Interview with his son Jean on October 20, 1996, in New York*

Rufus Stillman Rufus was working as a journalist when Andrew Gagarin, the president of the Torrington Manufacturing Company, hired him. Rufus eventually rose to the position of president and chairman himself, changing the name and logo to Torin in the process. In addition to the three Stillman residences, Breuer was at Rufus's instigation to design seven buildings for the company all over the world, as well as Andy Gagarin's own house; an elegant lakeside cottage for Rufus's father-in-law, Harry Caesar; a summer house in Wellfleet for Rufus's brother Edgar; four school buildings in and around Torrington; and a laboratory building for Yale, where Rufus had studied. *Interviewed July 20, 1995, in Litchfield, Connecticut*

Jeff Vandeberg After studying at the universities of Nebraska and Michigan, Jeff joined Breuer following a brief stint with Ira Kessler. His present idiosyncratic practice includes the much-praised Chelsea Market in lower Manhattan. *Interviewed July 28, 1995, in New York*

Paul Weidlinger Long one of America's most distinguished structural engineers, Paul was, like his good friend Lajkó, born in Hungary. Twelve years younger than Breuer, Paul first met him in 1930 when Breuer was visiting Paul's architect father in Budapest: "He knew who he was. I considered him a god." Paul went on to study both architecture and engineering at the ETH and worked for such distinguished designers and architects as his ETH professor Alfred Roth, fellow-Hungarian László Moholy-Nagy, and Le Corbusier before coming to America to teach at Harvard and MIT. He designed a summer house for himself in Wellfleet at Breuer's urging with "crits" from Corb, Gropius, and Chermayeff. Lajkó's advice was the most practical: "Don't pave the road." In his pioneering work on blast protection for the Department of Defense, Paul worked closely with many of the great physicist-mathematicians at the Rand Corporation, including John von Neumann, whom he quotes: "To be a genius, you have to be Hungarian, but it's not enough—you have to work." Paul died in 1999. *Interviewed August 15, 1995, in New York*

Paul Willen When Paul was getting a masters degree in Russian Constructivism at Columbia University, he met Val Michelson. Paul had taught himself Russian and was eager to practice on Val. During the summer of 1958 Paul worked in the field office at Saint John's helping Val with shop drawings and returned to study architecture at Pratt Institute at Val's suggestion. After a brief interview, Breuer hired him in 1962 for three months "on probation"— a frequent condition that would avoid having to give two weeks' notice in the event of a "blood bath." Paul left the office in 1965; he remembers his going-away party as featuring the unrolling of a sheet of yellow tracing paper on the drafting-room floor in lieu of a red carpet. He surfaced in the *New York Times* in the early 1990s as chair of a local AIA committee that challenged Donald Trump to improve his Upper West Side development. He ended up proposing a much-acclaimed alternative scheme—Riverside South—that was finally adopted by Trump, who hired him to oversee its development. *Interviewed November 1, 1995, in New York*

Jane Yu Born in China, Jane received her architecture degree from the University of Shanghai in 1954 before leaving with her family for Hong Kong. She eventually entered the United States as a political refugee and worked for Harry Weese and C. F. Murphy in Chicago before coming to New York. We hired her in the summer of 1963, and with a few interruptions, Jane stayed with the firm until 1980. For most of that time she was in charge of interior design, but her architectural training allowed her to pitch in at almost any point of any job. *Interviewed August 20, 1995, in New York*

Index

Page numbers in *italics* refer to illustrations.

Photography Credits

Numbers refer to page numbers.

Bill Allen/*New York Times* Pictures from the Archives of American Art: 71
Archives of American Art, Smithsonian Institution, Marcel Breuer papers: 6, 26, 33, 34, 48, 195, 200
Archives of the Roosevelt Library: 229
Patricia Layman Bazelon: 236
© Ellie Beckhard: 290
Walter Besneglieri from the Archives of American Art: 205
Kurt Blum: 193
Marcel Breuer: 84
Robert F. Gatje: 38, 41, 72, 83, 95, 109, 131, 139, 214, 219, 223, 237, 251, 257, 271
P. E. Guerro: 81
Yves Guillemaut: 98, 145, 158, 239, 267, 268, 270
Lee A. Hanley: 89
Hedrich-Blessing from the Chicago Historical Society HB 30662-A: 122
Lucien Hervé from the Archives of American Art: 46
Shin Koyama: 206, 225
Nicholas L. Ludington: 256
Wolfgang K. Mackrodt: 173, 256
Joseph Molitor from the Avery Architecture and Fine Arts Library, Columbia University in the City of New York: 217
Frits Monshouwer: 54
Robert Mottar: 108
© Hans Namuth Estate Collection, Center for Creative Photography, University of Arizona: 4, 105

Bob Noble, Staff Photographer, *New York Herald Tribune*, Queens Borough Public Library, Long Island Division, *Herald Tribune* Morgue from the Archives of American Art: 198
Arnold Rosenberg: 262, 280
Alfred Roth: 13
Ben Schnall: 43, 78, 170, 181, 182, 183, 186, 187 top, 190, 194
Rufus Stillman from the Archives of American Art: 36
Ezra Stoller © Esto; all rights reserved: 31, 57, 187 bottom, 199
Official United Nations Photo/Department of Public Information: 40
Jan Versnel: 86, 116
© Nick Wheeler: 285, 286